Big Kids, Bigger Feelings

Navigating **Defiance,**
Meltdowns, and **Anxiety**
to Raise **Confident,**
Connected Kids

Alyssa Blask Campbell, M.Ed., with
Rachel Stuart Lounder

HARVEST
An Imprint of WILLIAM MORROW

hc.com

FIRST EDITION

Title page illustration © Adobe Stock
Other illustrations throughout by Beki Rohrig

Library of Congress Cataloging-in-Publication Data has been applied for.

ISBN 978-0-06-341560-7

Printed in the United States of America

25 26 27 28 29 LBC 5 4 3 2 1

Rachel: *To Nora and Abel.*
This book is for you and because of you.

Alyssa: *To the big kids with big feelings.*
You are not too much for this world. Your ability to
feel so deeply and express your needs is a superpower.

Contents

Introduction

The Significance of Middle Childhood

Middle childhood is ripe with change: friendships blossom and shift, peer influence emerges, emotions become more complex, and bodies start to grow and develop in new ways. Children begin to form a clearer sense of identity, figuring out who they are and where they fit within their social circles, families, and the larger world around them. Social and emotional development accelerates alongside academic learning—just as kids move from simple addition to long division, they're also grappling with a more nuanced understanding of themselves and others. These years are marked by a deepening capacity for empathy and self-awareness, yet they're also a time when insecurities and self-doubt may begin to surface, shaped by kids' growing awareness of how others perceive them.

For parents, these years can feel like uncharted territory. The emotional outbursts you thought were reserved for toddlerhood resurface, but now they're accompanied by eye rolls, defiance, and attitude. It's a time of budding independence but also lingering dependence—children are starting to navigate the world on their own terms, testing boundaries and making decisions, but they still need us as their anchor. They may assert their desire for autonomy by rejecting your ideas or pushing back against your rules, yet they continue to crave your support, understanding, and guidance in ways that aren't always obvious.

These years also introduce a new set of challenges: managing peer relationships, coping with academic pressures, and handling the complex emotions that come with growing up. As they seek approval from friends and begin to explore their own interests and values, children are laying the foundation for who they will become. In this book we will equip you with the tools to understand your child's behavior, uncover the root causes of conflict, and support you in becoming their attuned leader.

Meet Your Authors

ALYSSA: After publishing *Tiny Humans, Big Emotions* with Lauren Stauble, requests immediately started to come in for a book that would address these same issues of emotional intelligence for an older age range. "Where is the book for how to navigate this with elementary-school-age kids?" "This makes sense for my preschooler, but I'm at a loss for what to do to help my fourth grader."

As a research nerd and consultant working with kids from birth through age sixteen, I was jazzed to get to work on what is happening inside the brains and bodies of kids in kindergarten through fifth grade. I love being able to dive into the science and share it in ways that make sense. I believe so deeply that it takes a village to raise kids, and I'm happy to pop into your village to turn research-based information into practical strategies for raising emotionally intelligent humans. My goal in all the work that I do, whether in the classroom or in workshops with parents and educators, is to distill data into real-life application. Bringing that into my work here in this book has been a gift.

A bit more about me: I have a master's degree in early childhood education; I co-created and researched the Collaborative Emotion Processing (CEP) method for building emotional intelligence; and I am a mom to two kids who are very different humans. When it came to writing this book, I knew right away that I wanted a coauthor who is a parent raising elementary-school-age kids so that we could really highlight the realities and practicalities beyond the research.

Enter Rachel. Rach has been the copywriter for Seed & Sew since 2018 and is one of the nerdiest humans I know. She loves to dive into research and understand the science behind why and how things happen, and she has two kids, who are five and nine at the time of this writing. She will share a bit about herself and her why behind this work and then we will let you know what to expect from us here.

RACHEL: I'm a mom of two, cancer survivor, and research lover. My fundamental approach to parenting and parenthood has been to always want to know the why. Why do behaviors happen? What's happening developmentally? Why am I reacting this way to my kids' behavior?

When my knee-jerk reaction to their behavior is to get triggered and angry, understanding the brain science behind my response helps me to be a more compassionate, empathetic human. My interest in fostering emotional intelligence for kids is twofold: I want my kids to know how to handle adversity and emotional pain. But it's bigger than that. I want that for all kids. I want children to grow up in a world where their partners, friends, and colleagues are emotionally aware. I want empathy and respect to be the norm in their relationships. I want them to know that conflict is a normal part of life and how to move through it.

There was a time in the early days of parenthood when I thought I could protect my kids from the hard stuff. Then I got cancer when my oldest was a month shy of turning two. I very quickly realized that I could not shelter her from the hardships of this life. That's when my interest in emotional intelligence and children's emotional wellness really took off. When I was given the opportunity to join Seed & Sew, it was a no-brainer. I love sharing research-backed strategies with other parents who are in the trenches, because I'm right there with you. When Alyssa asked me to write this book with her, it was another easy yes. There is so much information about babies, toddlers, and teens. But what about my nine-year-old who is rolling her eyes at me and slamming her bedroom door repeatedly? What the heck is up with that? My hope in sharing this book with you is for you to feel seen, validated, and supported in the unique challenges of middle childhood. I hope that you come away from this book knowing what to do with your nine-year-old and those behaviors and emotions you weren't expecting until the teen years. And I want you to come away knowing that you aren't alone and you've got a place to turn when the going gets tough.

Although we are two different humans, we are very used to writing a first-person narrative, as we've shared a voice through Seed & Sew for years. For simplicity's sake, we will use "I" throughout this book to share stories with you. We hope you can find yourself and/or your children in them.

What Can You Expect from This Book?

As parents, the elementary school years can challenge us in unexpected ways. They can bring back memories of our own childhood struggles, fears, and pain. We want so badly to protect our children, to make life easier for them, to ensure they grow up happy and well-adjusted. But how do we help them through the inevitable challenges they'll face?

I think about a day recently when my nine-year-old daughter, Nora, was strangely quiet when I picked her up from school. An enthusiastic conversationalist, most days she talks from the moment she wakes up until the moment she falls asleep at night. This was markedly different. I tried to start a conversation with her, but her answers were short, and her demeanor withdrawn. We were about halfway home when she quietly told me that she was having trouble with a classmate at school. A girl in her class had been scribbling on Nora's papers, hiding her school supplies, and threatening to lie to the teacher to get her in trouble. This had been going on for a couple of weeks.

There was a part of me that wanted to march into school and address it right away with her teachers. Or I'd call the girl's parents and let them know about the kind of human their daughter is. I'd do whatever it took to make sure that child left my daughter alone. This part of me wants to fight like hell to protect my daughter from experiencing the hurt, pain, and social stressors that I experienced as a child. Could I save her from all of that if I stepped in to stop it? this part wonders. It makes sense that we want to protect our children from experiencing hard things. It's natural to feel protective of them, and to view their experiences through the lens of what we experienced as children.

The reality is that our children will experience social pain. Listen, as a mom of two, I know how hard it is to accept that truth. If I could wave a magic wand and have my children not experience emotional or physical pain, I'd do it. I want to wrap them up and protect them from the hardships that are out in the world that I know about all too well—grief, feeling left out, embarrassment, fear, anxiety, disappointment, or maybe worse, feeling like a disappointment. And frankly, these feelings don't end in childhood: I recently found myself leaving a friend's dinner party replaying all the things I had said and wondering if her other friends liked me. This stuff doesn't go away and it would be a dream if we could save our children from this pain and angst. But even if we could do so, it wouldn't actually be helping them.

Our brains are designed to learn from the past, make adjustments, and try to avoid future pain. You only touch the hot stove once before your brain clocks it and says, "Don't touch that when it's on; it's hot." Even if we don't have conscious memories of the challenges we faced in elementary school, our brains have been storing the information for years to try to prevent us from feeling pain. Maybe it wasn't even something that happened to us, but instead something we witnessed—a classmate getting made fun of, cliques of kids leaving peers out intentionally, or the secondhand embarrassment of watching someone get talked about behind their back for wearing that outfit.

As parents, we can't take away the challenging but formative experience of navigating childhood and all of its social messiness. But we have the opportunity to give our children what many of us didn't have: the skills to navigate the inevitable social stressors that will happen in this life. Right now, it's a conflict with a classmate and they can come home to us and talk about it. Fast-forward fifteen or twenty years when we aren't there to solve their problems. What will happen when they have a conflict with a colleague or their boss? What skills will they have for self-advocacy and self-esteem? We get to build the foundation for that now during this unique period of development when kids are starting to spread their wings but are still coming back to the nest each day.

We do not believe in a one-size-fits-all approach to raising humans. If you're a parent of more than one child, you have likely experienced this firsthand—one approach may work well for one child but not at all for another. We will provide sample strategies and scripts you can use as jumping-off points, but what is most valuable is understanding what your child needs in a given moment to feel connected, safe, and secure. Most important, in this book we will aim to provide just that: a blueprint for how your unique child experiences the world around them and what would be most supportive from you in response. We will share resources and QR codes throughout, and all of them can be found at www.seedandsew.org /bigkids to access at your convenience.

Here is what we won't do in this book. We will not give you one specific approach that works for all children. We will not provide you with a short-cut. We will not deliver you a child who is obedient, always collaborative, and consistently regulated. By the end of this book, we will leave you with the tools to navigate the tough behaviors, understand what's happening in your child's body and brain, and respond. We will help you navigate the messiness of being human and create a world with your child where neither of you is expected to be perfect.

Who Am I? How Do I Fit into This World?

During middle childhood, children start to develop a clearer understanding of themselves and the world. Their interactions and experiences shape how they see themselves. This is why social interactions become extremely important to them during this time. You might observe that your child begins to pay more attention to their friends and peer relationships rather than just focusing on you and your family. Suddenly, there is an entire part of their world and their life that is separate from yours.

In early childhood, we have a lot of control over what our child's daily life looks like. We might be home with them, or perhaps they're with a sitter or at a day care or preschool program where we get frequent updates and communication about their day-to-day life. We know what's going on with them often down to the tiniest details. Middle childhood is a different ball game. They head to school in the morning, and when we see them in the afternoon and ask them how their day went, we might get a "fine" or "okay." There is so much happening for them socially and with their peer groups that we aren't privy to, so many things they are experiencing that we aren't directly a part of.

This isn't just a period of growth for our children; it's also a period of growth for us. It's hard to lose our sense of control over their daily routines. It can be hard to allow them to have a social world that is separate from us. We have to learn this brand-new balancing act of allowing them to have new experiences without being overly protective, while also being a safe place for them to turn to when they need us. We might notice in ourselves a sense of disappointment or sadness as their independence grows and they have a world that doesn't always involve us.

Knowing that a child's world is now more peer focused than ever before, it makes sense that the need for inclusion increases exponentially during this time. Wanting to be liked, wanting to be picked for the team, wanting to be included at recess, needing to feel a sense of belonging all come into focus in a new way. We are going to see them experience hurt, rejection, and embarrassment in social settings in ways we haven't seen before.

Jason is an energetic, sensitive, sweet third grader. He has recently become more and more focused on doing what his friends are doing. He frequently asks for playdates, and he's adopted his friends' mannerisms, suddenly dressing, walking, and talking the same way they do. He's feeling pressure to fit in socially in a way he hasn't before. His parents have noticed him paying close attention to the outfits he chooses for school, and how he styles his hair. He even asked for a new backpack to match one of his friends'. He seems to be feeling a new sense of pressure to fit in with his peers.

When it's time for basketball tryouts, Jason doesn't want to go, even though he asked his parents to sign him up, knowing tryouts were involved. He fights it every step of the way. At dinnertime his parents let him know he'll need to change into his basketball clothes as soon as he finishes eating. He seems to ignore them. He hems and haws at the dinner table. Pushes his food around his plate, gets up and down from the table, does anything besides sitting and eating.

When he does finally head to his room to change clothes, he's irritated about the way his shorts fit. He gets in an argument with his mom over what shoes he's going to wear. He shouts at her and slams his door in her face. Every bit of the process feels like a tug-of-war, his parents trying to pull him toward the door and off to tryouts, and him pulling back to stay at home. At this point his parents feel frustrated. He asked to play basketball. They let him know that tryouts were part of it, and he said he wanted to join. Why is this such a fight? What is going on?

As they're driving to the gym, his mom asks him about the situation.

"Jason, what's going on tonight? Why don't you want to go to tryouts?" she asks him. "No matter what happens, Dad and I will be proud of you."

Jason is quiet for a couple of minutes, but as they get closer to the gym he opens up. "I'm worried about what my friends will think if I don't make the team. Once the season starts, everyone spends all their time at practice and games. If I'm not on the team, they'll never be able to hang out with me. And maybe they won't even want to hang out with someone who can't make the team."

Jason's mental dialogue regarding basketball tryouts is a perfect example of what is happening internally for kids during this developmental stage. They're asking questions about themselves and about others:

Where do I belong?
What are the social norms here?
How do I fit into my peer group?
What do I need to do to be accepted?

In a dream world, our kids would always make the team, would never feel disappointment, and wouldn't have to worry about what their friends think of them. In the real world, they will experience rejection and pain—and it's not our job to protect them from it. It's our job to equip them with the tools to navigate it and to know that our love for them is unconditional—team or no team, we love them just as they are.

What's Your Role in This Phase of Your Child's Development?

Jason didn't make the team that year. After the call from the coach came, he cried, feeling disappointed and embarrassed. When he found out that his two best friends did make the team, he slammed his bedroom door, saying he wasn't going to school the next day. Naturally, it was hard for his parents to witness him experience this. They recognized that his school refusal was stemming from feelings related to belonging and inclusion. But even with that perspective, what were they to do? Often, we find ourselves trying to problem-solve for our children in these moments. What could we have done differently? When he said he didn't want to try out, should we have listened? Should we call the coach to figure out where he went wrong so we can try to fix it?

I'm giving you permission to stop second-guessing yourself. It's not your job to solve these problems. In fact, a situation like Jason's isn't actually a problem, per se. It's an opportunity for growth.

A New Way to Think About Big Feelings

Before we delve further into why this is an opportunity instead of a problem—and, more important, how to handle this in the moment—it's helpful for parents to take a step back and think about your own childhoods. How did your parents or the adults in your life respond when you experienced something hard as a child? I grew up in a "Dust yourself off and get up" family. "There's no need to get upset about it" was frequently heard in my childhood. We didn't have the research about emotions then that we have now. Today we know that in order for a child to cope with their emotions, we have to allow them to feel them. If we ask them to suppress or ignore their feelings, they won't learn to process them. But when

I was a child, it was culturally and socially expected for us to suppress our emotions, put on a smile, and move on.

This isn't the fault of previous generations, but truly a lack of research and information—just as we do today, they did the best they could with the information they had.

Now that we have a better understanding of how developing minds understand and process emotions, we can be more sensitive to those needs, and we need to also be careful that we don't swing that pendulum too far the other way to try to prevent hard feelings or experiences—the everyone-gets-a-trophy approach. There's a middle ground where kids experience hard things and then have a safe adult and a safe space to express, be with, and move through their feelings without rushing them away. That's what we'll be working toward in these pages.

Knowing that many of us grew up in spaces where emotional vulnerability was discouraged, it makes so much sense that we feel discomfort watching our children experience hard things. Of course it's difficult for us to hold space and allow them to feel, because many of us aren't even sure how to do that for ourselves. I wish I could go back in time and let my parents know that they didn't have to try to prevent me from feeling the hard stuff. You can't prevent it. You can't wish it away or plaster on a smile and hope the sadness disappears.

Though I can't go back to tell them that, I can share that message with myself and with you. We don't have to control every experience our children have; we don't have to prevent them from experiencing pain. We don't have to, and we can't. They will try out for the basketball team and not make it. They will be left out from a classmate's birthday party. They will navigate conflict with their peers. They will feel and experience many different emotions during these pivotal years. Our job is to be in it with them and to teach them how to cope—not to make it go away.

When Jason refused to go to school after learning he didn't make the team, his outburst was a symptom of the underlying emotional pain. He didn't need to be reminded that he had to go to school; he needed his parents to understand that he was experiencing something really hard. He needed them to allow him to feel those hard feelings, and be in the experience with him. Maybe he needed to hear his mom say, "Bud, I saw how hard you worked at tryouts tonight. It really stinks to work hard and not make the team. It makes sense to feel overwhelmed about going to school tomorrow. I'm here to help you through it."

There's another important component to Jason's story. In addition to worrying about the tryouts and what potentially not making the team would mean for him socially, he was in conflict with his parents. When they let him know at dinner it was almost time to get ready to leave the house, he ignored them. When it was time to get dressed, he turned it into an argument. He shouted at his mom and slammed a door in her face. He didn't listen or cooperate for most of the process. This is another hallmark of middle childhood. Suddenly, our child's world doesn't revolve around us anymore and as a result there is more pushback, more fighting for independence, more complex behavior challenges.

Brain Development During Middle Childhood

When toddlers and preschoolers are defiant or disrespectful, we have the neuroscience to explain it. They don't have well-developed impulse control yet, so even when they know they shouldn't do or say something, they truly can't stop themselves. They need us to co-regulate with them, to hold boundaries, to physically stop them from hitting, kicking, and biting.

In middle childhood, children enter a new realm. The brain of a child in this developmental period does have the capability to control impulses sometimes, like door slamming or shouting at a parent. Note the word *sometimes*. The part of the brain responsible for impulse control, the prefrontal cortex, is still quite underdeveloped during this stage of childhood. The bulk of its development happens in adolescence. So while it's possible for kids in middle childhood to access self-control, they're exercising a part of their brain that is years away from full maturation. With that in mind, it makes sense that they still need our scaffolding and support to regulate and respond with intention. We have a whole chapter on how to respond to disrespect and defiance, both in the moment and outside of it, to give your child tools to thrive in the world and in their relationship with you.

How and Where Can I Express Emotions?

Kids are learning how and where they can feel and express emotions both at home and out in the world. The goal is for them to know that all feelings are welcome and that not all expressions of those feelings are acceptable. We add another layer of complexity with the concept that some expressions are okay in certain environments and not in others.

When they're angry, how do we want them to express that anger?

Are we okay with them shouting at us and slamming a door in our face?

What do we want them to do instead?

What are we modeling for them when we're angry?

Leila is a kind, thoughtful, emotionally attuned fourth grader. She is increasingly aware of how her peers perceive her and worried about standing out or being different. She really wants to be liked and to be accepted in her social sphere.

It's soccer season and a game day. Leila is getting ready for school and needs to pack her uniform in her backpack. She can only find her shorts. Her mom agrees to look for the shirt and bring it to the game that afternoon. Leila heads off to school.

Leila's mom can't find the uniform shirt. She finds a different shirt that is the same color and brings it to the game. The coach isn't concerned and says the other shirt is fine. Leila's mom is thinking, *No big deal—we'll find the uniform shirt later and this will work for today. Maybe it'll even be a teaching moment about taking more responsibility for your things.*

She brings the shirt to Leila and tells her to go change. Leila shouts at her, "WHAT?! I can't wear that! I need my uniform shirt." The teachers and students in the hallway at school notice the shouting and turn to watch. Leila's mom tries to quietly reassure her that the coach said it was okay, and it's only one game. It will be fine. "IT'S NOT FINE!" Leila yells. She bursts into tears and runs away from her mom and into the bathroom.

Leila's mom goes into the bathroom to try to figure out what is going on. Leila tells her, "Mom, I can't wear that. I NEED my uniform shirt. I'm not going to play in that stupid shirt!"

Leila's behavior in this story is a great illustration of what kids are observing and learning about themselves, their emotions, and the social implications of experiencing a conflict like this in front of others. We're going to look deeper at two parts of this interaction between Leila and her mom: Leila's need to feel a sense of belonging with her peers, and her understanding of what emotional expression is acceptable in front of them.

When Leila's uniform shirt went missing, her mom did her best to figure out a quick solution and ran it by her coach. To her—and probably to you—this seems like it is not a problem, right? It's just one game, and the shirt was the same color and style—most people probably wouldn't even notice the difference.

But that's not how Leila saw it. I remember one morning in my early twenties: I was getting ready for work. I was running late and couldn't find my blazer. I was feeling a ton of pressure to look put together because this was a new job and my boss and coworkers always looked extremely professional. I tore our apartment apart looking for the missing blazer. When my husband suggested that I just wear a blouse instead, I shouted at him and started crying out of frustration. Sure, it was just a blazer. And to him and most outsiders, it probably didn't seem like a big deal. But the real reason I was so upset wasn't because of the blazer; it was really about wanting to feel like I belonged at my job, like I was good enough for this new position, like I was worthy of respect. My husband's well-meaning attempt to reassure me sent me over the edge. I didn't feel like he really understood the situation or how high the stakes felt for me at that moment.

My blazer is Leila's uniform. Yes, it's just a uniform jersey; yes, it's just one game. But it's also so much more than that for Leila. It's about her need to feel accepted by her peers, to fit in, to belong. That need for belonging felt so acute for Leila in that moment that the thought of standing out or looking different sent her over the edge.

Let's take a deeper look at another aspect of this situation. At the suggestion of wearing a different shirt, Leila shouted at her mom. Her teachers and classmates, who were in the hallway at the same time, all stopped and turned to watch. When Leila started crying, she ran away from her mom and into the bathroom.

I think back to when my kids were toddlers, and they were losing it in the grocery store. They would yell, cry, even scream. People would sometimes stop and look. My toddlers didn't notice or care if people were watching. They were swept up in those big feelings, and while they certainly wanted me to notice and support them, the eyes or opinions of others weren't even on their radar. Not so for kids in middle childhood. The eyes and opinions of others are 100 percent on their radar; in fact, they might be the only thing on their radar sometimes.

While a younger child may have started crying from frustration and then reached out to their parents for support, Leila started crying and ran away from her mom. Leila is learning that crying is acceptable only in certain environments. Perhaps she's noticed that when her classmates cry at school, other kids make fun of them. In a dream world, any human would be able to cry anytime they felt sad. In our world, that's not the reality. There are social consequences for certain types of emotional expression. We're going to dive deep into this in Chapter 7 as we look at peer pressure and social belonging more closely.

In this book we are going to tackle the challenges of middle childhood together and we're going to do it in a way that's never been done before. Yes, you'll leave with tools for navigating the tough behaviors, the social challenges, the complex emotional changes, and everything in between, but you'll leave with much more than that.

We're going to dive into the neuroscience of behavior, the why behind all the tough stuff we see at this age. Middle childhood is often overlooked, while there are a ton of resources for navigating adolescence. When we skip over this important period of development, kids and parents enter adolescence without the tools they need. Middle childhood is the time to build a foundation of connection and collaboration in preparation for adolescence. We build these skills now so that as our kids continue to change and grow, we've got a toolbox to pull from.

Chapter 1

What Is Emotional Intelligence?

E motional intelligence has become such a buzzword. How cool is that? We get to raise kids in a time when people are talking about this stuff—stuff that in my childhood was chalked up to things like defiance and disrespect from children, and a caregiver's lack of control over a kid's behavior. As jazzed as I am about emotional intelligence hitting the zeitgeist, we need to back up a little and chat about what it even is, what it means, and how it shows up in everyday life.

A relatively new term, *emotional intelligence* was defined by Daniel Goleman in 1995 as "the capacity for recognizing our own feelings and those of others, for motivating ourselves, and for managing emotions well in ourselves and in our relationships."[1] We break his definition into five components: self-awareness, self-regulation, empathy, motivation, and social skills.

Emotional Intelligence: A Skill Set to Navigate Your Internal World

When you envision what you want your children to be like as adults, you may yearn for kind humans who know how to control their words and body and who can navigate social spheres and situations. Or, as my dear friend put it, "I'm just trying not to raise a jerk." We want kids who will ultimately be able to navigate the world outside of themselves, but in order to do that they need to develop a skill set for navigating their internal world first.

Self-Awareness, Self-Regulation, Self-Control

When I was eleven years old, I was kicked out of Mrs. Joliet's English lesson for rolling my eyes. When I got home and my mom asked me about it, I told her, "Mom, I'm literally not in control of my face." "Well, no one else is, Alyssa, so you're going to have to get in control of your face," she replied. She wasn't wrong. I was responsible for my words and actions, but the logistics of *how* to get in control of my face seemed impossible.

Part of my struggle was that I lacked self-awareness over my body and the way it responded to and interacted with my environment. How do you get in control of something you don't even know is happening? This is why self-awareness is the key to developing the other components of emotional intelligence. When we can notice what is happening inside of our bodies as we are experiencing it, then, and only then, can we regulate our nervous system to choose how to respond.

At age eleven, I wasn't aware of the signs that always preceded my eye roll: my heart starting to race, my armpits growing sweaty, my face getting red, and my jaw tightening. In fact, it wasn't until I was an adult, in my mid-twenties, that I started to build the self-awareness skills to notice those internal signals that said, "Buckle up, an eye roll [or choose your behavior here: sassy comment/sarcasm] is on the horizon." If we want to see a shift in children's behaviors, it's imperative that we start by building their self-awareness of what's happening inside their body before the behavior explodes on the surface. We will dive deep into this later in the book—stay tuned.

Self-awareness is essential to hone the ability to pause after our initial, unconscious reaction to a trigger, and then consciously manage our response. That ability to pause is the difference between our reactive self and our responsive self. Once we've honed this self-awareness skill and can notice that initial reaction that's out of our control, we can focus on what *is* in our control by regulating the nervous system so we can access the ability to choose our words or behavior.

Let's head back to Mrs. Joliet's English class. The assignment was to write and give a presentation with an in-depth analysis of a character of our choosing from *Charlotte's Web*, which we'd read as a class. I'd worked hard on my poster board for the presentation and rehearsed my prepared speech over and over, riddled with anxiety about having to read it in front of the class. When it was my turn, and I was in the middle of reading "Templeton was very selfless," Mrs. Joliet chimed in to correct me, "Do you mean selfish?" The rush of embarrassment surged, my face got red, my heart pounded, and every part of my body oozed sweat . . . then I rolled my eyes, "Yeah, whatever, selfish, I mean," I said anxiously, wanting to be anywhere but in front of the whole class feeling like the dumbest human on the planet. "Head into the hallway, Ms. Blask. We don't do eye rolls here," she said, ejecting me from the spotlight.

The goal of becoming more self-aware isn't to change our initial reaction (the red face, pounding heart, sweat of embarrassment) but to recognize the signs; once we notice those cues, we can learn how to regulate the physiological reaction enough to choose our response. In other words, in order to prevent that eye roll and the "whatever" in my response, I needed to be able to notice my physical sensations and catch that pause after my physiological symptoms surfaced so that I could control my next response. Self-regulation is the key to preventing that spiral further into dysregulation or distress. I needed to build in self-regulation tools in order to cope with my feelings in that moment. Only after the awareness and regulation pieces were in place would I be able to access self-control. Expecting kids to demonstrate self-control without first nurturing their self-awareness and self-regulation is like asking them to read before teaching them the alphabet. Throughout this book, we'll offer strategies to help kids build these essential skills, tailored to meet their unique needs, so they can foster the ability to make intentional choices instead of being driven by automatic reactions.

Learning to self-regulate is not a one-size-fits-all process—what works with one child may not with another. We will support you with different techniques to build this skill throughout this book.

Understanding Empathy

Empathy doesn't just happen—it's built on a foundation of self-awareness, self-regulation, and self-control. To really connect with someone else's feelings, we first have to understand and manage our own. If we're not self-aware, it's hard to notice how our emotions or actions affect others. If we're not able to regulate those emotions, big feelings can take over and leave no room for anyone else's experience. And without self-control, we might react impulsively in ways that shut down connection. These skills all work together to help us show up with empathy, which is key to building strong relationships and navigating the world with kindness.

My husband recently worked really hard on a bid project, dedicating hours to preparing it after the kids went to bed and into the weekends. After all that time and work, his bid was not chosen. Not long after, I overheard a conversation between him and a nine-year-old child in our life who plays travel soccer, who had shared how disappointed and upset he was after his team lost the season. "Oh man, that stinks, buddy. I've seen you out back practicing and working your butt off. I'm sorry your season ended that way."

Think about how you might have responded in this conversation: It's nine-year-olds' travel soccer. As an adult, it might be easy to dismiss this and say, "It's no big deal; you'll get them next season." From an adult perspective, a child's soccer league may not be perceived as important as a business deal that, after all, has real-world financial and professional ramifications. But to the nine-year-old child who put hours into training and competing, losing the season was, indeed, a very big deal and a major disappointment.

After my husband's recent failed bid, he knew what it felt like to work hard at something and not have it pan out the way you wanted. Fostering empathy in children begins with responding to them in an empathetic way. This doesn't mean absorbing their emotions or solving their problems for them. To truly show empathy, we must first recognize and manage our own emotions, allowing us to be present with our child as they navigate their feelings. It's so easy in the hustle and bustle of everyday life to look at a child's problems and dismiss them as minor or inconsequential in comparison to the challenges we face as adults. If we want children to grow up to be empathetic adults, it starts in childhood with the small stuff. Because the small stuff isn't small to them.

In this book we will dive into myriad ways to foster empathy in your child, but one key distinction to make up front is that it's not our job to decide if someone should be experiencing the emotion they're feeling. It's not our job to judge whether or not that child should be upset about not winning the soccer tournament. They're already feeling it. We get to empathize with what they're feeling, not why they're feeling it.

A Growth Mindset

A growth mindset is the belief that through learning, hard work, and persistence, we can develop new skills, talents, and knowledge. Carol Dweck's work on growth mindset illustrates that praising children's intelligence—"You're so smart" or "You are really good at math"—can decrease children's intrinsic motivation.[2] Dweck also highlights that praising effort—"You tried really hard on that" or "When you couldn't figure that out, you did a great job continuing to try different ways to make it work"—can increase motivation.

Why is this important? Dweck's research showed that the kids who were praised for their intelligence self-selected only easy problems they knew they would succeed at in order to continue to get the praise for the outcome. However, the kids who received the effort praise were more likely to choose harder problems they knew would continue to teach them more. They felt secure in taking a risk, making mistakes, and continuing to try and problem-solve because they knew their value wasn't connected to the end result. They were less focused on being perfect and more focused on continuing to grow and learn.

When we use tools like reward systems to try and get a specific outcome—"If you are quiet in the hall every day, then at the end of the week you get to pick from the prize jar"—we will see temporary change when the adult is looking, but it rarely leads to long-term skills or behavior change. Kids working for the prize jar will learn to be quiet when adults are around as long as there is a prize at the end of the week. Take away the prize or turn the adult's gaze and the behavior will pick right back up.

The goal is to foster intrinsic motivation instead. In this book, you will learn how to instill intrinsic motivation so that the kids are quiet in the hall because they want to be respectful of their peers, who are trying to learn in the other classrooms. Extrinsic motivation asks, "Are you proud of me?" Intrinsic motivation says, "I'm proud of me." This is a mindset that will benefit your child for life.

Social Skills

One area of emotional intelligence that is in the forefront for this age group is social skills. Babies start off focused only on themselves, toddlers move into parallel play near other humans, preschoolers move into learning how to engage in collaborative play with peers, but it's in the kindergarten to fifth-grade range where inclusion and belonging become crucial to survival. Research has demonstrated that kids who feel a sense of community or school belonging are less likely to experience suicidal ideation.[3] As kids are in this phase, we get to help them learn when certain behaviors are appropriate and when they aren't. We get to foster the skills necessary for them to connect with others while getting to know themselves more. Social skills will guide them through the foundations of being in relationships with other people and learning how to find their inner moral compass in those relationships. Buckle up, because we are going to dive deep into social skills with you.

When our children have the ability to notice what is happening in their body, gain control over their self-regulation experience, and are driven to continue to grow and evolve, then they can move through the world as kind, respectful, thoughtful, engaged people. Supporting a child's emotional intelligence shifts the way they are able to show up in relationship with the world at large, with you, and ultimately with themselves.

Attachment Theory

Our attachment to our primary caregivers forms the core of what we come to believe about the world around us and how we relate to it, especially relative to our physical and social safety and survival.

I recently watched a video of a competition with people who had to walk across a tightrope to reach a platform, and if they made it, they would get a luxury vacation and a large chunk of money. They were harnessed for safety, but otherwise free to fall off the rope. Their family members were on the home base platform and the prize was on the other platform; all they had to do was walk from one platform to the next without falling. At any point, they could push a button on their vest and be pulled back to safety with their family, giving up the prize. The first person started going, eyes on the prize, got partway, and then aborted the mission, pushing the button to return to safety.

As I watched each person navigate the tightrope, one thing was clear when they reached the platform—whether they went back to their family or made it to the prize: the look on their face said relief that they were safe and secure. This is a good way to think about attachment and how at the root of attachment is the question "Am I safe?"

John Bowlby and Mary Ainsworth were pioneers in attachment theory research, which shows that the way primary caregivers respond to their child's needs shapes the child's sense of safety and trust in relationships. This includes addressing emotional needs, such as how caregivers respond to a child's dysregulation and distress. These responses play a crucial role in shaping a child's understanding of emotions, their ability to experience and express feelings, and their sense of emotional safety.

There are four attachment patterns: secure, avoidant, resistant, and disorganized, which we'll explain in greater depth in a moment.

In her book *Raising Securely Attached Kids*, licensed therapist Eli Harwood outlines the ways that a child's attachment pattern affects the way they process emotions and interpret their environment.

Secure attachment means you feel like you can turn to your parents with your hard stuff and they can handle it. You know what to expect from them because they've consistently shown up for and with you when you were in distress. As Eli puts it, "We learned to *reach* and *receive* when we were upset, scared, or in a state of distress."

Avoidant attachment happens when you have parents who consistently respond in a way that is anxious, cold, or dismissive. When the going gets tough, they are not there to support you. You know what to expect from them, but what you can't expect is for your emotional needs to be met.

Resistant (often referred to as anxious) attachment is marked by inconsistency. You aren't sure if your parents will be warm and welcoming or anxious, cold, or dismissive. You don't know what to expect. Because they are unpredictable, you learn not to share your hard stuff with them because they might not be able to handle it.

Disorganized attachment occurs when your parents or primary caregivers are a threat to your safety. The threats can include abuse, neglect, trauma, or chaos in the home. When faced with a threat, you learn to shut off, disconnect, and get as quiet and small as possible when facing tough feelings or challenges, or you blow up, assert dominance, and try to appear as big and powerful as possible. While all attachment patterns can be changed with work and intention, disorganized attachment is the hardest to alter.

All these attachment reactions are about safety. The child is learning, *When am I physically, socially, and emotionally safe?* Attachment patterns create a set of rules we believe and apply to all our relationships, even outside of our parents and caregivers. If it isn't safe to be vulnerable at home with the people who are supposed to love us unconditionally, then is it safe anywhere?

Our goal in this book is to help you nurture a secure attachment relationship with your child. If you didn't grow up that way, you're not alone—it's estimated that only about 50 percent of us grew up with secure attachment. Luckily, it's never too late to shift attachment patterns, especially because we often repeat what we know and experienced in our own childhood (or swing the pendulum to another insecure attachment pattern). Throughout this book, we will support you with ways to nurture a secure attachment relationship so that when your kids experience hard things they run to you, not away from you.

Connecting with Your Child

When we feel connected in our relationships, we are able to feel safe, leading to increased collaboration and cooperation. Connection, however, is not one size fits all. Early on in our relationship, my husband wrote sticky notes and put them in places I would pass in my morning routine. They said things like, "I love how much you care about the world" and "The world needs what you have to offer. Remember to take up space." Now, with two kids and busy lives, those sticky notes look like little texts here and there that say, "Hey, thanks for taking care of the kids' summer camp scheduling. I'm grateful to get to figure this out with you." These notes fill my cup. I feel loved, valued, and seen when I read them. But if I reached out to him with thoughtful touchpoints like those, even though he would appreciate them, it isn't what fills him up the most. We have a connection mismatch; my preferred way of receiving connection isn't his. I have to be mindful and intentional to connect with him in the way he needs, not the way that I need and that feels the most natural to me. Everyone gives and receives connection in different ways, and this can apply to our kids too. When there's a mismatch with them, it can be easy to miss the mark or feel like they're not seeing or appreciating our bids for connection.

Think of it this way: every human has their own unique "connection blueprint"—a way of feeling seen, valued, and loved that's deeply personal to who they are. Our role as parents is to become compassionate "detectives," curious and open to discovering what makes each child feel

Examples of Connection

- **Let them be the expert:** Show interest in something they're into and let them teach you. "You know way more about Pokémon than I do—can you show me how to play your favorite one?"

- **Move together:** Get active in a way they enjoy, whether it's a bike ride, hike, or shooting hoops. It's a good way to connect without too much pressure to talk.

- **Learn a new skill together:** Try following drawing tutorials, practicing a new sport, or making new food together.

- **Ask them interesting questions:** Encourage them to open up by showing you're interested in their ideas. "If you could create your own class at school, what would it be about?"

- **Reminisce together:** Share your favorite memories about what they played, words they said, or things you did together. "When you were two, you would say 'boo-berries' instead of 'blueberries'! We would buy blueberries just to hear you say the word. We loved it so much."

connected. There's no single formula for love and connection that works for every child; instead, connection comes from meeting our child where they are and engaging in ways that resonate with their unique personality, interests, and experiences.

You might notice, for instance, that one child lights up when you spend one-on-one time together, while another feels most secure through physical affection or words of affirmation. Rather than relying on categories or assumptions, you can take cues from your child's everyday behaviors and reactions, listening carefully to what they're trying to communicate. This might mean experimenting—offering quality time, shared activities, or gentle words of encouragement—and observing what resonates for them. With this mindset, connection isn't about "getting it right" every time;

it's about staying curious, open, and willing to try different approaches to deepen understanding.

What's even more important is that our child's needs may change over time. As they grow, the ways they experience love and security may shift, and when we remain adaptable, we're showing them that connection is a constant but evolving part of our relationship. Building this foundation means tuning in to their individuality and meeting them where they are, which in turn teaches them that they are worthy of love just as they are.

What's powerful about this approach is that it can grow with our child over time. Our child's needs aren't fixed—they're likely to change as they grow. The ways they feel secure or connected will evolve, and our flexibility as parents helps us keep up with these changes. By staying open and curious, we build a relationship that adapts and deepens over time. This foundation, grounded in meeting our child where they are, also shows the child that they are valued and loved just as they are, at every stage.

Why Does This Matter?

My daughter wouldn't stop antagonizing my son. I'd told her at least five times to leave him alone, but she wouldn't. I was running out of patience. "Okay, since you won't listen to me, you're off screens for the day tomorrow," I said.

Later, after my kids were in bed for the night, I was thinking about my daughter and *why in the world* she wouldn't leave her brother alone. How many times did I have to ask her? As I thought about it, I realized something. My daughter has a high need for connection. It's almost like filling a leaky cup. Every day, she asks for playdates or to see her friends. Her nervous system is regulated when she's connected to other people. My son recharges with alone time, so their needs are in opposition.

She wasn't intentionally bothering him or being defiant, she was trying to get her needs met. Sure, taking away screen time got her to stop for today, but what about tomorrow when she is seeking connection again? She'll go right back to bugging her brother to try to get him to connect with her. The punishment wasn't going to teach her how to meet that need in a way that worked for our family, and it would also cause a cycle of frustration—the more she tried to meet this need for connection, the more I'd continue to try to punish her without changing the behavior for the long term. By getting frustrated and exasperated by her bid for connection and punishing her for it, I was inadvertently sending her the message that her needs were inconvenient and unwelcome, that she'd better suppress those needs or else I'd be taking things away from her.

There's an alternative to this cycle of frustration though—and it lies in emotional intelligence. If I could help her identify when her nervous system was asking for connection through building self-awareness skills, and give her options for how to meet that need (come talk to me, ask to FaceTime a friend, etc.), then she would have a skill set for the next time it came up.

Research shows that parents are the primary predictor of their child's level of emotional intelligence.[4] How we respond *does* matter. When we help kids cultivate EI, we set them up for positive outcomes across the board. Kids with higher levels of EI are more likely to succeed academically,[5] less likely to engage in risky sexual behaviors,[6] less likely to use drugs,[7] less likely to be victims of bullying,[8] and less likely to experience anxiety and depression.[9]

Now, I want to be clear: I didn't screw up my kid when I took her screens away. Was it in alignment with my values as a parent? No. Did it fracture our relationship and jeopardize her emotional wellness? Also no. Building emotional intelligence in our children is not about responding with intention *every time*. That's not possible and it's not even the goal. Part of building these skills for our kids is modeling them, and that includes modeling what it looks like to make mistakes and navigate repair. Conflict and mistakes will be a part of your relationship with your child.

Dr. John Gottman is a psychologist and researcher known for his groundbreaking work on emotional intelligence and connection. His work emphasizes the importance of communication, emotional attunement, and conflict resolution in building strong, lasting relationships. In his book *Raising an Emotionally Intelligent Child*, Gottman shows that even when parents do not respond with intention and attunement all of the time, they can still build emotional intelligence and cultivate positive outcomes for their children. I like to think of this work as a practice. Never will I ever get to a point in my parenting where I'm like, "Okay, I did it. I'm emotionally intelligent and so are my kids so we're never going to experience conflict or mess up again." That's not the reality of being a human. Yes, the way we respond matters. It matters in a big way *and* it's important to know that hiccups and mess-ups are all a part of it.

When we can support our kids with tools for self-awareness, self-regulation, empathy, social skills, and motivation, it shifts how they will experience life and the challenges to come. Nearly one in three teens ages thirteen through eighteen experiences an anxiety disorder.[10] Equipping our kids with a skill set to understand how their brain and body work, how to navigate their emotions, and what to do when they experience something hard—from failing a test to being made fun of at school to traumatic events—is truly life changing. They can navigate the ebbs and flows of relationships and learn how to have healthy conflict. They can build skills for perseverance, resilience, and grit. They can learn that the goal isn't the absence of hard things, but rather the tools to navigate whatever comes their way in life. Once they cultivate self-awareness about their own feelings and insecurities, they can learn to recognize these same feelings in others, and learn what to do when those insecurities are projected onto them. We can raise humans whom we continue to be in relationship with and who know they have a safe place to turn to when they need it. This book will help you strengthen your tools for emotional intelligence alongside your child's. The future is emotionally intelligent, and you are raising the future.

Chapter 2

Helping Children Understand and Process Their Emotions

It was my least favorite time of day. The hours between four and eight p.m. in our house on weeknights can be a real doozy. I had just wrapped up a really busy day at work, picked up the kids from school, and was diving into dinner prep. Usually, I try to wrap up work early enough that I can eat a snack and have ten minutes of quiet time before getting into the after-school routine. This day I had been so focused on a task at work that I didn't have time for anything other than sprinting out the door. I barely made it to school on time for dismissal.

I'd gotten us home and was standing at the counter chopping dinner ingredients while my kids alternated between talking to me and playing with each other (read: arguing, fighting over toys, and yelling at each other). I washed their lunch boxes while I waited for their pasta to cook. The pasta timer went off and I drained it and threw the sauce on while refereeing yet another argument. I felt like I was on a timer, just waiting for a bomb to go off. I was always rushing to get dinner done before the kids got hangry and started snagging snacks that would spoil their appetite for dinner. I was interrupted approximately ten thousand times by the dog and the fighting. I was already hangry myself. My husband texted me to let me know he was running late. *Great*, I thought to myself sarcastically. I plated our dinners and sat down with the kids. I'd missed the cutoff and they were cranky. They complained about what I'd made for dinner. Requests for ketchup, ranch, and for me to pick out the "green stuff" were coming at me faster than I could respond. I hadn't even taken a bite of dinner yet.

My husband walked in the door and although I was irritated that he was late, I breathed a sigh of relief. I had backup! I could tap out if I needed to. I could eat my dinner and not be a waitress for a minute. Or so I thought. He told me something had come up at work that he still hadn't finished, and he needed me to tackle bath- and bedtime prep with the kids. Typically, this would be no big deal—we both work, and this comes up from time to time for both of us. But in that moment, I was pushed over an edge I didn't even realize I was teetering on. I lost it. I got snappy and sarcastic and rude. I stormed out of the kitchen—my dinner untouched and my kids looking at their dad like, *What is happening?!*

We've all been there, right? It's the perfect storm of overstimulation, hunger, and unmet expectations. I was mentally drained that day, and my kids' fighting and noise was further draining me. I hadn't eaten before school pickup, and I was hungry. I was trying to meet the needs of my kids while ignoring my own. Then I expected my husband (who had no idea I was feeling overwhelmed) to meet those needs, and when he couldn't, I lost it on him. I'm in my thirties, I've been working on building my emotional toolbox for fifteen-plus years, in therapy and with other modalities, and I still lost my cool. I spoke really unkindly to my husband while my children watched. I have the brain development and emotional intelligence to respond with intention and yet I didn't. I was operating on autopilot, didn't pay attention to the warning signs in my body, and couldn't access self-control when I was triggered.

Think back to a time when you've yelled, snapped, or shouted. What led up to that moment? What needs were unmet? Why didn't you have the capacity to respond with intention at that moment? Now think about your child. When they are snappy, rude, or they shout, what is your assumption? Do you find them defiant? Disrespectful? Do you find yourself thinking that they're too old to behave that way? That they should know better? You're not alone. Culturally, we tend to accept the idea that adults sometimes lose their cool because they're under-resourced, but when children lose their cool, we default to disrespect and defiance. Let's look at the science of self-control together.

Self-Awareness, Self-Regulation, and Self-Control

Before we can access self-control, we need to be able to self-regulate. Before we can self-regulate, we need to be aware of our dysregulation. If we want our children to move through the world with intention, it starts with these skills.

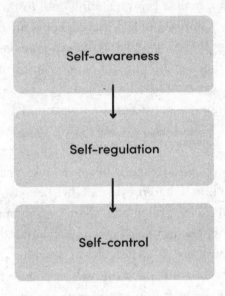

Self-awareness is the ability to recognize different body sensations and, sometimes, the emotions that are driving them. In my case, if I had paused to notice what was happening in my body, I would have felt that I was hangry and overstimulated. I would've noticed my stomach pulling, my agitation increasing, my shoulders raising toward my ears, and my jaw clenching. Instead, I was operating on autopilot, powering through, and I missed the signs.

Many of us come into adulthood believing that hard emotions are bad, something to be avoided, based on the way we were raised. Think about a time you were upset as a child. How did the adults in your life respond to you? Many of us were taught to suppress, to distract, and to mask—to put on a happy face for the comfort of others. With that in mind, it makes sense that when we're operating on autopilot, we default to trying to suppress our emotions. Until we can't anymore. Until they come exploding out of us. Many of us are still learning what it feels like when those hard emotions are building because we've gotten so good at trying to pretend that we aren't feeling them. It's okay to not be okay.

Once we're aware of what's happening in our inner world, when we're both recognizing and allowing the feeling, then we can work toward self-regulation. Self-regulation is the ability to create a pause between the initial reaction and the response. What does this look like in the moment? Let's think back to my losing my cool on my husband. In the absence of self-regulation, I defaulted to an autopilot reaction—it happened subconsciously. Before I even realized it, I was loud, snappy, and rude.

What would this have looked like if I'd self-regulated? First, it requires self-awareness. I notice my heart beating fast, my voice speeding up. Ahh, I'm overstimulated and annoyed that my expectation of tag-teaming the evening with my husband was not met. Once aware of how I am feeling, I can practice self-regulation, the ability to pause between my initial internal reaction and the thought to take ownership over what happens next. Self-regulation allows us to move out of autopilot and to consciously choose how we want to move forward. Perhaps I could have paused and taken a couple of deep breaths. Maybe I could have focused my attention on the floor beneath my feet, the feeling of the chair supporting my body, and grounded myself in the present moment. There are many strategies for self-regulation, and we'll cover them in depth in the next chapter, with real-life ways to do this work for yourself and with your child.

Self-regulation and self-control

Self-regulation and self-control are often used interchangeably; they are linked, but they are two distinct processes. Self-regulation is the inner work of creating space between the stimulus and the response. It's the literal calming so you can choose what happens next. Self-control is the act of choosing to respond with intention. For me in that moment with my husband, self-control would have involved making the choice to speak with kindness and respect to him. Rather than get snappy and sarcastic, a self-controlled response might have sounded like, "Hey, I'm feeling over-whelmed and hungry right now. I need to step away and eat my dinner in the quiet, and then I can come back and tackle bath- and bedtime. Can you tap in for dinner with the kids and then wrap up your work after?" or "Before you head back into work mode, I need five minutes by myself. Can you please tap in here?"

Sometimes we encounter a mindset from parents when it comes to kids' emotions and meltdowns that we as parents shouldn't "feed into" their tantrums. This is rooted in the idea that if we pay attention to our children's hard feelings, we will reinforce the challenging behaviors that often accompany them. Imagine if you were having a tough day and you snapped at your partner. Now imagine that your partner refuses to talk about your experience and emotions because they don't want to "feed into" you losing your cool. Having your partner ignore or shame your hard feelings doesn't help you to not lose your cool again, it just makes you feel alone in your experience. If our goal is for kids to be self-aware humans, we have to allow their hard feelings to exist so that they can learn to recognize them in their bodies. They (and you) aren't failing for feeling.

There are two aspects of this thought process to break down and exam-ine. First, it conflates hard emotions and dysregulation with undesirable behaviors. Although we often see difficult behaviors arise during a child's hard emotions, the two are not the same. A child isn't slamming the door because they're frustrated. They're slamming the door because they're frustrated and they are still learning how to notice frustration when it's building (self-awareness) and how to find the pause to regulate their body (self-regulation). Without those two foundational skill sets, they can't choose their words and actions (self-control). Second, it relies upon the idea that ignoring challenging behaviors (and the underlying emotion and need) will make the behavior stop. The truth is that when we ignore a child's challenging behaviors during a meltdown, what we are actually ignoring are the emotion and need that are driving the behavior. We can ignore, punish, or shame behavior all day long, but if our child doesn't have the skills to navigate those hard emotions, the challenging behaviors will inevitably pop up again. When we ignore, we are simply showing

What we see:
An eight-year-old uses a strong attitude, "talking back" to their parent.

What we don't see:
The child hasn't eaten for three hours, is overwhelmed with the school day transitions, and is feeling disappointed about missing out on a playdate.

them what *not to do* without equipping them with the tools for what *to do*. Instead, we can teach kids the skills to understand their emotions so that rather than suppressing them, they can recognize them, regulate, and access self-control. The first step in learning to accept your child's emotions is to separate the dysregulation and emotion from the behavior.

Spotting the Need Behind the Behavior

Mateo is a highly energetic and social ten-year-old boy. He loves to connect with others, talk, and play. He thrives in a big group of peers. Mateo has a five-year-old younger sister, Rosie. His sister is quieter, more cautious, and prefers to play alone or in a small group. Her social battery drains quickly, and you'll often find her seeking respite in her room to recharge.

Mateo's parents were becoming increasingly frustrated because their afternoons and evenings had become dominated by Mateo's demands and disruptions. When Mateo's mom picked him up from school, she found herself dreading the car ride home. From the time Mateo got in the car until they were home, he would antagonize Rosie, trying to get her to respond to him. He would pinch her, flick her arm, or whisper things that would get under her skin. It wasn't unusual for Rosie to be crying out of frustration by the time they got home.

Mateo's mom would attempt to separate the kids when they got home to give each one some time to decompress, but Mateo hated it. He would shout at his mom and repeatedly slam his bedroom door. He would come out of his room and try to negotiate with her. She would eventually let the kids play together again, and before long, Mateo was antagonizing and Rosie was crying.

If Mateo wasn't trying to get a rise out of Rosie, he was making demands of his parents. If his mom was trying to make dinner, he would ask her to do things or get things for him, and if she asked him to wait, he would get into something he wasn't supposed to. If his dad was home, Mateo expected his undivided attention regardless of what else was going on or what responsibilities his dad might have to attend to. If he didn't get his way with his parents, he would go back to teasing Rosie.

It felt like Mateo needed constant supervision or things would go off the rails. His parents were mentally exhausted by it and frustrated that at ten years old, he was still acting this way. It sometimes felt like they were dealing with a three-year-old, not a ten-year-old! They talked to Mateo, read to him, and played games with him. They made sure to spend quality time with him, but it felt like pouring their efforts into a leaky cup. It was never enough. They began to resent Mateo's behaviors and found themselves wanting to spend less time connecting with him. It became a cycle: Mateo asking for attention, his parents feeling frustrated about it and giving him less attention, and Mateo asking for attention in ways that were more and more triggering for his parents.

We are often triggered by a child's behavior, assigning meaning to it from our social programming and childhood experiences. We see behaviors and we have a default reaction to them before we even notice that it's happening. Mateo's parents saw his behaviors as attention seeking. They felt he was disruptive, demanding, and antagonistic. They began to resent the behaviors and pull away from Mateo, which ultimately resulted in his exhibiting more difficult behaviors. When he asked them to play, they found themselves responding with things like, "Well, if we weren't constantly breaking up fights between you and Rosie, we'd have a lot more time to play with you."

Let's look at Mateo's story through a different lens. All behavior is communicating a need. When we see attention-seeking behaviors, what we are really seeing is connection seeking. Humans are social animals. Social connection is a physiological need. How much connection we need depends on how our nervous systems work—we'll dive into this in the next chapter! Mateo is asking his parents to help him get his needs met in a million frustrating and inconvenient ways. When we were working with Mateo's parents, his mom expressed that sometimes it was hard for her to view connection as a valid need. Intellectually she could understand that all humans need connection, but in the moment with Mateo she found herself annoyed. She felt inconvenienced. She was struggling to meet his needs because she was still caught up in the behavior and, frankly, didn't want to connect with him in those moments. As we dove deeper, Mateo's mom shared that when she had been seeking connection in her childhood, her needs were dismissed. She was labeled as dramatic and demanding. She was ignored or punished for seeking attention. She began to believe that her need for connection was a want, not a need.

Mateo's mom is not alone. Many of us were raised with narratives around attention-seeking behaviors. Many of us did not have our connection needs met because they weren't recognized as needs. We were labeled or shamed or punished. It makes sense that Mateo's mom was triggered. Unknowingly, Mateo's need for connection was bringing her painful childhood experience to the surface. When Mateo sought connection, she didn't see a physiological need, she saw a dramatic and demanding child because that was the messaging she had received in her own childhood.

What comes up for you when you think of the need for connection? Does it feel the same or different from the need to eat or sleep? Does it feel the same or different from the need to take a break from stimuli? The truth is that social connection is just as vital for our health as what we eat and how much sleep we get. In fact, former US Surgeon General Dr. Vivek H. Murthy has cited loneliness as an epidemic that is leading to devastating health outcomes: "[Loneliness] is associated with a greater risk of cardiovascular disease, dementia, stroke, depression, anxiety, and premature death. Its mortality effects are equivalent to smoking 15 cigarettes a day."[1] Over time, we've learned that connection is crucial for not just our mental wellness, but also our physical health. It's a need just as great as those of our physical body.

The goal isn't for children to stop having needs or expressing emotions. The goal is to help them build awareness around their needs and emotions so they can communicate them in a prosocial way. Mateo isn't antagonizing Rosie or annoying his parents because he wants to cause strife in his family. He is communicating in the only way he knows how. He needs support in building skills to express his needs in another way. Imagine how differently things would have gone in Mateo's family if instead of antagonizing his sister, he was able to go up to one of his parents and say, "I really need some connection right now." For a child to access that kind of self-control, they need to first build self-awareness and self-regulation skills.

The Collaborative Emotion Processing (CEP) Method

When it comes to building emotional intelligence in kids, Lauren Stauble—author, researcher, and early childhood educator who coauthored *Tiny Humans, Big Emotions* with me—and I found that the biggest factor is us, the adults showing up with these kids each day. Many of us didn't grow up in emotionally supportive households or cultures, learning how our brains process stimuli around us and what regulates our unique nervous systems. We often were taught to suppress versus express emotions and often felt responsible to help the adults in our lives stay or get regulated.

Lauren and I teamed up to co-create the Collaborative Emotion Processing (CEP) method and researched it with Angela Garcia, M.A., teacher and researcher, in 2018 to provide a guide for building adults' emotional intelligence alongside our kids'. Our findings suggested that, with training in CEP, teachers and parents become more aware of their emotions and/or there is an increase in the number of coping strategies that they know to offer young children. Teachers and parents reported being less overwhelmed when they were using the CEP method.

The CEP method is made up of five components, all with a foundation in mindfulness.

1. Self-awareness

Self-awareness is the ability to recognize and understand your own emotions, thoughts, and behaviors.

Imagine you've had a long, exhausting day at work, and when you get home, you feel irritable. You're thinking about all the things that you still need to do: cook dinner, pack lunches, spend time with your kids. Your partner comes into the room and asks you a question and you just *snap*. All your frustration and overwhelm comes exploding out of you.

Now reimagine the scenario. As you're thinking about dinner and packing lunches, you notice that your chest is feeling tight and your shoulders are tense. You notice that your body and mind need a minute before moving into the evening routine. Your partner walks over to you and asks you a question and you say, "Hey, I'm feeling really overwhelmed and tense at the moment. I need a few minutes to myself and then we can come back to this."

This is self-awareness—it helps you respond with intention rather than reacting automatically.

2. Uncovering implicit bias

Implicit bias refers to the unconscious attitudes or stereotypes that influence our perceptions, actions, and decisions without us being aware of them.

It was the first week of school and I was ushering my kids through the door at home. "Please empty your lunch boxes and put them in the sink," I said to them. My five-year-old started on the task, but my nine-year-old started to melt down. "I'm so tired! I just want to rest," she said. *Your brother is four years younger and he's doing it*, I thought to myself. That thought showed my implicit bias around age. There was a part of me that didn't feel compassion or grace for my daughter because I felt that she was old enough to handle the task. The truth is, she *is* old enough to handle the task, and outside of the stress of back-to-school, she takes care of her lunch box with no problem. It's not about her age but rather her regulation and capacity in the moment (stay tuned, we'll be diving deeper into regulation and capacity throughout this book).

Implicit biases are often in conflict with our explicit attitudes. I don't actually believe that nine years old is too old to have hard feelings, need a break, or have a low capacity for tasks, stimuli, or stress. However, social programming from my own childhood has created a bias around age that sometimes impacts my initial reaction. Implicit biases often pop up in adulthood around age, gender, race, socioeconomic status, physical appearance, ability, and more. You can find more about uncovering implicit biases on page 198.

3. Self-care

When we talk about self-care, we likely mean this in a different way than the self-care you've seen touted on social media.

As parents/caregivers we are stuck in a catch-22: we need self-care in order to effectively parent, and because we are parents it's hard to access effective self-care. Often, self-care is framed as a weekend away, a long luxurious bath, or a mani/pedi—most parents can't imagine finding the time or money to make those things happen. Self-care within the CEP framework is different; it focuses on nervous system regulation. Some simple ways to implement self-care in your daily routine: hydrate, eat enough food, find a way to move your body that feels good. Setting boundaries is also a form of self-care. Are there things you can say no to in order to create more space for your regulation? Scan the following QR code to take our quiz to better understand what you are sensitive to and what is regulating for you.

This quiz will help you customize self-care for your nervous system. For instance, proprioceptive input (deep muscle pressure) and touch are

regulating for me, so my self-care can include wearing my baby or snuggling into my kid while we watch a movie. My husband is dysregulated by touch and can get touched out. Self-care for him usually involves vestibular input (movement) or a break from sensory stimuli. He sits in an office chair that swivels and has a little bounce to it so he can get vestibular input in throughout the day. If there are two chairs in a room, one that swivels or rocks and one that is stationary, he always chooses the one that moves and I always choose the one that doesn't. Our nervous systems have different needs. Understanding your unique needs will allow you to customize self-care for yourself.

There are two types of self-care: proactive and reactive. Proactive self-care is what we do from the moment we wake up, and all throughout the day, to support our capacity for self-regulation. Imagine if we woke up and didn't eat food until we were hangry and stayed in that pattern all day. It would be hard to navigate the world. Instead, we eat before we are hangry so we have the capacity for managing the day. The same goes for all the sensory systems. We aim for proactive self-care every couple of hours throughout the day to support our ability to access regulation and self-control when stressors arise, like the defiant eye roll. This can be simple, like going to the bathroom alone without a phone and taking deep breaths for the minute while we are in there. My nervous system thanks me when I sit and breathe without doing another thing for a minute. I added a walking pad under my desk because movement throughout the day is helpful for me. I alternate between sitting and walking now. I have earplugs that I wear at home, especially during the last few hours of the day, because I'm sensitive to sound and being around kids is inherently loud at times. I will tell the kids that my brain needs a break while I'm getting dinner ready and that I'll have my headphones on while listening to music or podcasts. They know if they need me they can come tap me for help. These are ways I proactively practice self-care.

When you know what regulates your nervous system proactively, you can tap into those same types of things reactively in the moment to regulate and calm. I will squeeze my fists and let them go or wrap my arms around my body for a big hug to myself. I will say a mantra to myself as I take deep breaths. Sometimes I will tell my kids, "I'm going to calm my body so I can support you."

4. Scientific knowledge

Scientific knowledge helps us understand child development and use that information to guide how we respond to children. It gives us the answers to many of the whys we face in parenting: Why does my child behave like this? Why are they so upset over small things? Why do they sometimes sneak around or hide things from me? Why does every situation feel like a struggle?

By exploring brain development, how the nervous system works, and the latest research on children's behavior, we can gain a clearer picture of what's happening in our child. This knowledge helps us understand that many behaviors are completely normal for their age. When you understand *why* your child acts a certain way and have tools to respond effectively, it becomes easier to react with empathy and patience. You'll feel more equipped to handle tough moments, making parenthood feel less overwhelming and more intentional.

5. Adult–child interactions

This refers to what happens in the moment between you and your child. The first four parts of CEP are designed to help us understand the meaning behind our child's behavior; see what feeling or response that behavior might trigger in us; manage our own self-care so that we're more likely to stay self-aware, self-regulate, and respond with self-control; and gain a better understanding of the science behind childhood development and behavior. The first four steps prepare you for this fifth step of response, the goal of responding with more intention. What are helpful ways to show up with our kids so they can build these skills too?

In the next section we are going to outline the Five Phases of Emotion Processing to explore this in more depth. This is a framework to guide you through emotion processing. This framework isn't just for kids; it's for any human who is working to build emotional intelligence and cope with their emotions in a healthy way. As you move through interactions with your child, remember that there is no perfection in parenthood. You won't always be able to emotion-coach or respond with intention and that is okay.

CEP is not a script you apply to make your problems disappear. It's a practice that will invite you deeper into your relationships with your children (and most likely the adults in your life too) by responding with intention and purpose. CEP isn't the absence of hard things; it's a method for being with and moving through the hard things so they don't become all-consuming.

The Five Phases of Emotion Processing

When we were creating the Collaborative Emotion Processing (CEP) method, Lauren Stauble and I developed the Five Phases of Emotion Processing. These will guide you through emotion processing whether you're two, twelve, or forty-two years old. We generally move through the phases sequentially, but not always at the same speed. The five phases are a tool for understanding how to help your child build their self-awareness skills and move into regulation and problem-solving. It is not realistic to move through these phases every single time there's dysregulation or a hard feeling. You will not always respond with intention. You won't always have the time, resources, or capacity. That's okay. Perfection is not a requirement in this work. In fact, it's a disservice to children to even attempt to model. Instead, we get to do something so much more powerful for them by showing them what it looks like to make mistakes, acknowledge accountability, and continue to show up to connect with one another.

Let's look at what the five phases might look like for Mateo and his

Allowing Kids to Feel Might Sound Like . . .

- "It makes sense to be frustrated. That didn't feel fair."

- "Tell me more about this."

- "It makes sense to be mad about that. If you need to yell, you are welcome to yell outside or in your room. I'll be here when you're ready to talk."

- "Do you want me to sit here with you? Okay, I'll be in the kitchen if you change your mind."

Bonus Tip: For older kids, these verbal bids may not be what invites them to share their feelings. Sometimes too much talking is dysregulating. I might grab some playdough or beads to string and quietly work in a communal space. If the child doesn't join me, I don't make a big deal of it. But if they do join me, my goal is to sit quietly, working side by side with them. If they choose to talk, the space is available for them, and sometimes, it's the silence that is most validating.

family. The first step in emotion processing is to allow the emotion without trying to stop it or immediately solve the problem. Remember that allowing an emotion is separate from allowing behaviors. Picture this. Mateo starts bothering Rosie. She wants to be alone in her room to play, but he just won't let her. He starts doing his usual small annoyances to try to get her to respond to him. Mateo's mom would typically respond to Rosie's frustration, separate Mateo, and make him have some time alone in his room. This time, she uses it as an opportunity to build new skills.

Phase 1: Allow the emotion

Mateo's mom: "Hey, bud, I noticed that you were trying to play with Rosie and she's wanting alone time. Please come out of her room. I can help you."

Recognizing Perceived Emotion Might Sound Like . . .

- "Cleaning your room is a big job. It can feel overwhelming to have such a big job to do."

- "I have been *so* busy with the baby this morning. I wonder if you've been wanting my attention too?"

- "I hear you shouting my name. Are you feeling frustrated waiting for me to respond?"

Here we see that Mateo's mom is addressing the behavior by removing him from Rosie's space, but in a connected way that allows him to feel emotion without shame or punishment. This builds self-awareness skills.

Phase 2: Recognizing the perceived emotion

"It's hard when you really want to play and Rosie doesn't. I wonder if you're feeling left out or lonely right now." When we acknowledge what we see and address what might be fueling it, we help our child tune in and get curious, deepening their self-awareness skills.

Phase 3: Security

One of the key components to feeling safe to feel hard things is knowing that the emotions won't last forever. We want our kids to know that they come and go kind of like clouds in the sky. We can help illustrate this for kids with social stories. This might mean sharing a story from your childhood when you felt the same emotion and how you got through it. Mateo's mom might share with him: "Mateo, when I was your age, I always wanted to play with the girl who lived next door to me. Every day after school I would go and knock on her door and ask her to play. Sometimes we played together, but lots of times she couldn't or didn't want to play. I felt lonely and really wanted someone to talk to and play with. I went home and asked Nana for help. I told her I was lonely. She was busy making dinner,

Feeling Secure in Hard Feelings Might Look Like . . .

- Acknowledging that the feeling won't last forever.

- Knowing that you can trust your body to feel a feeling without getting stuck.

- Accepting that all feelings that show up are valid.

- Turning to people who support you in hard feelings.

but she let me call my cousin on the phone. Even though I didn't get to play with my neighbor, it felt really good to have someone to chat with. After that, whenever I felt left out or lonely, I told Nana, and she helped me. Our feelings don't stay forever. They all come for a little while and then leave."

Phase 4: Coping strategies

There are two types of coping: coping mechanisms and coping strategies. Coping mechanisms are like pressing pause on an emotion. They're a temporary fix to numb the feeling, something we often use to make the discomfort of a hard emotion go away. They are excellent for survival and aren't inherently bad.

We all turn to mechanisms by default if we are not working to build and practice coping strategies or if we don't have the capacity to access a strategy in the moment. Coping mechanisms give us a quick dose of dopamine, tapping into the reward center of the brain for temporary relief, but they don't address the underlying need. Coping mechanisms can include scrolling social media, shopping, substance use, gossiping, teasing, and other forms of distraction.

Coping strategies help to calm the nervous system for longer periods of time, allowing us to move into processing the emotion and problemsolving. Coping strategies can include breathing, moving your body,

Examples of Coping Strategies

- Going for a walk

- Engaging in art (painting, drawing, collage, etc.)

- Swinging or rocking

- Seeking connection from a friend or trusted adult

- Taking space alone

- Reading a book

- Kneading/squeezing playdough

- Asking for help

- Going outside

- Mindful breathing, perhaps together with a caregiver

lifting heavy things, deep pressure (like lying under a weighted blanket), receiving a massage, talking to a safe person, stepping outside, and noticing where your body is, what it feels, and what it sees. Find a more comprehensive list above.

The goal isn't to never use mechanisms. Mechanisms can be helpful tools and are sometimes necessary to move into coping strategies. When my nine-year-old daughter is in the thick of anger she gets resistant to talking. If I try to get her to open up to me, she escalates. What she needs in those moments is a mechanism. Mechanisms work on the reward system in the brain and give us a quick hit of dopamine. That dopamine hit can be the bridge to help us feel ready to access a strategy. For my daughter that sometimes looks like a game of Mario Kart, or the chance to look through some photos on my phone. After that dose of dopamine, she's more likely to feel ready to talk through those hard feelings and move into truly regulating her body.

In Mateo's case, he was already tapping into a coping mechanism. He was antagonizing Rosie to get a reaction out of her. He was getting a quick dopamine hit from that, but his underlying need for connection was still unmet. The goal is to help Mateo learn how to use a strategy that helps get his underlying needs met. We help kids learn to self-regulate by first

Problem-Solving Prompts

- "Hmm, this is tricky. I'm not sure how to solve this."

- "I wonder what would happen if . . ."

- "What do you think we should do?"

- "How could we solve this?"

- "What ideas have you tried?"

- "What ideas won't work?"

- "Who could we ask for help?"

- "How can we make this feel good for everyone?"

co-regulating with them. You can scaffold this growth for your child as they work to build these skills. In Mateo's case, his mom might have said, "I'm cooking dinner, but I can tell you need some connection right now. Would you like to help me cook or FaceTime Nana?" If Mateo's mom wasn't busy cooking dinner, she might have offered to read with him or play a board game or some other connecting activity.

Phase 5: Moving on

At this point, we are ready to problem-solve or let it go. Let's think back to Mateo. He's moved through the first four phases of emotion processing, and let's imagine he was able to call his Nana on FaceTime and meet that need for connection. Now what? Now Mateo's mom has an opportunity to talk this through with him and think about how he could navigate it the next time he's feeling lonely or left out. With his body regulated and his needs met, Mateo is ready to collaborate with his mom to come up with a plan for next time. We can support problem-solving by asking our child the right questions rather than solving the problem for them.

Problem-Solving Examples

- "It looks like you both wanted to use the scooter. Hmm, I'm not sure what to do here." Wait as the children give you ideas. If they don't provide anything that works, try: "I wonder what it would look like to take turns. How might that happen?"

- "You keep on trying, but that origami box just isn't working. Who could we ask for help?"

- "It felt really lousy when he said that to you. How could we solve this? What do you need from him to make it feel right?"

We might notice that a new emotion, like embarrassment, surfaces when Mateo's mom attempts this conversation. In this case, she can acknowledge that: "I'm wondering if you don't want to talk about it because you're feeling embarrassed. Sometimes it's uncomfortable for people to see our hard stuff. I get that. I love you all the time, not just when you're happy and calm."

Kids are incredible problem-solvers when their needs are met and can often come up with solutions we wouldn't have thought of. Remember, emotion processing is a skill that will take time and practice. Just like we don't read to babies expecting them to read back to us, we can't give kids the sample language once or twice and expect them to be always fully self-aware and self-regulated. Just as literacy skills take years to build and fully develop, emotional literacy is a long game too.

Maybe you read Mateo's story and it resonated with you. Perhaps you read it and are thinking to yourself, that would never go over with my kid. Here's the thing: emotion processing isn't a prescription. It's not a "do this and you'll get this" solution. It's a skill set, and the way we build this skill set will vary from child to child. We're going to dive into some science in the next chapter that will help you identify your child's needs and create strategies for emotion processing that fit those needs as well as those of your family. At the end of the day, the most important thing we can remember in this process is that the goal is to be in a connected relationship with one another, with all the messiness that comes with that.

What Emotions Am I Safe to Feel?

The goal for kids is to know that they can be their whole, messy, vulnerable, human selves with us. They can break down to us when they're scared. They can turn to us when they're full of rage. We can handle it when they're sad or lonely. This doesn't mean that they can slam doors, yell at us, or disrespect us (hang tight—we will dive deep into behavior challenges in later chapters). Each time we respond to an emotion, we are sending our kids messages about which emotions they are safe to feel. Which emotions do we welcome? Which ones do we try to shut down?

Remember how Mateo's mom responded to him? She connected with him right away and she also set a behavior boundary. She wasn't going to allow Mateo to continue antagonizing Rosie. She reminded him of the importance of respecting Rosie's space and separated him from Rosie by inviting him to come with her so she could help him. What she communicated to Mateo in that moment was that what he was doing was not okay, but what he was feeling was totally normal and okay.

Mateo is going to learn that there are spaces in life where he isn't safe to feel all his emotions, that there are people who can't handle all his hard stuff. That's okay. That is a part of building emotional intelligence— cultivating the social skills to know what is appropriate where and with whom. He might learn that expressing sadness around Oma results in a dismissal of his feelings or feeling frustrated around Papa comes with an attempt to distract from the feelings. He's going to learn to differentiate. What you have is the opportunity to show him that all his feelings are safe to be felt with you. And hear me out: it's also okay if you're still working on that.

Both of my parents grew up in households where there was no space for sadness. Their sadness was met with responses along the lines of, "You're okay," "Get back on that horse," and "It could be worse." Consequently, both of my parents learned that sadness is not a safe emotion to experience.

They, in turn, met my sadness with the same dismissal and distraction. Now, when my children feel sad, my first instinct is to make it go away. Sad = bad. I'm still learning how to be with my own sadness without turning to a coping mechanism like a quick scroll through Facebook Marketplace to distract myself and temporarily numb that deeply uncomfortable feeling. I don't even have to buy anything. A simple "Is it still available?" message gives me the dopamine hit I need to get a break from feeling the hard stuff.

So, when my children are feeling sad, fuhgeddaboudit. In that moment, I want them to know they will be okay and have to fight every urge to tell them they are okay. When I do this, my child will correct me, "I'm not okay right now." You don't have to get it right all the time. You don't have to have the capacity for all your children's feelings all the time. You're going to get impatient, need a break, feel overwhelmed. You are human. You aren't failing. The beauty is in what we do and say later. "Hey, bud, earlier when you were frustrated with your homework I too was frustrated. Sometimes when I'm frustrated, I have a hard time slowing down and being kind. I'm going to keep working on that. I'm not mad at you for having a hard time. I love you."

Building a Foundation of Emotional Literacy

Remember Leila's story? Leila lost it on her mom in the hallway of her school because her mom didn't bring the right uniform shirt for her soccer game. What would it look like to help Leila learn to navigate that differently? How do we respond in the moment to her behavior and emotions? How do we build skills outside of the moment to support Leila the next time she navigates something socially stressful?

Leila's mom was embarrassed by Leila's reaction and was tempted to jump right to making sure Leila knew it was not okay to talk to her like that. Relatable, right? When those challenging or embarrassing behaviors pop up, especially in public, the desire to make sure our kids know it's not acceptable is so real. In that moment though, Leila is living in her amygdala, her "feelings brain." She's not able to access the part of her brain that is able to learn a lesson or receive feedback. Talking about the behavior will happen later. The goal for responding in the moment is to send Leila a message about her emotions. To let her know it's okay to feel frustrated and anxious about having the wrong shirt, that hard feelings come and go, and that she can tap into coping and navigate the tough stuff.

So, what really happened with Leila that day? Leila's mom held space for her emotions knowing that they would talk about the behavior later. "Honey, it makes total sense to want your uniform shirt for your game. I know it can be stressful to feel like you're the only one who looks different." She gave Leila a moment to just feel without the pressure of needing to suppress or move on from the emotion. They didn't have time to move through the Five Phases of Emotion Processing because Leila's game was starting soon. "Your game starts in ten minutes. Let's walk down to the field together. If you're feeling nervous, I'll be right there with you." Leila walked down to the field with her mom, still teary-eyed and nervous. She was fidgety with her shirt and clearly uncomfortable. Her mom didn't try to make Leila's feelings go away or solve her problem for her. She let her know it was okay to be uncomfortable and that she wasn't alone. Leila's teammates were totally unfazed by her different shirt and Leila ended up playing a great game.

Later, at home, after Leila had time to eat dinner and play outside, Leila's mom circled back to what had happened at school. "Leila, I want to talk about what happened at school today. You're not in trouble and I want to help you with tools for next time you're feeling that way." Leila nodded her head but didn't say anything. "It seemed like you were really worried about your friends noticing your shirt and maybe afraid of not being accepted or liked if you didn't have the right uniform shirt on." Leila nodded again. "It makes sense to want to feel liked and included. I feel that way too sometimes." Leila's mom gave a couple of minutes for that to sink in, opening the door for Leila to share when she was ready.

"I just really don't like it when I stick out. I don't want to look different. You made it seem like no big deal, but it was a big deal to me."

"You're right. I didn't think about how it might make you feel to be the only person on your team dressed differently. There's a lot of pressure to fit in at school, huh?" her mom asked. Leila nodded again.

"There are probably going to be more times where you feel like you stick out at school, or like you don't necessarily fit in with certain peers. It's okay to feel nervous when that happens, and I can help you work through it if you share it with me. It seems like it's helpful for you to talk it through."

"Yeah, I like talking about it and hearing when you've felt nervous. Have you ever felt like you don't fit in?"

"Totally. When I was in school, I wasn't very athletic. I really enjoyed art and reading. At my school, it was harder to make friends if you weren't into sports. I felt like an outsider sometimes."

"So what did you do?" Leila asked.

"I talked to my mom and asked her to help me. She helped me come up with some ideas for connecting with my peers. She also helped me understand that sometimes I wasn't going to fit in. I wasn't always going to be liked. She gave me some ideas for what I could do when I felt sad and left out. I sometimes wrote in my journal. Sometimes I just needed to talk about it."

Leila nodded quietly, absorbing what her mom was sharing.

Her mom continued: "It's important to me that we speak to each other with kindness, even when we're feeling the tough stuff. I wonder how we could navigate it differently next time. I don't want you to shout at me."

"And I don't want you to make it seem like worries are no big deal," Leila replied.

"That's totally fair. I'll work on treating your emotions as something important because they are. Since you said talking this out has been helpful, how about next time you're feeling nervous about something, instead of shouting at me, how about you pull me aside and let me know you need to chat? I'll know that means that this is something important to you and I'll help you."

"Yeah, I can try to do that," Leila replied.

Did you notice that Leila's mom waited until after Leila had eaten and moved her body before diving into that conversation? We're going to cover regulating the nervous system in depth in the next chapter because it's such a crucial part of this work. We can't teach kids about what to do differently next time until their body is regulated and they have access to their full brain, not just their "feelings brain." Leila's mom also prefaced the conversation with "You're not in trouble." Talking about behavior is often hard for kids. They know they aren't supposed to yell, slam doors, and talk disrespectfully. They often enter conversations feeling a sense of guilt or embarrassment. Letting them know they aren't in trouble is a way to help them feel safe and open the doors to vulnerability.

Leila's mom helped her daughter to recognize what she was feeling in the moment when she lost it over the shirt. She was feeling nervous and like she needed to fit in. Talking about their experience and helping kids put a name to the emotion is part of helping them build self-awareness. Leila's mom validated Leila's emotion and normalized it by sharing about a time that she felt similarly. She noticed that talking was helping Leila and she brought that to Leila's attention too. Talking with a safe person is a coping strategy for processing emotions. Noting for Leila that talking helps her feel calm is helping her to build her future self-regulation skills. She's building the foundation for learning what helps her calm down when she's feeling something hard.

In the story when Leila's mom shared about her own experience navigating peer relationships, she noted that sometimes she did feel left out, and she wasn't always going to be liked by everyone. That was a helpful way to let Leila know that the goal isn't to be liked by everyone. Sometimes we won't mesh well with another human and that's okay. The goal isn't to help our kids be best friends with all of their peers. The goal is for them to have the skills to navigate complex peer dynamics and the ebbs and flows of social groups at this age.

Right now, it's a uniform shirt. Flash-forward to parenting a teen and the stakes get higher. Think about the things you might have been exposed to as a teen. Were your friends drinking? Did they smoke? Were they having sex? Did you feel pressure to try things because you wanted your friends to like and accept you? Did you feel safe enough to talk to your parents about it?

If we want to raise kids who will bring us their really hard, scary, vulnerable teenage stuff, we get to set the stage for that now. We get to be a safe place for them. We get to help them tune in to what is happening in their body and brain when they're feeling the hard stuff. We get to help them build the skills to process those emotions, so they aren't stuck in them. We get to support them in learning to be self-aware, so they can self-regulate, so they get to choose what they do next—rather than making rash decisions because they don't know what to do with their emotions and they don't feel safe to turn to us. Stay tuned for Chapter 7 where we dive deep into peer relationships, peer pressure, and bullying.

Chapter 3

Why Can't They Control Themselves?

Henry, eight, and Flynn, six, are brothers. Ever since Flynn started kindergarten last year, the drive home from school in the afternoon has become a dreaded chore for their mother, Anna, who doesn't understand why they can't seem to stop themselves from fighting every single day. No matter what she says to them, it continues.

Today, she picks them up, and Henry starts sharing excitedly about his day. He talks a mile a minute, enjoying this connection time with his mom. After about five minutes of Henry talking, Flynn asks to listen to the radio. Anna turns on the radio. They listen together for a few minutes and then Henry starts talking over the radio to share more about his day with his mom. Flynn asks Henry to be quiet because he can't hear the song. Henry complains because he's trying to talk to Anna. It quickly devolves into an argument.

"I want to talk to Mom, you don't get to decide that I have to be quiet," Henry tells Flynn.

"It's too loud when you talk and the music is on. I just want to listen to the music," Flynn replies.

"You're such a baby, Flynn. You always have to get your stupid way!" Henry shouts.

Flynn starts crying and screams back, "Just SHUT UP, Henry. Just BE QUIET."

Anna turns off the radio and reminds both boys that they need to speak to each other with kindness. They continue to fight. Some days Anna loses her patience and shouts at them. Today she just does her best to tune them out while she's driving as her adrenaline skyrockets and she tries not to explode. They're almost home when Henry hits Flynn, and Flynn retaliates by scratching Henry. Both boys are crying by the time they pull into the driveway.

Henry and Flynn's mom feels really defeated about this pattern between her sons. It happens at home too, but is always more pronounced in the car, where they have no place else to go. She can't understand what is so difficult about getting along for a twenty-minute drive. Why fight over something like the radio? Why fight to the point of hitting and scratching each other? They know better.

We're going to look deeper at this dynamic through the lens of the nervous system, and it's going to give us a whole new perspective on what's happening for each of the boys.

Understanding the Nervous System

All day long your nervous system works to keep you safe. It notices everything happening around you at all times and asks, "Am I safe?" As you're reading this, maybe the washing machine is making some noise in the background. Your nervous system tells you, "No need to pay attention to that, you're safe." Now if your smoke alarm suddenly went off, your nervous system would yell, "THAT'S IMPORTANT! PAY ATTENTION! DO SOMETHING!"

Our nervous system is *always* taking in information around us. It takes in the sound of the dishwasher running, the way the sweater feels on our body, the corner of the rug that sticks up, the smell of the hand soap we use to wash our hands, the sunlight coming through the blinds, cars driving by, the movement of someone as they walk into the room, and so on—and filters it. The stimuli are cumulative, adding up throughout the day. Think of your nervous system as a funnel—all the information comes in at the wide opening at the top, or mouth, and then has to filter out through the narrower bottom, or spout. We all have an internal funnel that processes stimuli we encounter every day, and the width of the spout is different for each of us.

This matters when it comes to how we process the world around us. If you take a funnel with a small spout and a funnel with a larger spout and you pour sand into each of them from the mouth at the same rate, the one with the smaller spout will get backed up and start to overflow before the one with the larger spout.

Humans with a smaller funnel spout are really good at noticing the details, allowing just a few specks of sand to pass through at a time. They can also get overwhelmed by stimuli and overflow with sand more easily. The ones with a larger funnel spout can filter stimuli faster, with more ease, and often miss details.

This constant work of the nervous system can be compared to apps running in the background of your phone. From the moment your phone is turned on, it starts to drain its battery. The more apps that are running and the more you use them, the faster your phone battery dies. Certain apps will drain it faster than others. Sending a text might be like walking by a piece of mail on the counter: your brain registers that information, but it isn't very draining. Streaming a video could be like your kids screaming while you're making dinner with a child pulling at your pant leg and the microwave timer beeping; your brain gets overwhelmed with the sensory experience and starts draining quickly. We can recharge the phone to avoid that red battery alert signal, or we can wait until it crashes, plug it in, and wait while the system restarts.

The same is true for our nervous system. We can recharge it proactively throughout the day to keep it out of the red zone and manage the cumulative effects of sensory stimuli, or we can wait until it crashes as the sights, sounds, tastes, smells, and touch experiences of the day inevitably add up and we explode, recharge it, and give it time to restart. We're going to dive into how to proactively recharge your own and your child's batteries, as well as how this can vary from person to person depending on how hard they work to filter information (how wide or narrow their funnel spout is).

One of my children has a large funnel spout and one of them has a small one. My daughter's funnel spout is large. She can take in a ton of information around her and easily filter it out. She can be sitting at the table doing her homework while I cook in the background and chat on the phone, her brother plays loudly with cars, and her dad is on a Zoom call for work. As information comes into the top of her funnel, it slides right through, allowing her to be surrounded by stimuli and not feel overwhelmed for a while.

My son's funnel spout is small. He notices the smallest details. He hears the dog barking three houses down the street, is constantly aware of the texture and feeling of his clothing, and notices if even one of his stuffed animals is out of place. If he is sitting at the table working on something for school, he needs a quiet environment—no phone calls, no video calls, and no one playing loudly nearby. All that stimuli would add up and overflow his funnel spout because only a few tiny grains of sand can move through it at one time. Even in the scenario where he's simply playing with cars while his sister does her homework, he will be the more likely child to say, "Mama, it's too loud. Stop talking on the phone." His battery drains faster than hers does.

Stimuli add up as the day goes on, so our capacity for tasks and experiences can vary depending on how much stimuli we've already had to filter. For example, my elementary-school-age kids will brush their teeth independently in the morning before school with very little resistance. They often do it without even being reminded. Teeth brushing in the evening is a totally different story. They've both been filtering information all day long and they're tired. I remind them to go brush their teeth and they either don't respond or they whine. I have to physically walk with them to the bathroom and get their toothbrushes loaded for them. Most nights I end up doing half the brushing too. They know how to brush; they show me that every morning. However, in the morning—with their batteries charged—they have the capacity to brush independently. In the evening—after processing the world all day long—they're out of capacity. Their funnels have overflowed, their batteries are drained, and a task that *should be* simple, becomes hard.

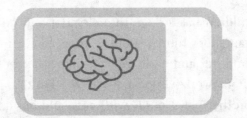

- Sleep
- Food
- Quiet
- Dark spaces
- Moving our bodies
- A long hug
- Connecting with someone we love
- Going upside down
- Spinning
- Swinging
- Dancing
- Deep breaths

- Hunger
- Tiredness
- Changes in routine
- Unknown expectations
- Things or people moving in our environment
- Sounds
- Clutter
- Screens
- How things feel or taste
- Experiencing emotions
- Experiencing other people's emotions

The Sensory System

As children we learn about the five senses: taste, touch, smell, sight, and sound, but there are four other senses in our bodies that are vital for how we move through the world and what triggers us to lose control or what recharges us. We used to identify only eight total systems, but practitioners now more commonly recognize a ninth sense in sensory integration: neuroception. Let's dive into all of them.

Proprioceptive sense

The proprioceptive sense is body awareness—feeling where your body begins and ends. This is how we put on a shirt without actively thinking

Examples of Proprioceptive Input

- Animal walks: bear walk, crab walk, snake slither

- Jumping and crashing onto a soft surface or a pile of cushions

- Tug-of-war

- Deep pressure massage

- Tight hugs

- Wheelbarrow walking

- Carrying heavy things

- Working out: push-ups, planks, squats, etc.

- Using a foam roller

of each step: put my arm through the hole and push, put my other arm through the other hole and push, and pull it up over my head. The body learns this pattern and can do it without even thinking about it.

Humans with low proprioceptive awareness might try to sit next to someone and accidentally sit on them. They might be like a bull in a china shop sometimes, unaware of the things around them or how close they are to them as they move through a room. You might notice them bumping into things that seem obvious, or being too physical with peers. This is sometimes mistaken as aggression or misbehavior, but kids with low proprioceptive awareness often *truly don't see or feel* how close they are to their peers.

They may also crave proprioceptive input and need it every sixty to ninety minutes throughout the day. We all need some proprioceptive input to recharge and some of us need more than others. For long-term development and short-term recharging, we benefit from deep pressure (such as arm squeezes and hugs), heavy work (think CrossFit for kids—lifting or pushing heavy things), or big muscle movement (such as jumping, push-ups, or wheelbarrow walking). Throughout this book, the proprioceptive sense will be referred to as the "big body play" sense because that is how we tend to see it show up at these ages.

Vestibular sense

The vestibular sense is awareness of movement, balance, and coordination. It lets our body know where our head is in relation to the rest of us. This helps us navigate the world without falling down and helps us understand if we are upside down or right side up. We all have a different tolerance and need for vestibular input. Kids who are regulated by vestibular input might enjoy going on a swing, spinning around, or doing cartwheels. My son is vestibular seeking and will often flip upside down on the couch to watch TV or seek out games in which he gets to flip or spin. When your vestibular system is underresponsive you might feel wobbly, bump into things, or be unstable on your feet. Someone who is vestibular sensitive might get motion sickness easily, feel dizzy after just a little spinning, or tend to avoid the swings.

Examples of Vestibular Input

- Swinging
- Spinning on an office chair
- Jumping on a trampoline
- Lying in a hammock
- Riding a bike

- Hanging upside down
- Jumping rope
- Rocking
- Riding in a wagon
- Doing yoga inversions

Interoceptive sense

The interoceptive sense is the perception of sensations inside the body. It lets us know when we are hungry, full, tired, or thirsty, or if our heart is beating fast. As children are building self-awareness, they are tuning in to their interoceptive sense to notice what is happening inside their bodies. These sensations give them clues to how they are feeling or what emotion they might be experiencing. If I say I have butterflies in my stomach, you know that feeling and that it means I'm feeling nervous or excited. We can help kids tune in to more internal body clues to be able to notice how different emotions feel in their body. This is a crucial step in kids being able to access self-regulation and then self-control. Some people have a sensitive interoceptive sense. They can be kids who go from zero to one thousand when they start to get hungry or tired. All of a sudden they're *starving* or *exhausted*.

Neuroception

This is the body's system that detects threats versus safety. Have you ever been in a place where you could feel someone looking at you? Your neuroception was saying, "Hey, pay attention." I think of this as my Spidey sense. Neuroception allows you to read the energy in the room. Humans who are neuroceptive sensitive are keenly aware of the energy and other people's feelings in an environment and are often referred to as deep feelers. They can present as deeply empathetic or codependent. It can be very challenging for their nervous system to calm if someone else in their space is dysregulated. The other person's dysregulation feels like a threat to their nervous system. Sometimes they can subconsciously fall into people-pleasing patterns to try and keep the peace to alleviate the stress on their nervous system. An adult's tone, body language, and self-regulation play crucial roles in how this child will respond to them.

A Unique Sensory Profile

Every human has a unique sensory profile. This means that the way we take in the world around us (our funnel spout size) is different for each of us. The inputs that drain our battery will vary from person to person. Likewise, the inputs that charge our battery will vary too. I am a human who loves deep pressure. It recharges me. I could get a deep tissue massage for four straight days and still want more. I love it when my big dog lies across my body and I can feel his weight on me. I'll often lie on my belly on the floor and ask my kids to walk on my back. All of those are examples of proprioceptive input and touch. Those are the most regulating inputs for me.

My husband is very different. He often finds deep pressure input draining. He doesn't like massage, tight hugs, or having the dog or kids sitting on top of him. He regulates through movement. He's always moving. Running, jumping, playing outside with the kids. I sometimes joke and call him a bobblehead because when he's playing or joking with the kids, he will subconsciously be wiggling his head a little bit. These are all examples of vestibular input, and that is what's most regulating for his body. Vestibular input is more draining for me. I get dizzy and uncomfortable when I spin, jump, or do things that change my head position too much or too quickly.

When we know what we are sensitive to (what drains us) and what we are seeking (what regulates us), we can take care of our nervous system proactively by anticipating what will be draining and tapping into recharging activities. I seek touch for regulation, so if I'm upset, a hug is calming or someone I love putting their hand on me feels good. My son is touch sensitive, so if he is dysregulated and yelling or crying and I offer a hug or put my hand on him, he escalates further. What's draining for him is regulating for me. This is not one size fits all, which is why we are here to guide you in figuring out how your nervous system works, and also how your child's works. This will be key for knowing what tools will be helpful for your child proactively throughout the day as well as reactively in the hard moments.

Sensory Mismatches

When there are different or opposing sensory needs, we call this a sensory mismatch. This can happen between a parent and child, siblings, peers, etc. My husband and I are a sensory mismatch. The things that recharge me are draining to him and vice versa. My two children are a sensory mismatch. My daughter is a sensory seeker, needing more input than other humans to feel regulated, and my son is sensory sensitive, feeling overwhelmed by sensory stimuli faster than others.

We're going to dive deeper into what those terms mean by revisiting Henry and Flynn's story. Anna describes Henry as a very talkative, social, energetic child who loves to hang out in big groups and connect with others. She describes Flynn as a quieter, more cautious kid who is happy to hang out at home. While Henry will often ask, "Can we see our friends after school today?," Flynn tends to want to go home and decompress with some independent play.

The way that Anna describes her sons helps us get a better understanding of how their nervous systems work. Henry is a sensory seeker. He has a bigger funnel opening. He finds it easy, even fulfilling, to be in a big group. The sounds and sights of a social hang aren't draining for him. He loves to chat. He wants to connect with others as often as possible. He also loves to climb and tap into big body play. He's drawn to physical play because his body needs it in order to feel regulated.

Flynn is sensory sensitive. He has a smaller funnel spout. His quiet and cautious demeanor stems from his observant nature. He notices all the small things happening around him. Sometimes he is referred to as shy, a term Anna empowers him to wear proudly, like a superpower. He works extra hard to filter information so he can be present to what is happening, and with the intention he brings to the environment, he excels at detecting and retaining details. He recharges with quiet time, with less stimuli. Sometimes we notice that sensory-sensitive humans are not dysregulated by stimuli if they are in control of it. For instance, someone else vacuuming is too loud for them, but they can listen to music that they put on at a loud volume.

How does this connect to the boys' fighting in the car? Let's think back to what triggered their argument. Both boys had just processed an entire school day. When they got in the car, they both were likely working with a low battery. Henry started trying to meet his needs by talking to his mom, processing the day with her, and finding connection through verbal communication. A few minutes later Flynn had asked to listen to music, sound he could control and predict. Henry listened to the music for a few minutes and then started talking to his mom over the music. Flynn asked Henry to stop talking and things escalated from there. At that moment, the boys' sensory needs were in opposition to each other. Henry was seeking more input, more talking, more connection with his mom. He was trying to recharge his battery that way. Flynn was also trying to recharge his own battery, by asking for no talking—just music. In fact, his asking for music in the first place was likely a response to needing the talking to stop. The argument continued because neither boy was able to access what they needed for regulation.

When we are navigating sensory needs, the goal is first to understand how our children's sensory systems process information in order to build skills to meet those needs. We can teach kids strategies for regulation, depending on what makes sense for their unique sensory profile. It could be muscle input (proprioceptive), movement (vestibular), connection (neuroceptive), or a sensory break with some downtime. Sometimes it's a combination. If you're reading this and feeling daunted by the task of identifying your child's sensory needs, you're not alone. It's a lot to think about. Start with our free regulation quiz by scanning the following QR code. The quiz will ask you a series of questions and use your answers to identify specific inputs your child would find most regulating. Moving forward we'll refer to those inputs as regulating activities.

Proactive Versus Reactive

One question I often ask myself as a parent is "Am I setting them up for success?" If my child showed up to a sleepover without pajamas, a toothbrush, and clothes for the next day, I wouldn't be setting them up for success that night. So we work together to have everything they need going into the sleepover. Maybe once they're there, the plans change and they get to go swimming with their buddy, but don't have their swimsuit. Now we figure out a plan to get them a swimsuit and continue on with their sleepover. I helped my child proactively by packing the things I knew would be needed for their sleepover. I pivot to support my child reactively when the plans change. We approach nervous system regulation similarly: we focus on both proactive and reactive regulation strategies. This means that we can use regulating activities both as a part of our typical daily routines and as a calming strategy in the heat of the moment.

I know for myself, I need a combination of proprioceptive inputs and sensory breaks throughout the day to remain regulated. The dog in my lap, a twenty-minute strength-training workout, and something crunchy to eat (jaw movements = proprioception) are staples in my daily routine. Those are my proactive regulating activities. My reactive regulation tends

Suggesting Regulating Activities Might Sound Like . . .

- "Wow, this is frustrating. I'm going to take a second to breathe before I keep trying. Want to do silly breaths with me? Let's blow our lips like horses."

- "We're about to be in the car for a while. Let's see who can do ten jump squats the fastest."

- "This gathering is *so* loud. I'm going to pop outside for a little walk. Want to join me?"

to lean toward needing a sensory break. I'm most likely to lose it on my kids when I'm overstimulated and don't step away.

Reactive regulation for me often looks like stepping into the bathroom and locking it for a few minutes to take some deep breaths and ground myself. I might even turn off the lights and run cold water over my hands and face if I'm really on edge. Sometimes my kids are standing outside the door and trying to talk to me. I let them know, "I'll be out in just a few minutes to help you. I need to calm my body so I can treat you with kindness." I do my best to focus on my breathing, the feeling of my feet on the ground, and the coolness of the water on my skin. Bringing myself back into the present, letting my nervous system know I'm safe. Using the free regulation quiz linked in the previous section, you can get an idea of what regulating activities would be most helpful for your child. If you're wondering how you're going to integrate these activities into your already packed schedule, stay tuned—we're going to dive into that before we wrap up this chapter.

Sometimes we might know what our child needs at the moment but not be in an environment where it's easy to meet that need. This is where accommodations come in. Anna might know that what Flynn needs is to take space and be in an environment with less stimulation. However, they're in the car with nowhere for Flynn to go. How can she meet both boys' opposing needs while they are trapped in a small space? It might mean that Flynn has access to headphones to listen to his music without the outside noise. This accommodation would allow Flynn's needs to be met, without having to try to silence Henry, who is also working to meet his own needs.

When our child's nervous system gets back to regulation, then they can access more of the skills we know they have. Navigating how to change the behaviors we are seeing requires the belief that all behavior is communication of a need. We get to play detective to determine that need.

Examples of Accommodations

- Chair bands

- Stress-free clothing (soft material without tags or seams)

- Lightly tinted sunglasses

- Weighted lap pad

- Chewing gum

- Balance ball seats

- Headphones

Born That Way

When Anna was asked to describe her sons as infants, she described Henry as a laid-back baby who slept on the go and didn't cry unless he was hungry—even his hunger cry was more of a whimper. It was easy to integrate Henry into their family because he was so content to be along for the ride. While Anna was expecting the transition to parenthood to be really hard, it actually felt pretty seamless.

When Flynn came along two years later, it was a different story. He cried unless he was in a baby carrier or a swaddle being bounced. They survived the first few months of his infancy by wrapping him up in a stretchy wrap, Anna bouncing him on a yoga ball, while Henry sat on the couch next to her watching cartoons. Flynn hated the car so they rarely drove anywhere. Sometimes Flynn would cry so hard that the only way to calm him was to take him into a completely dark room, blast white noise, swaddle him, and bounce him while loudly shushing in his ear.

She remembers one day, when Flynn was about two weeks old, her dad called her to check in. She told him she was bouncing Flynn on the ball to stop his crying. Her dad responded, "You know, Anna, you can't just bounce him on that ball all day. He needs to learn how to be put down." Anna remembers feeling a rush of guilt and confusion. Was she creating this? Was she setting Flynn up to need bouncing for the rest of his infancy?

Would she ever get off this ball? Would she ever have time to connect with Henry again? All these questions, combined with her sleep deprivation and overall physical exhaustion had Anna completely overwhelmed. She described that time of her life as exhausting and isolating.

Anna's experience with her boys illustrates something important to note and understand. As parents we do not create or shape a child's sensory profile—they are born that way. Anna didn't do anything to "make" Henry a laid-back baby—it's simply who he is. His large funnel spout made it easy for him to take in the world around him and remain regulated. In the same way, she didn't do anything to "make" Flynn a sensitive baby. His small funnel spout, which allows him to be attuned, observant, and detail-oriented, made the world very overwhelming for his newborn self. There are common comments from the peanut gallery about birth order and how second (third/fourth/fifth/etc.) children just have to learn to go with the flow and that's why they're so chill. The truth, however, is that the way children process stimuli in the world plays a *huge* role in their ability to go with the flow and be regulated in varying environments. The way they integrate the sounds, textures, sights, smells, tastes, and internal experiences from being awake and alive will exist from birth and factor into what it looks like to support them proactively and reactively with regulation each day. The goal isn't to change them, but instead to help them cultivate awareness and regulation strategies to thrive.

Task Demand and Capacity

Remember that story about me losing it on my husband when I was hungry and overstimulated? At that moment the task demand I was facing (cook, feed kids, break up fights, pack lunches, etc.) was greater than my nervous system's capacity. There was too much going on, too much pressure building inside for me to take any more. We can increase capacity in ourselves and our children by focusing on the following five things we call FACTS. They are the cornerstone for regulation and have a large impact on our ability to regulate.

Food
Activity
Connection
Tune-out
Sleep

Food

We've all been there, right? The hangries strike and suddenly we're losing it when we trip over that toy in the hallway, or the dog comes inside with muddy paws, or our partner is home late. Hunger causes shifts in the nervous system that are similar to what happens when we feel anger, fear, or sadness.[1] Predictable, consistent eating opportunities create safety for the nervous system. The goal is for each snack and meal to contain carbs, fat, and protein. This helps fuel a child's growing body and encourages blood sugar regulation and satiety. A meal schedule with food offered every two to three hours helps kids tune in to their hunger cues and eat the right amount for them. For some kids, eating intuitively when meals are offered is easy and natural. These kids seem to eat whatever is in front of them when they're hungry. However, for others, eating isn't so intuitive. There's a common myth that kids will always "eat when they're hungry," but this isn't always true for those with sensory sensitivities or challenges.

Mindy was making dinner for her two kids—pasta, broccoli, and mandarin slices. She plated the food and set it down in front of Peter, age six, and Belle, age ten. Belle dove right into the meal, but Peter hesitated. He was wiggly in his seat as he pushed his food around his plate. "Buddy, what's up?" Mindy asked him. "My nose is all stuffy, and it's hard to eat. I don't know if I can eat this," he replied.

"But my nose is stuffy too," Belle interjected, "and I'm eating it!" Belle had always been a good eater, but Peter not so much. *Why such a drastic difference? Is Peter just picky?* Mindy had wondered over the years.

It's easy to look at Belle and Peter and think that Peter is just being difficult and choosy about food, when in reality it's a difference in their nervous systems. Peter's interoceptive system is sensitive so he's hyper aware of the sensations in his body. When his nose is stuffy, it makes swallowing feel different and uncomfortable for him. Belle isn't sensory sensitive and while she notices her stuffy nose, it doesn't make her so uncomfortable that eating is a challenge.

Sensory sensitivities can affect eating in myriad ways. If the environment is overstimulating for a child, it may be hard for them to sit and eat a meal. If the child is touch sensitive, how food feels in their mouth can play a big role in their ability to eat it. If a child is interoceptive sensitive, they may have a hard time eating if they have to poop or are feeling tired. When we can support kids' regulation, we can help them be set up for more success around meal and snack times.

For all kids, but especially sensory-sensitive kids, it's important to offer at least one food at every meal or snack that feels safe for your child. This may look different when your child is sick. Under normal circumstances Peter would have eaten the dinner his mom made him, but when he was feeling sick, it became a challenge. Being flexible during illness can help lower stress for both you and your child. A note: Being open to flexibility doesn't mean that there are no boundaries around food, and it doesn't mean that you become a short-order cook.

At breakfast the following day Peter is still sick. Mindy makes the kids toast with peanut butter and smoothies. She's thinking that the smoothie will be a safe food for Peter while he's not feeling well. "Mom, I still don't feel well. Can I just have ice cream for breakfast? It will feel good on my throat."

"Ice cream isn't on the menu this morning, buddy."

"Why nnnnnnooootttttt?" Peter whines.

"Because ice cream will give your body quick energy, but not long energy. Your body is working hard to get rid of your sickness. It needs long-energy foods to do its job."

"Well, I'm not eating this toast. I don't know why you even put it on my plate."

"That's fine. You don't have to eat it."

It's okay to set boundaries around food and for your child to get mad about it. In this case, Mindy made sure to offer Peter a safe option, and then let him have his feelings about not having ice cream. Being flexible and offering safe foods doesn't mean it's a free-for-all. Kids feel safe when they know there are boundaries in place—even if they get mad about them.

The goal is for kids to understand how food works in their bodies because before you know it, they are accessing food for themselves outside of your house. Notice how Mindy explained why ice cream wasn't a breakfast option? This helps Peter become aware that food impacts our energy levels and how our bodies work. She also didn't get ruffled when he said he wouldn't eat the toast. The more we can communicate safety and regulation with our nervous systems, the easier it will be for our kids to eat in our presence. This means not putting pressure on them. We can help kids learn which foods give them sustainable energy and which foods are more for fun (often quick-energy foods), and help them understand that a wide variety of foods is necessary for health.

A note: Peter was annoyed but wasn't totally off the deep end during that conversation—he was able to hear it even though he didn't love it. If he had been in full meltdown mode, his mom could validate his experience and allow his emotion with as few words as possible. "You really wish you could have ice cream for breakfast. I get that, bud. It isn't available right now." If you're in the heat of the moment with a fully melting kid—that's not the time to explain how food works. The learning part of their brain is offline if they're melting like that. Finding a time to chat about food when your child is regulated is ideal. Prepping meals or baking together can be a good time for this. Later, when they're regulated, you can go back to the earlier example to explain more. If you grew up in a "because I said so" household, it can feel uncomfortable to wait to explain the why until later. A part of you from childhood that didn't feel seen or heard may surface inside your head wanting you to explain everything now so your child feels seen or heard. That makes sense. You can notice that part of you and its goal of not repeating the "because I said so" pattern and help that part know you will come back and explain more when your child is regulated enough for that conversation.

Scripts for Talking About Food

- "Oh, you're really eyeing those chips. Let's have something that fills your body with lasting energy first."

- "I haven't had any green food yet today! I remember that green veggies have lots of vitamins that my body needs."

- "Your plate has strawberries and toast. We're missing something with protein. We need that for our muscles! Should we add some eggs?"

The above scripts are some examples of how to talk to kids about how food fuels their bodies.

Activity

I had a full workday ahead of me when we got the alert that the kids' school had a snow day. They were elated to get a bonus home day and asked to watch a movie and have breakfast on the couch. Totally. What a win-win. I can dive into my workday while they cozy up with a movie. One movie turned into playing on their Switch and before we knew it, it had been hours since they'd moved their bodies. Cue the bickering. One thing after another from one sibling being annoying to their getting easily frustrated trying to level up in their game. The volcano was erupting. After fielding complaints, I hit my limit and said, "That's it. Screens off. Go outside." The complaints grew and escalated until finally they were outside. After about forty minutes my daughter came in to grab food to bring out for her and her brother. What? Is this kindness and collaboration I see? Ahh, the power of movement in activity!

Just like our bodies need food on a consistent schedule we also need regulating input consistently. Proactively recharging our nervous systems works best if we are actively moving our bodies every ninety minutes to two hours. Here's the thing though—you don't have to carve out time specifically for activity; you can integrate it into pockets of time you already have. When we're getting ready to leave the house for school, I typically help the kids get dressed first. Then I go get dressed. There's a five-minute period when I'm busy getting dressed but they're all set to go. At that time I might throw a couple of pillows or the beanbag on the floor and encourage them to jump from the couch to the pillow pile while they wait for me. When they get home in the afternoon, I usually offer up a quick activity before we dive into our evening routine. I might have them take turns dragging each other around the kitchen island on a blanket or offer different ways for them to watch a show like sitting in a beanbag, in an office chair that spins, or in a swivel chair. They might jump on the pogo stick or shoot hoops in the driveway. Three to five minutes at a time is all it takes to reap the benefits. The benefits, however, are cumulative. They add capacity to our nervous system, allowing us to navigate emotional regulation with more ease.

Connection

I was packing lunches for a beach day. I just wanted to get us out the door so we could enjoy the warm weather. It felt like the kids were nonstop alternating between "Hey, Mom, look at this!" and "Look what I just made!" or "Mom, watch this!" I was bustling around gathering up snacks and waters and would look up at whatever they were showing me for a quick second and then try to get back on task. Soon, my son was at my side with a pile of the kinetic sand, showing it to me for what felt like the hundredth time. "Buddy, I see it. I've already seen it like ten times. You're going to make a mess. Just let me get us packed for the beach." He dropped the sand on the floor and shouted, "I don't want to go to the stupid beach anyway!" He stomped to his room and shut his door with a bang. My first thought was to address the word *stupid* or the door slamming. As I was walking to his room, I paused. He had been trying to connect with me all morning and I'd only been half paying attention because I was rushing to get us out the door. He didn't need me to tell him that he shouldn't say *stupid* or slam his door. He already knows that. His capacity to regulate was inhibited because his need for connection hadn't been met.

As we've discussed, our nervous systems are wired for connection. Connection is a human need and yet in our culture we often treat it as a *want*. When my younger child needs quiet and my older child won't leave him alone because she's craving connection, I'm quick to categorize her desire for connection as something negotiable. *Why does she constantly want someone's attention? Why won't she just leave him alone?* Those are the things that come up first for me. Interestingly, those are phrases I heard from adults when I was a child. I really have to pause and notice when I'm reacting from that place instead of seeing that behavior as communication of a connection need.

Connection doesn't need to be an hour of undivided one-on-one time. It can be as simple as noticing something helpful the child does, chatting with them about their day, or going for a walk together. Do you remember Mateo's story from Chapter 2? His mom's response to his need for connection is a great example because she was busy when he needed connection. So relatable, right? She said to him, "I'm cooking dinner, but I can tell you need some connection right now. Would you like to help me cook or FaceTime Nana?" It's okay if you don't have the time or capacity for a game or to read. It's okay to invite them into your task or give them another way to get their need met, like FaceTiming a friend or family member.

Tune-out

When Adara got home from school with her kids, it felt like everything was happening at once. Shira had basketball practice in an hour and was whining about having to do homework on practice night. Meanwhile, Ari was complaining that he didn't want the soup simmering in the Crock-Pot for dinner. The sounds and demands from both kids, combined with the pressure of getting Shira's things together and feeding the kids before heading back out, quickly became overwhelming. Adara's mind was swirling.

All she wanted was to lie in a dark room for five minutes, free from noise, whining, and background voices—somewhere no one needed anything from her. Her body was overstimulated, and she knew she needed a break. Stimuli build up throughout the day, and taking intentional breaks or downtime helps the nervous system process and engage without hitting a breaking point. Adara was overdue for one.

She looked at her kids and said, "I need a minute. I'm going to put my AirPods in and listen to a song in my bedroom by myself to regroup, and then I can come help you." The AirPods allowed her to control the noise, drowning out the background sounds, while retreating to her bedroom gave her a chance to turn off the lights, close her eyes, and have a moment free of touch or demands. It was the pause she needed to catch her breath and reset.

Things that we wouldn't necessarily think of as being "stressful" can actually be sources of stress for the nervous system. In his book *Self-Reg: How to Help Your Child (and You) Break the Stress Cycle and Successfully Engage with Life*, Dr. Stuart Shanker identifies "noise, sights, touch, smells, and other kinds of stimuli; pollution, allergens, and extreme heat or cold" as stressors to the nervous system. Think about the things your child might encounter during their day. What sights and sounds are they navigating at home and at school? What does their classroom environment look, sound, and smell like? Those inputs are slowly draining their battery as the day goes on. If your child has a smaller funnel spout, you might notice that these stressors drain their battery more quickly. We can't eliminate these biological stressors, but we can help our children recharge by building in opportunities for them to have downtime and tune out. Downtime might include going into their bedroom and reading or listening to calming music. It might be building a blanket fort and giving them a quiet toy or activity to do. Some families have used a play tent or even a cardboard box with a blanket over the top to create a quiet spot for a child to hang when they need less stimulation. Ideally, this area can be consistently available so that they can access it as needed.

Sleep

Our town was doing a fundraiser for a local family who had lost their home in a fire. There was an auction, a spaghetti dinner, and a street dance. A part of the road was blocked off, a dad volunteered to DJ, and glow sticks were handed out. The kids were so excited to get to stay up past their bedtime and dance outside in the street with their friends. They had an amazing evening and it was all great until it was time to go home and everyone crashed and seemed to melt down. My plan was to get them home to bed, and reset tomorrow. Except that when they woke up the next day it continued. The whining, the fighting, the pushback—what the heck? You just woke up. But they'd just woken up with an hour and half less sleep than they normally got. They were still tired and now their capacity for regulation was much lower than usual.

Researchers from the University of Maryland School of Medicine (UMSOM) have linked lack of sleep in children with greater incidences of mental health problems like depression, anxiety, and an increase in impulsive behaviors.[2] Elementary-school-age children should get nine to twelve hours of sleep per night. "Children who had insufficient sleep had smaller volume in certain areas of the brain responsible for attention, memory, and inhibition control, compared to those with healthy sleep habits," says study lead Dr. Ze Wang.[3] Sometimes we see a connection between how a child filters sensory input and their sleep needs. If your child tends to be a large funnel spout kid, you might notice their sleep needs are on the low end of the spectrum. Conversely, a sensory-sensitive child (smaller funnel spout) might need more sleep in order to fully recharge.

Having a consistent bedtime and wake time can help regulate your child's circadian rhythm, making it easier for them to fall asleep at bedtime and wake refreshed in the morning. Consider using blackout shades to help facilitate easy initiation of sleep if it's still light out at your child's bedtime and to protect their sleep if the sun rises before their desired wake time. Research shows that consistent sound, like white, pink, or brown noise can help drown out outside noise, supporting a deeper, more restful sleep. Screen use within an hour of bedtime can prevent the production of melatonin, the sleepy hormone that supports the initiation of sleep. Keeping phones and screens out of bedrooms is a way to regulate screen use. It can be helpful for kids to listen to an audiobook or meditation to fall asleep. For children who struggle with anxiety, keeping a journal to offload their thoughts and feelings before bed can be a supportive tool for processing the day.

Balancing Task Demand and Capacity

Zeke's parents were at a loss. Zeke had just come home from school with his report card. It was the end of the first quarter of fifth grade. Each night Zeke had told his parents he had done his homework and was all set for the next day. They made sure to ask if he needed any help and he always said he didn't. His report card told a different story. Zeke had over fifteen missing assignments. The note from his teacher said he was doing well in the classroom, but that homework was often missing or not finished.

Why didn't he tell them he was having trouble? They'd never had a problem with him lying before. At least not on a consistent basis like this. His parents didn't understand what had changed. Plus, they made sure to have him take care of his homework before he did anything else. As soon as he walked through the door, it was homework time. They wanted him to be able to get it done so he could enjoy the rest of his evening. They wondered where they had gone wrong.

As the next quarter started, Zeke's mom committed to sitting down with him each day after school and getting his homework done. Each afternoon it was an uphill battle. He couldn't remember which assignments needed to be done. He was easily distracted and quickly frustrated. He would eventually lay his head on the table and stop responding to his mom's prompts to get it done. He continued to turn in half-done assignments, and his parents' feelings of helplessness and frustration increased.

On the surface it might seem like Zeke is lazy or unmotivated. His parents are really concerned about his lying too—which makes total sense. They're doing their best to make sure he's successful at school, and somehow this is the result. So what's going on at the root? Zeke's story is a great illustration of what happens when a child's task demand is greater than their capacity.

This was the first quarter of fifth grade and his teacher noted that he was doing well in the classroom. What he was experiencing when he got home was restraint collapse. Restraint collapse is what happens when we hold it together all day and then lose it when we finally get to our safe space. We often associate after-school restraint collapse with meltdowns, big emotional outbursts, or disrespect. It doesn't always look like that though. It can also be avoidance and withdrawal, as Zeke's parents were experiencing with him. With the stressors of a new school year, the increased academic rigor, the new social dynamics, and the pressure to hold it all together in class, Zeke gets home and has nothing left. His battery is drained—his capacity gone. He isn't lazy, unmotivated, or lying to be deceitful or defiant. He is exhibiting signs of dysregulation.

His parents try their best to set him up for success by encouraging him to get his work done right away when he gets home, so he can have the rest of the day to play and relax. He tries but he just can't. He knows what he needs to do for homework, but he has nothing left to give. Unknowingly, Zeke's parents are increasing his stress after school by having homework time happen immediately. They want so badly for him to succeed, but they just don't yet know what he needs to be successful. When we're looking at what kids need to be set up for success, we're going to refer back to FACTS.

Using FACTS, Zeke's parents restructured Zeke's afternoon routine. Through the process of elimination, they honed in on what aspects Zeke might need. Zeke had always been a solid sleeper, so they could eliminate S (sleep). He also walked home from school, so they didn't think a lack of activity was the problem. That eliminated A (activity). That left Food, Connection, and Tune-out. They started offering food right away when Zeke got home from school. He sat and had a snack and talked or played tic-tac-toe with his mom. Then she encouraged him to take some downtime in his room. They came up with what that would look like together.

"Zeke, we're going to start giving you some relaxation time after school. When you get home, I'll make you a snack and hang with you for a bit. Then it will be relaxation time. What do you think would help you relax after school?" his mom asked him.

"Playing Mario Kart?" he suggested.

"I really want to give your brain a break from bright lights and sounds. Mario Kart has both of those. Do you have any other ideas?" she replied.

"I could build Lego?"

"Perfect. Your after-school relaxation time can be Lego time."

After Lego time, it was homework time. His mom sat down with him and helped him. With his basic needs met, he was able to stay focused for a longer period of time. His frustration tolerance was higher. He still needed some reminders and support from his mom, but it was getting done.

Fast-forward a few months. The new routine is now well-established. Every day after school Zeke has snack and connection time with his mom and then his Lego relaxation time. Next, he moves on to his homework. Except now, he's doing it unprompted. He rarely needs reminders, and if he has a challenge he can't work through, he'll bring it to his mom to ask for help. With her support, he's able to work through even the most frustrating homework problems.

Using FACTS, Zeke's parents were able to meet his needs so that he could be successful with his nightly homework. While they thought that getting homework done right away would be best for Zeke, what he actually needed was food, connection, and time to tune out first. They implemented snack time, with his mom there to connect with him. Emotional connection is key for kids to be collaborative and cooperative (we're going to dive deeper into emotional connection in the next section). His mom was setting the stage for a regulated homework time by filling his emotional cup first. Note that it wasn't a long, drawn-out activity. It was simply a few minutes of his mom being present to him, being available to chat or play a quick game.

Next, he got a stimulation break. They worked together to figure out what it would look like. Zeke's first suggestion was screen time—which makes total sense. When you're mentally exhausted, vegging out in front of the TV sounds so appealing. There's nothing wrong with vegging out in front of a screen, but it's not a good fit for all kids if you're looking to regulate the nervous system (more on this in Chapter 9). Zeke's mom explained why screens weren't an option, and she and Zeke continued to brainstorm. His next suggestion was Lego, which his mom agreed was a great option.

At first Zeke's mom was remained there to support him through his homework. Eventually though, Zeke was doing it independently. Not only that, but when something challenging did pop up, he was regulated enough to ask for help and then stay on task to work through it. Zeke went through an incredible transformation, from lying, avoidance, and missed assignments to regularly completing his homework independently.

Your Child's Emotional Bank Account

We were rushing to get out the door for school. We'd all woken up late and needed to get on the road in the next five minutes. Getting dressed had been a battle. I tossed the kids some toast while getting their lunches into their backpacks. My son started complaining about how his socks felt and I'd already changed them once. I could feel myself getting irritated and snappy.

"You guys, I've said it at least three times now. Get your shoes on, NOW," I said to them.

"I don't want to go to school! I hate school," my son replied.

"Sorry you hate school, but it's time to go. Get your shoes on, I'm getting in the car."

"NO. I HATE school. I'm not getting my dumb shoes on because I'm never going back."

I grabbed their backpacks and walked out to the car. Both kids were still in the entryway and still without shoes.

"Are you kidding? What is happening this morning? Just get your shoes on. Come ON." My frustration was building. Why did everything have to be a battle? "Just get in the car, you can put your shoes on while we drive."

After I dropped the kids off and had a minute to reflect on our morning, I realized something. Typically in the morning we are all awake early enough that we don't have to rush. Usually my son crawls into bed with me and sits with me while I wake up and drink my coffee. My daughter joins us and we have a little chat about the day ahead, or something else that might be on her mind. They each have the time and space to connect with me in their own way—and I try to be sure their emotional cups are filled before we enter the hustle and bustle of getting ready and out the door. On this particularly challenging morning, we had woken up late. I had started the day in a rush. I didn't connect with either one of them, and instead, my first interaction with them was my listing off all the things they needed to do.

We are wired for emotional connection. Without it, our nervous systems do not feel fully safe or regulated. When our emotional bank account is empty, we don't have the capacity for collaboration and cooperation. Imagine for a moment that you've just woken up. Your partner immediately starts rushing you, reminding you that you're going to be late for work. You start getting ready, but your clothes feel uncomfortable. You go to change and your partner gets irritated with you. "Hurry up!" they half shout at you. You're already feeling the stress of needing to get ready quickly, and their irritated tone isn't helping. You're still groggy, and you can't find your jacket. You rush around and finally find it. Your partner is already walking out to the car and they shout over their shoulder, "LET'S GO!" Now you're becoming irritated. You get in the car and your partner starts talking about the house project you've been working on together. He

Prefrontal Cortex
Logical thinking part of the brain, used in problem-solving, making conscious, regulated choices, and conflict resolution.

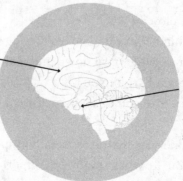

Amygdala
Survival part of the brain, which uses the instincts to fight, flee, freeze, or fawn to try to stay alive and feel safe.

asks you if you can stop at the hardware store to grab something. You're immediately annoyed. *The audacity to ask for something after the way our morning went*, you think to yourself. *You've got to be kidding.* After the morning you just had, your nervous system is sounding the alarm. You're in your amygdala, the feelings part of your brain. You're not accessing the prefrontal cortex, the part of the brain required for logic and problem-solving. You can't enter into chatting about the project with your partner until you can move out of your amygdala and access the rest of your brain.

It's the same for kids. My kids weren't cooperating that morning getting ready for school because they *couldn't*. They didn't wake up and decide to be difficult. They woke up and had needs that I didn't have the bandwidth to meet that day. They felt disconnected from me and their nervous system alarms were going off. Before I could ask them to get ready and get out the door, they needed their emotional bank account filled. When I didn't have the capacity to do that, they were unable to cooperate with me and we had a me-versus-them morning. The goal isn't that we are always connected and collaborative. Relationships involve this ebb and flow of connection and disconnection. We can reconnect later and acknowledge how off the morning felt. In the moment, if we have the capacity, we can state the experience. "Wow, we woke up late and the morning routine is all off. It feels uncomfortable and we are all having a hard time with each other this morning."

Often the way that children express love is how they like to receive love. Think about what your child does when they want to interact with you.

Do they snuggle up close to you?
Do they do something helpful for you?
Do they want to play a game or sit down and chat?
Do they create a piece of art for you?
Do they tell you they love you or say something kind?

Typically, there is one way that is especially important and impactful for them. Pay attention to what might be important to your child by noticing how they express their love to you. Filling a child's emotional cup doesn't require tons of time, or one-on-one undivided attention, but it does require some intention. Notice what fills their cup and focus on making small connections throughout the day in ways that mean the most to them. Think quality over quantity.

Obedience Culture

A well-behaved child isn't always an *emotionally well* child.
And an emotionally well child isn't *always* well behaved.

—ELI HARWOOD, M.A., LPC[4]

Many of us were raised in obedience culture. We were expected to do as we were told, no arguments. If we didn't, we were disobedient, defiant, disrespectful. Our parents wanted us to listen to them—and I totally get that. I also want my kids to listen to me. I don't want my kids to ignore what I say or do the opposite of what I ask of them. The allure of obedience makes total sense. It can feel so exhausting when kids constantly push the boundary or always need to know the why behind something. It would be so nice if every once in a while they just said, "Sure, Mom," and complied with the boundary being set. The reality is that if I want to raise kids who understand their sensory and emotional needs, and know how to meet those needs, they have to be allowed to advocate for themselves now and push back against "authority" in the safety of our home to learn how to do so respectfully. While expecting and requiring obedience can work in the short term to manage behaviors, it can actually work against your long-term relationship with your child.

Let's think back to Zeke for a moment. He wasn't getting his homework done, even when his parents had reminded him and even when they sat down and tried to help him. Imagine for a moment that Zeke's parents didn't recognize or address the needs of his nervous system, but rather focused on making sure he obeyed them at all costs. Every night they sat down together and made Zeke get his homework done. Punishment and obedience culture often go hand in hand, so imagine that his parents threatened to take away all of his screen time if he didn't complete his homework every day after school. Zeke would continue to struggle from lack of capacity. If he was able to complete the homework, it wouldn't be his best work. When each afternoon was a struggle for Zeke, his parents would increasingly see him as disobedient and defiant. The homework might get done, but Zeke's self-worth would diminish and his relationship with his parents would suffer.

Obedience culture is often a breeding ground for perfectionism and anxiety. Perfectionism is linked to higher rates of psychological struggles, like behavioral and peer challenges.[5] If you make a mistake, if you take a risk, if you are not perfect, you're in trouble. There's no room for dropping the ball, being accountable, and maintaining connection and safety in the relationship if every time your child doesn't obey, you assert dominance and control. Want to know what's even more impactful and powerful? Curiosity. I wonder why they disobeyed. I wonder what's coming up for them. Are they afraid of not fitting in? Of not having friends if they listen to that rule? Are they overwhelmed with what's on their plate? Are they struggling with something personally and need support? Curiosity leads to connection, which often aligns behavior with values.

"No one is going to want to play with him if he's always telling people what to do like that and never using manners," a friend of mine vented about her child. If someone comes up to you and says, "I need that pen" versus "Can I please have that pen?," your nervous system may react differently to the two phrases. One might put you on the defensive or in attack mode, with the other leaving you feeling secure and safe. How we say things can affect how others perceive us and can lead to opportunities for success. Dr. Stephen Nowicki's book *Raising a Socially Successful Child: Teaching Kids the Nonverbal Language They Need to Communicate, Connect, and Thrive* dives into how our tone and body language are a part of communication; in fact, nonverbal communication is often more powerful than what we say with our words. For some children this can be learned through how you speak to them, what you model in how you communicate with folks when they are around, and through what they observe others doing. For other children those nuances in modeling can get lost and they might need more specific examples of language to use or nonverbal gestures to consider for social success. The goal isn't for all kids to be robots, communicating in the same way, but rather for all kids to have the toolbox they need for the success they're interested in. If they want to enter a peer group, join the soccer team, or participate in drama club, we can equip them with the ways to communicate that can set them up for success. We start by helping them learn what to communicate and then move into how.

On the drive to Jordan's house for a pool party, Juno's mom, Erin, reminded Juno of their family rule when visiting other people's homes: to ask kindly if they want or need something. Last time they were there, Juno had taken it upon herself to pop into the kitchen pantry and grab a snack. Erin had been embarrassed when Juno emerged with chips and salsa at the pool, having taken them without asking, and Jordan had said, "Those are my chips."

"Hey, Juno, when we are at Jordan's, if you need anything, you can ask Mrs. McNeil. Remember to say please when you ask," Erin had gently reminded her.

About an hour later, Erin overheard Juno say, "Mrs. McNeil, I'd like to get some juice from the fridge."

"Sure, go ahead," Mrs. McNeil replied.

On the way home, Erin acknowledged that she was proud of Juno for asking for the juice, and then added, "It can feel kind to the other person if you say please when you ask or thank you when you get the juice. We can practice those next time." First, they worked on what to say, and next, they would work on how to say it. Building these skills would help Juno navigate social situations and access what she needed in a prosocial manner.

We can punish, shame, or otherwise force kids to obey, but it won't set us up for a long-term relationship of collaboration and cooperation. If you're reading this, I know that you want to have a trusting, connected, emotionally healthy relationship with your child. I know that you want your child to listen to you because they want to hear what you have to say, not because they are afraid of what will happen to them if they don't.

Chapter 4

You're Old Enough to Know Better

Luis and Mace are brother and sister. Luis is ten and Mace is six. Luis's parents describe him as high energy and easily distracted. His body needs a lot of movement to be regulated. He's been called a "busy body" by his teachers. Mace tends to move through the world more slowly. She's observant and detail-oriented. Her nervous system regulates best with reduced stimulation and she needs much less big body play than Luis.

Their dad, Andy, is struggling with their morning routine and getting out the door for school. When it's breakfast time, while Mace sits and eats, Luis is up and down from the table constantly. If he sees a marker nearby, he'll start doodling. If there's an action figure on the counter, he'll grab that and start playing. Andy will remind him to eat and he'll take a few bites and then get distracted again. This is the type of behavior Andy would expect from Mace, given that she's only six, but not from Luis—he's old enough to sit still. Yet Mace is the one sitting at the table eating while Luis is all over the place.

It's the same trouble with getting dressed and brushing teeth. Andy explains that Mace is six, so she still needs some help. He lays out her clothes for her the night before and then she'll get dressed on her own. He loads her toothbrush and then she'll brush her teeth. She has a checklist with pictures in her room that she follows in the morning, and Andy is available to help her through it as needed.

While Andy is trying to support Mace, Luis is constantly interrupting. He can't find the pants he wants, he can't find comfortable socks, his favorite shoes have mud on them. "Bud, you're ten. This shouldn't be so difficult. Just get dressed. Mace is already ready to go," Andy says. "Yeah, because you helped her! Her clothes are already out every morning. It's easy for her!" Luis shouts back.

While Mace goes and gets her shoes on, Luis is still barefoot trying to find socks. Andy tells Luis it's time to get in the car. Mace heads out to the car while Luis starts trying to wipe the mud off his sneakers. He decides he needs a different pair of shoes altogether. He runs back to his closet to find them. Mace is already in the car and buckled in. The clock is ticking and they're going to be late. Andy is running out of patience. "Luis, LET'S GO! It shouldn't be this hard. You're too old for this—you know how to get ready. You need to start listening to me in the morning. You're going to be late to school!"

When we look at a child's behavior, it's very easy to use their age as a benchmark for what we can expect. In some respects this is totally appropriate. I still expect to have to keep a close eye on my kindergartner when we are in a parking lot or crossing a street. Sometimes I even need to hold his hand, depending on his regulation level. If I feel like his battery is low (and subsequently his access to impulse control), I'll hold his hand. However, with my fourth grader, I trust that she can navigate a parking lot safely without me having eyes on her constantly. She knows how to look both ways for cars and can cross the street safely if she needs to. It makes sense to have different expectations based on a child's age, but it gets tricky when we start to expect children to stop having needs or stop expressing those needs by a certain age—this is what we call age bias.

Let's look at how age bias is showing up in Andy's response to Luis and Mace. Mace is six, so when she needs extra support moving through the morning, her parents expect it. They've done an incredible job of setting her up for success by laying out her clothes, loading her toothbrush, and giving her a visual guide in case she needs help remembering the steps required of her. Luis is ten and when he has trouble in the morning, it annoys his parents. They expect more from him. He's older, he's been in school longer than Mace, and he's had much more experience with the morning routine—shouldn't he be able to handle this? This is the fallacy of age bias—it tricks us into believing that age is the best way to determine which behaviors we can expect from a child. What we actually want to look at when determining what we can expect is the child's nervous system and level of regulation.

The way that Luis and Mace are described by their parents gives us important information about their nervous systems. Luis is a child we would describe as a sensory seeker. He needs a lot of input to be regulated. He's kind of a whirlwind, always moving, always getting into things as he's trying to meet that need for himself. Mace moves through the world more slowly; she's attentive to details and very observant. She needs less input and movement to be regulated and it's easier for her to stay focused on a task—like getting ready in the morning. To add another layer to this dynamic, Mace is only six, so her parents expect to have to support her. They've set her up with a visual checklist, they lay out her clothes, and they load her toothbrush for her. These supports help her to move through the morning routine without getting drained or overwhelmed. Luis at age ten, with his unique nervous system needs, also needs support moving through the morning. Just because he's older doesn't mean that those nervous system needs don't exist anymore.

Andy tries changing Luis's morning routine with his nervous system needs in mind. First thing in the morning, Luis has access to movement. He has five minutes to jump on his bed, work out with Andy, spin on Andy's office chair, or have a dance party in his room. He has a small poster in his room with his four movement options and he gets to pick one each morning. Next, he eats breakfast. He sits next to Mace, but his chair is different. He has a chair band around the legs of his chair and he kicks the band back and forth as he eats. After he eats, he goes to the bathroom, where he finds his toothbrush loaded and a sand timer. He turns the timer and brushes until the time is up. He hops down the hall to his room and puts on the clothes that he and Andy laid out the night before. He looks over to his door and checks his visual checklist. He still needs to put on his shoes and then he'll be ready. He chose his shoes last night and they're ready next to the door. He puts them on and heads out to the car.

With Andy's support, Luis's mornings have completely changed. With more access to regulating movement throughout his morning routine, Luis now has the capacity to accomplish his tasks. Andy provides additional support with visual aids and helps Luis lay out his clothes and shoes the night before. When Luis goes to the bathroom to brush his teeth, his body is regulated, and with his toothbrush loaded and a timer ready for him, it's not draining for him to get his teeth brushed. Every small thing that Andy has added to their mornings, from the chair band to the checklist, stacks up to create a huge change for Luis. With his needs met, the mornings are no longer a battle.

We don't grow out of needs. We have the opportunity to provide systems of support to help each other thrive. My friend was just sharing how she was thirty-seven years old when she realized she needed to meal-plan her family's dinners for the week, otherwise she would wind up scrambling every afternoon and evening trying to figure out what to make with what she had on hand. When she plans the meals out over the weekend, she can get the right groceries and then the rest is all laid out on the magnetic fridge calendar. No guessing or remembering required. We get to help kids develop systems for success. Luis wasn't trying to be late and unable to focus every morning; he just needed a system that would set him up for success.

Meeting Them Where They Are

Imagine that you're teaching in a third-grade classroom. Your students are reading early chapter books. You have a new student, and they've been placed in your classroom based on their age, but they don't know the alphabet. You're not going to hand them a chapter book. You're going to start with the alphabet and help them build the skills they'll need to *eventually* read chapter books. You understand and accept that this will take time, regardless of the fact that they are "old enough" to know how to read. While we readily accept that reading requires us to meet a child where they are and build from there, we often struggle to grasp the same concept when it comes to emotional development. Why is this such a challenge for us? Many of us come into adulthood and parenthood with social programming that shapes how we perceive emotions and behavior through the lens of a child's age.

Think about what you saw and heard as a child. How did your parents or caregivers respond to a crying baby? Was it different from how they responded to a toddler or an older child? Many of us were held to higher (and unrealistic) expectations as we got older. When we shouted or cried from frustration but were "old enough to know better," we weren't met with empathy and understanding. Our caregivers weren't able to see past the behavior to the underlying need. We learned that we wouldn't get the support we needed when we expressed emotions in certain ways, so we learned to suppress our emotions. We learned to mask. Those experiences shape how we perceive *our* children's needs and behaviors and what biases we bring into our parenting. We all have biases. The goal isn't that they never pop up in our parenting; the goal is that we can start to identify them and begin to rewrite those narratives and create new patterns in our relationship with our children.

I can really relate to Andy's reaction to Luis. "You're too old for this" or "You're old enough to know better" were lines I heard frequently in my childhood. That deeply ingrained bias often pops up as my first reaction when I feel torn between my five-year-old and my nine-year-old. We were getting ready to go for a hike and my son was irritated with his socks. While he was kicking off his boots and half shouting about the "stupid" socks, my daughter was telling me about a conflict she was navigating with her friend. I was trying to find different socks and was only half listening, nodding my head and saying "mhm" while rummaging through a laundry basket. "Mom, are you even listening?!" she asked me. "I'm doing my best. Can't you see I'm trying to do two things at once? Can you just wait for a second?" I replied. "You're so mean. You're only helping HIM." She pointed her finger at her brother. "I hate this family!" she shouted. "Do you really think talking to me like that is going to make me want to help you?!" I replied. She stormed out to the car, slamming the door behind her.

Age bias was coming up for me at that moment, big-time. My son had shouted at me and said "stupid" and I'd been able to look past that and work on meeting his needs. According to the biases I hold around age, it was easy for me to accept that he had lost access to kindness and patience because he was dysregulated. For my nine-year-old, I had a different perspective. I was only looking at her behavior through the lens of her age. She needed my emotional support with a social conflict, and when I couldn't give it to her in the moment, she got frustrated. My age bias popped up and I immediately classified her as "old enough to know better" than to interrupt me while I was trying to respond to her cranky brother, and then to get snarky with me when I wasn't able to be present to her. The truth is that she was dysregulated by a social stressor and then when she reached out to me to help her, I was unable to authentically connect with her, which increased her dysregulation. It makes sense that she got snarky with me; she's human. It's not a fair or developmentally appropriate response to expect a nine-year-old to never react from a place of dysregulation. Heck, that's not a fair or developmentally appropriate response for any human, adults included. If I can accept that my five-year-old has needs that sometimes feel inconvenient, and that his expression of those needs will sometimes be from a place of dysregulation, I can also accept that from my nine-year-old.

Something to note from that interaction: It's okay that I didn't have the bandwidth in the moment to actively listen to her while I was tending to her brother. It's okay to not be able to be emotionally present to your child at the drop of a hat. It's not possible to do that or even necessary. My inability to be present in the moment wasn't the issue. The issue was that my bias prevented me from seeing her need for what it was and responding to that. Instead, I saw only the behavior, the unkind words, and I lost my cool. It would have been a whole different ball game if she had said, "You're so mean! I hate this family!" and I had responded with, "Ugh, I'm so focused on finding these socks, I can't give you my full attention. I know this is important to you and I really want to listen to you. Let me get us out the door and we can chat about this in the car."

Teach Them What They *Can* Do

"It's kindergarten behavior," the fifth-grade teacher told me. "Crying?" I inquired. "Yeah, fifth graders should know how to solve problems. They shouldn't still be crying about them." While fifth graders should absolutely have problem-solving skills, expressing a hard emotion through tears doesn't indicate the absence of those skills. Remember the Five Phases of Emotion Processing from Chapter 2? The first phase is allowing the emotion. Being allowed to feel is a prerequisite for moving through the rest of the phases, including problem-solving or moving on.

When we tell children they're too old to cry or that they should know better than to shout or misbehave, what we're actually communicating is that if they lack the skills to express their emotions differently, they need to hide or suppress those emotions because it's too inconvenient for us. What if we send a different message? What if we respond with empathy, regardless of a child's age? What if we let their nervous system know that they are safe? What if our actions say, "It's okay to feel. It's okay to have needs. You're safe with me and I will teach you how to express in a way that will help you be successful in this world."

Building emotional literacy doesn't happen in the heat of the moment. As we learned in Chapter 3, we first have to communicate safety to a child's nervous system. Remember how I snapped at my daughter after she told me I was mean and she hated our family? Even if I had been able to stay calm, and respond in a better way, it still wouldn't have been a teaching moment. Not yet, anyway. She was coming into the scenario dysregulated. She wasn't ready to learn. I wasn't able to respond the way I wanted to that day, so later on when we were both calm, I entered into repair with her. "Hey, love, remember earlier today before the hike when I snapped at you? I'm sorry. I should have taken a moment to breathe so I could speak to you with kindness." She nodded quietly. "It makes total sense that you were frustrated when I wasn't fully listening to you. It's hard when I get distracted taking care of your brother sometimes."

"It's so unfair! He takes so much of your attention," she replied.

"Sometimes being the big sister can be tough, huh?"

"Yeah. It can," she said quietly.

Before I dove into chatting about her behavior, I wanted to own my mistakes and let her know that I understood what she was feeling at that moment and that her feelings were valid. This pours into her emotional bank account and adds to our connection. Once I knew she felt safe and validated, I circled back to her behavior. "When you need my attention and you're frustrated with me, instead of calling me mean or saying you hate our family, how else could you let me know?" I asked her.

"I don't know. I didn't feel calm enough to be kind," she replied.

"That makes total sense. I didn't feel calm either, and then I got a little snarky too," I said. "Something that helps me get calm so I can be kind is to take a couple of deep breaths or scrunch my shoulders up to my ears and then release them down a few times. I'm going to try to do that next time. What do you think could help you feel calm?"

"I feel calm when I can take space, but I couldn't take space because we were getting out the door," she said.

"Hm. That makes it tricky. Can you think of anything else that helps you feel calm?" I asked.

"I could use my headphones. Can we keep them in the car so I have them when I can't take space?" she asked.

"Absolutely," I replied.

A note on making mistakes and repairing: Nobody is doing this perfectly. We are human and things will get messy. That is how being in a close relationship with another person works. There will be conflict; it might get ugly sometimes. Helping your child with their social and emotional development doesn't mean that you will live without conflict; it means that you're working to build the tools necessary to navigate it in an emotionally healthy way. When I could see past my daughter's age, own my mistakes, and lean into what she needed, it opened the door for me to teach her how she could get that need met differently next time. It gave me the chance to add to her toolbox, and to continue to help her build the skills she'll need to move through future social situations with success. It provided an opportunity for me to model how to make mistakes and reconnect with someone through accountability.

Developmentally Appropriate Behavior

When my oldest turned six, I noticed a distinct change in her. Suddenly, she no longer took what I said at face value. My telling her that something was true or right just didn't satisfy her anymore. She needed to know *why*. She needed to see it for herself. If I asked her to put on a jacket, she'd want to know why she needed one. If I told her it was cold out, she'd try to negotiate. If I insisted, she'd choose a jacket, not a sweatshirt, and she'd roll her eyes at me, the disdain radiating off her so thick I could cut it with a knife. She was beginning to understand that the rules of her world were not absolute, they were shaped by the adults around her—and she wanted her own voice and influence to have their place. She wanted to shape her own world. So she started experimenting. She used a sharp tone, she rolled her eyes, she got snippy with me. She was argumentative and dismissive. *Where did my sweet little girl go?*

Maria Montessori, a physician and founder of the Montessori education philosophy, identified middle childhood as the "age of rudeness." If you've ever been on the receiving end of the abrupt and abrasive communication of an elementary-school-age child, you know what she is talking about. Understanding that this is a part of your child's development doesn't mean that boundaries and expectations go out the window. It doesn't mean that you're allowing them to be rude, argumentative, or disrespectful (buckle up, we're diving into disrespect and defiance in the next chapter). What understanding typical development allows us to do is to see these undesirable behaviors for what they really are: a lack of capacity or an area where the child needs to build a new skill.

When we are looking at developmentally appropriate behaviors, we have to look through the lens of skill building and capacity. Rather than asking myself how old a child is in order to gauge my expectations, I ask myself: *Do they have self-awareness and self-regulation skills? Have they been taught to notice what is happening in their body? Do they have coping strategies to turn to?* If the answers are yes, my next question is: *Have their FACTS needs been met, allowing them the capacity to execute those skills?* The behaviors we might expect to see from a child who has been taught self-awareness and self-regulation skills, and who has had their FACTS needs met in that moment, are going to be vastly different than the behaviors we would expect from a child who hasn't yet built those skills or doesn't have the capacity to access them. Your child may communicate that they need support building or accessing a skill through various behaviors like melting down, pouting, complaining, sulking, slamming doors, using impermissible language, throwing things, withdrawing, or lying. This is not to say that these behaviors are permissible, but rather that it is within the realm of normal to see them surface.

We can acknowledge that challenging behaviors are part of childhood development while also helping children build the skills to meet their underlying needs. When we only wait for behaviors to pass instead of offering this support, those unmet needs often resurface in new challenging behaviors in the next stage of development. When your child's FACTS needs are met and their nervous system regulated, you can begin to help them learn what they can do next time, and how they can make a better choice in the future.

Expecting More from Children Than We Expect from Ourselves

I was loading the dishwasher while waiting on hold with the insurance company. I was trying to dispute a claim that had been coded wrong, while also trying to get the kitchen cleaned up so I could make lunch. My son was at the table working on a puzzle. It was a jigsaw puzzle and every time he pressed a new piece into place, he was accidentally shifting the whole puzzle and a few pieces would come apart. He was mostly able to fix it on his own and move forward, but as time went on, he was getting more frustrated with it. Just as he asked me for help, the insurance agent came onto the line. "Hang on, buddy," I whispered. "I can come help you as soon as I get off the phone."

"WHAT?!" he shouted. "Right when I ask you for help you have to get on the phone? I hate this puzzle!" He stomped away down the hall and started repeatedly slamming his door. I tried to pay attention to the agent on the phone, while the loud banging continued. Eventually I stomped down to his room, opened the door, and said, "Stop it! I just need to finish this conversation! I've been on hold forever, just let me get it done!" He went to slam the door again and I blocked it with my foot. I stood there, blocking him, while I finished the phone call. When I got off the phone, I was thoroughly irritated. "Sometimes I just need you to wait. I can't always help you at the drop of a hat. I had been waiting for a long time to speak with someone. I need you to have more patience."

Later that day we were getting ready to head to a school function. My daughter was receiving a sports award, and the event required semiformal attire. I'd helped each kid get dressed and gotten myself dressed. My son was building with Lego while I packed up the car. Typically I would have given him a five-minute warning, but time got away from me and now it was time to go. "Buddy, let's get shoes on. We need to get in the car now."

"Hang on!" he said. "I just need to add a couple of last pieces."

"Buddy, we need to go now. We're going to be late. Go get in the car please," I replied. I walked down the hall to grab my phone and purse and turn out the lights in the house. When I walked back into the living room, he was still building.

"We need to go NOW. I told you that. Stop building and get your shoes on. We're late!" I said with irritation.

"I just needed a minute. You can never wait for me!" he shouted as he went to get his shoes on.

His words sank in and it dawned on me: I ask him to wait all the time, including that same day when I was on the phone, but when he asks me to wait, I'm not willing to do that. When I tell him to do something, I want him to drop what he's doing and respond to me immediately. Yet when he expects me to drop what I'm doing for him, I get frustrated and give him a lecture about patience. If I have a hard time waiting, why do I expect him to be fine with it? Why are adults allowed to make mistakes, experience different emotions, and have needs that aren't convenient while holding kids to a different expectation? If adults yell when they're frustrated, why can't kids? If adults get angry when they're embarrassed, why can't kids?

Our kids see what we are modeling, and while we don't have to be perfect, we can't expect them to be perfect either. So sometimes you'll have a hard time waiting and sometimes they will too. Sometimes you'll yell when you're frustrated and sometimes they will too. Before expecting perfection from them, pause and ask yourself if you are holding them to different expectations than you hold yourself to.

Chapter 5

Responding to Disrespect and Defiance

Nadia is a bright, precocious, social eleven-year-old. She does well in school and is involved in several extracurriculars. Her teachers often remark that she is helpful, kind, and quick to follow direction. Lately, when Nadia's parents have listened to her teachers describe her, they've felt like there is no way they are talking about the same child. At home Nadia is moody, argumentative, and sassy. She's constantly rolling her eyes at the things her parents say. The tiniest thing can set her off into a rage spiral. She's unpredictable and unhelpful. Her parents are exasperated by her much of the time.

Nadia's mom, Amiya, recalls an argument they had recently. Nadia asked to play a game on Amiya's phone. Amiya said no because Nadia needed to take care of her after-school tasks first. Lately she had gotten into the habit of tossing her backpack on the floor and leaving her shoes in the entryway instead of unloading her bag, emptying her lunch box, and putting her shoes away. "Before you can use my phone, you need to empty your lunch box, hang your backpack, and put away your shoes," Amiya told her.

"No, I just got home from school and I'm tired. I'm not doing that," Nadia replied.

"Okay, well, it needs to be taken care of before you can use my phone," Amiya said.

"Whatever, I'll just watch the TV then." Nadia rolled her eyes at her mom as she said it.

"No, you aren't having screens until that stuff is taken care of," Amiya replied.

Nadia grabbed the remote and plopped down on the couch.

"I can take the batteries out of the remote or unplug the TV if it's too hard for you to listen," Amiya said.

"Ugh, you are the WORST!" Nadia shouted. "I wish I didn't have to live in this stupid house with your stupid rules." She stomped out to the entryway and chucked her shoes as hard as she could into the shoe bin. She grabbed her lunch box out of her backpack and threw it into the sink—breaking a small cup as she did so. She stomped to her room, slammed the door, and yelled, "STAY OUT!" as loud as she could.

Amiya is at a loss. She's worried about Nadia's behavior and needs it to change.

Allowing kids to feel and teaching them to process their emotions doesn't mean that behavior is a free-for-all. Treating children with respect is often conflated with being permissive, but that couldn't be farther from the truth. A key component of treating children with respect is having boundaries and teaching them how to move through the world in a pro-social way. It is a disservice to children to allow any and all behaviors. All emotions are allowed, that doesn't mean all behaviors are allowed.

Nadia is described as helpful, kind, and quick to follow direction at school. So what's the deal at home? Although it can be easy to forget this, kids are going through so much at school. In addition to the academic pressures, they're navigating the social hierarchy in their peer group and trying to find their place. They may be experiencing embarrassment or rejection as friendship dynamics fluctuate. There can be a lot happening beneath the surface that impacts their capacity in the moment. The goal is to communicate to Nadia that she is allowed to feel frustrated when her mom says no. She's allowed to be annoyed that she has to take care of her things before she can use her mom's phone and she's *not* allowed to speak disrespectfully. She needs a boundary to help her learn what the expectation is regarding how she speaks to her mom. In the last chapter we noted that children may communicate that they need support through various behaviors including disrespect and defiance. Nadia is communicating that she needs help building the skills to navigate these emotions without getting disrespectful toward her mom.

Amiya makes some changes in the way her conversations with Nadia are going. She outlines her expectations for how Nadia can express her hard feelings. She starts off when they are both calm, and circles back to the fight they had about screens.

"Nadia, I know you're tired when you get home from school, and I know it can be really frustrating to follow the rules sometimes. I get that. Moving forward, if you speak to me disrespectfully, I'm going to be done talking until we're both calm and can speak kindly to each other." Nadia nods her head in acknowledgment and they move on with their day.

A few days later, they get into another argument. Nadia left her backpack on the floor again and her water bottle had leaked onto the carpet. "Nadia, come here please. I need you to take care of this," Amiya said, pointing to the water bottle and the mess on the floor.

"I don't want to, it's just water, it will dry," Nadia replied.

"Nadia, please wipe it up with a towel, it will only take a second," Amiya said.

"Well, if it will only take a second, why don't you do it? If it's so easy, why do I have to do it?" Nadia's tone of voice became sassier as the conversation progressed.

"Nadia, I'm not going to continue to discuss this if you can't speak with kindness. Wipe it up and let's move on with our day."

"No, I'm not done talking. You're the one having a stupid attitude. Why do you make such a big deal out of spilled water? You started this whole thing and you're the reason I'm not speaking with kindness!" Nadia was digging her heels in.

"I'm going to take some space in my bedroom. I'm open to chatting about this when we're both calm," Amiya replied as she walked to her bedroom and closed the door. Nadia stomped down the hall and tried to open the door—it was locked. Amiya heard the knob jiggling and reminded Nadia, "I'm taking space for a few minutes. I'll be out shortly. When I come out, if you can be respectful, I'm happy to chat."

"UGH! Fine!" Nadia replied.

Later that evening before bed, Amiya circled back to what had happened earlier. "Nadia, it makes sense to feel annoyed sometimes when I ask you to do something. There are times when I need to do something and I really don't want to. I understand that. At the same time, I expect us to treat each other with kindness and respect," Amiya said.

"I know. It's just really hard for me to be kind when I'm mad at you," Nadia replied.

"Totally. When I'm in a bad mood, it's hard for me to be kind. I find it helpful to take space when that happens," Amiya said.

"I don't like it when you take space from me. I feel like I need to keep talking to you," Nadia replied.

"Yeah, it can be really uncomfortable to be in conflict and not fix it right away. I get that. I'm still going to take space when you're not able to speak kindly to me. It doesn't mean that I'm mad at you, or that I don't love you. I will always love you no matter what. Sometimes we just won't be ready to talk things out," Amiya reassured Nadia. "Later, when we're both calm, we can come back to whatever it is." Nadia nodded her head in acknowledgment.

"Today has been tough. Let's go tackle the spilled water together. If you wipe up the spill, I'll clean your water bottle and refill it for tomorrow."

"Okay, deal," Nadia replied.

Amiya has given Nadia clear expectations for how to communicate during a conflict moving forward, and has followed through on her word by taking space when Nadia is being disrespectful and holding that boundary even when Nadia pushes back. It's important for kids to know that it's okay to feel frustrated, annoyed, or mad and Amiya does a great job of normalizing those emotions. It's also normal and expected that they need us to teach them how to communicate those feelings in an acceptable way. This is another one of those emotional literacy skills that takes time to build. Nadia is still going to lose her cool sometimes—she's going to get sassy and snarky. She's going to have days when she has lower capacity and needs her mom to set and hold that boundary until she can speak with kindness.

You may have noticed that Nadia expressed some discomfort around

Instead of . . .	**Try . . .**
"I cannot handle this right now! I'm going to my room. Please don't talk to me."	"I'm feeling really frustrated right now. I'm going to my bed to calm my body. I'll be back in a few moments. You are safe here."
"Ahh! I'm so mad." Then you walk away, leaving the child in isolation.	"You are safe to cry in your room. I need to go to my room to cry too. I'm leaving you for a moment and I will be back."
"If you're going to cry, go to your room. That's too loud."	"I want to keep you safe and treat you with respect. I need a moment alone first before we continue."

Amiya taking space. Nadia mentioned that she didn't like it when her mom did that, and she felt like she needed to keep talking to Amiya. That was Nadia's way of saying, "It's uncomfortable for me to be in conflict with you and not fix it or talk it out right away." Amiya acknowledged how uncomfortable it can be and reassured her that their relationship was intact, even when they were in conflict, even when they weren't able to talk it out right away.

The goal isn't to never be in conflict with our children. Conflict is a part of being in a close relationship with another human. If you grew up in a household where an adult disconnected from you, ignored you, or gave you the silent treatment when they were dysregulated by your behavior, then you might feel triggered by taking space during a conflict. You might notice a part of you that fears abandonment if you pause, slow down, or take space. There's a huge difference between taking space to regulate and come back together to reconnect or repair and taking space to punish a child with disconnection.

Respect and Obedience

Culturally we have trouble differentiating between respect and obedience. So many of us are navigating parenthood with social programming that taught us that respect and obedience are one and the same. Obedience relies on fear and punishment. Respect is entirely different. Respect relies on mutual understanding, collaboration, and cooperation. If someone asked me if I want my kids to be able to think for themselves, my answer would be *yes*. It's almost a no-brainer for me—until my child is standing in front of me, thinking for themselves, and suddenly it's triggering narratives around obedience and respect. In our culture we are quick to label a child "disrespectful" when what we actually mean is that they didn't blindly obey exactly what we said. We have to ask ourselves: What is our goal for this child as they move into adolescence and adulthood? Do we want them to think critically, be innovative, and be able to recognize when something isn't right? If we do, we have to allow those skills to be built now—which means we have to let go of the idea that they need to automatically follow everything we say. This doesn't mean they get to be rude, scream at us, or call us names. It does mean that we have to be open to allowing them to disagree with us, and be willing to collaboratively solve problems.

It was eight thirty p.m. and Eli was still awake. His bedtime was eight p.m., but this happened sometimes, where he'd fight falling asleep. He'd fidget in bed, and talk or sing to himself. He'd come out of his room repeatedly. He needed to go to the bathroom, or he wanted to see what time it was, or he had one more thing to tell his parents. On this particular night, his dad, James, was feeling drained and ready to be "off" from parenting.

"Eli, you need to stay in your bed. Stop fidgeting and rolling around. Enough is enough. If you come out of your room again, you're not going to Joey's house tomorrow after school," James told him.

Eli stayed in his bed, but continued to sing to himself. After about ten minutes, James returned to Eli's room. "Eli, stop singing. Stop talking. If you want to go to Joey's tomorrow, you need to be quiet."

"I can't fall asleep tonight. I don't know why but I just can't," Eli replied.

"I told you to stay in bed and be quiet. I don't care if you're awake, but you need to listen to me or you can forget about your plans tomorrow," James responded.

"That is so unfair! I can't help it if I can't fall asleep. Singing helps me settle down!"

"No, singing is keeping you awake. I said be quiet—that means be quiet."

Eli started to tear up. His capacity was low—he was tired and it had been a full day. He wasn't sure why he couldn't fall asleep. He was so looking forward to hanging out with Joey tomorrow. The idea of his plans being canceled riled him up even more. He tossed and turned for almost another hour before falling asleep.

"I can't believe he fights it so hard," his dad said to his mom. "Why can't he just listen and go to bed?!"

James was conflating respect and obedience and expecting immediate compliance. In James's mind, Eli was purposefully fighting sleep. He was disrespecting his dad by coming out of his bedroom, fidgeting, talking, and singing. James wanted Eli to go to his room, not come out, not move, and not speak. If he did those things, James would know that Eli respected him.

How might this same scenario play out if respect was differentiated from obedience? Given the same circumstances, what if James had responded as follows:

"Eli, you've come out of your room twice tonight. What's going on?" James asked him.

"I can't fall asleep tonight. I don't know why but I just can't," Eli replied.

"Okay. It's really important for your brain and body to get rest. It's okay if you can't fall asleep. I expect you to stay in your bed though," James responded. Eli nodded and walked back to his room.

Ten minutes passed and Eli came out again. "I still can't fall asleep," he whined. "It's taking forever."

"Bud, I know it's frustrating when it takes a while to fall asleep. Your job is to stay in your room, even when it's hard."

"Why does it have to be bedtime?! I'm not even tired."

"Eli, you can walk back to your room on your own, or we can walk together." James started to stand up to walk Eli back to his room.

"Fine!" Eli huffed. He returned to his room.

Eli stayed in his bed but continued to sing to himself. After another ten minutes, James went to Eli's room. "Eli, I'm concerned that you're keeping yourself up with the singing."

"It helps me stay still in my bed when I sing. I really think it helps me fall asleep faster," Eli replied.

"Okay, if singing helps you, that's fine. Please continue to stay in your bed."

Eli sang for another ten minutes or so and then all was quiet. His dad walked down the hall and peeked his head inside Eli's room—Eli was asleep.

In the second scenario, you may have noticed that James continued to be firm on the boundary of Eli staying in bed, while being open to Eli's thoughts on why singing should be permissible at bedtime. Allowing Eli to think for himself and have ideas doesn't mean that bedtime doesn't happen. Bedtime is nonnegotiable. It does mean that Eli is allowed to advocate for his needs (singing helps him calm), and that the adult in his life is open to hearing those thoughts (which doesn't always mean that the adult allows the child's thoughts to influence the outcome, but the willingness to listen is important). Something to note about Eli and the singing: Eli couldn't pinpoint why, but he could recognize that his body calmed faster when he was able to sing. Fortunately, his dad was open to the idea because Eli had actually created a coping strategy on his own and was tapping into it. Singing impacts the nervous system and has been shown to reduce tension.[1] It's incredible what kids are capable of when we're willing to give them the time and space to think and have respectful dialogue.

This doesn't mean that every boundary or expectation is negotiable. You will have nonnegotiables in your life—things like health and safety boundaries that aren't up for debate. It was never up for debate that Eli needed to stay in bed. Your child might think brushing their teeth is not always necessary, but that doesn't mean you're going to collaborate with them on a plan for less brushing. You might be open to collaborating on ways to make brushing less stressful for them, but the brushing itself isn't up for discussion. The *what*—teeth brushing—is the firm boundary. The flexibility is in the *how*—giving them a visual timer, letting them listen to a song while they brush, etc.

Behavior Challenges in School

Lindsay got the call from school around noon. Her ten-year-old son, Luca, had been sent to the principal's office again. That was the third time this month. It was the same story—Luca was being disrespectful to his teacher. He'd turned in a math paper and she had returned it to him because he had written down answers but hadn't shown his work. He needed to redo the math problems and show how he was getting his answers. He refused to complete the paper again, and when his teacher reminded him that incomplete assignments would impact his grade, he replied with, "I don't care about dumb grades anyway!" At that point he was sent to the principal's office. Lindsay was beginning to really worry about Luca. He needed to learn how to behave in school. She worried his punishments would get more severe as he got older. She felt an urgency to get his behavior under control now while he was still young. She also felt embarrassed. What did the teacher and principal think about Luca? What did they think about her? Did they think that she allowed this kind of behavior at home? What judgments were they making about her family?

Parents of children who are struggling with behavior at school often feel helpless and overwhelmed. When you're not physically present with your child, you can't be there to stop behaviors or support their emotions. Here's the good news: you don't have to stop their behaviors at school. You can't. That's out of your hands. What you can do is influence and support your child at home.

"Hey, Luca, what's going on at school? Why did you get so upset about your math?" Lindsay asked him.

"It's so annoying! If I know the answer, why do I have to show everything? Also I hate how she says it so loudly in front of the whole class when she tells me I have to redo it. Everyone looks at me," he complained.

"Ugh, yeah. It is annoying to feel like you have to do extra work. It's hard sometimes to follow the rules when they don't make sense to you. I get that," his mom replied. "It sounds like you're also feeling embarrassed when she corrects you in front of the class."

"No, I'm not embarrassed. It's just dumb that she does that."

Luca's story is a great illustration of how academic and social stressors at school can drive maladaptive behavior. First, he's got the issue of not showing his work. To him, it feels like extra work to write out the process he's using to come to his answer. It frustrates him. Plus, he feels defensive and embarrassed when his teacher corrects him because his classmates can hear it and that is layered over his frustration. While Lindsay can't control what happens to Luca at school or how he responds, she can work to help him build tools for frustration and embarrassment at home.

"Buddy, think about what you do at home when you get frustrated with me. What usually happens?" Lindsay asked Luca.

"Sometimes I go play outside or I put my headphones on to listen to a story. You told me to do that stuff so I don't end up yelling at you because then I have to go to my room."

"Right, in our family if you can't speak with kindness, you have to take space until you're ready to be respectful. It sounds like at school, your teacher also expects kindness and respect. I wonder what you could do when you're frustrated or embarrassed."

"I don't know, but she doesn't care. She just gets mad at what I say and then sends me to the principal's office."

"Yeah, it might be tricky at school when it comes to your feelings. Your teachers might not realize that when you get defensive about your work, it's because you're embarrassed. They might just think you're being rude. Can you think of anything you could do to help yourself feel calm when you're embarrassed so that you don't say unkind things?" Lindsay asked.

Luca just shrugged in response.

"Hm, I wonder if you could ask to be excused to the bathroom and take a few moments alone to calm down before you talk to your teacher. Maybe then you'd be able to explain why you were frustrated or embarrassed without shouting or saying something that would get you in trouble," Lindsay offered.

"But what if I take too long in the bathroom and I get in trouble for that?" Luca asked.

"If that happens, I can support you. I can chat with your teacher about giving you time to calm your body. For now, let's just give it a try and if any issues pop up, you don't have to figure them out alone. I'll help you."

It's hard to relinquish control and know that our children will experience stress at school. It's even harder when that stress manifests as behavioral challenges. It's one thing to deal with disrespect from your own child in the privacy of your home. It's another to navigate your child's being rude in public and the embarrassment that can trigger for us as parents. I remember being at a school function and my son was angry with my daughter. The room was packed with students, parents, and teachers and suddenly my son loudly shouted, "Sissy! Stop it! I HATE YOU!" I firmly believe that there is no perfection in parenthood. I expect children to act out sometimes. I don't view children's behavior as a reflection of their parents—but when it comes to my own children acting out in public, I admit that I struggle. I worry about the judgment of others, I wonder if they are using my child's behavior as a measurement of my worth as a parent. I worry about my children being misunderstood or labeled.

Lindsay was worried about what people would think of Luca and their family too. It's so easy in those moments to fall into punishing or shaming children in an attempt to stop the behavior. Our embarrassment drives fear, which often triggers us to default to patterns from our own childhoods. Lindsay did an incredible job of looking past her own embarrassment and worry in order to connect with Luca and get to the root of what was happening. She encouraged Luca to think about how he copes with hard feelings at home and what the boundaries and expectations are within his family. She reinforced that those boundaries exist at school too and she gave Luca some suggestions for how he could calm in order to communicate with his teacher in a kind and respectful way. A few weeks after that conversation with Luca, Lindsay received an email from Luca's teacher noting that he was asking to go to the restroom more than usual. Lindsay explained that Luca was using going to the restroom as a way to step away and get calm. Luca's teacher liked the idea and actually came up with a hand signal that Luca could use in class to let her know that he was going to the restroom to get calm. His outbursts in class reduced and his ability to communicate with kindness and respect increased.

Racialized Anger Bias

Racial disparities in how behavior is perceived and handled are widespread throughout the American school system. A 2023 study showed that teachers in the United States were 71 percent more likely to report feeling anger as compared to concern when they read about a potentially challenging behavior of a Black student as compared to one of a white student.[2] These racial disparities start as early as preschool, follow children into elementary school, and continue through middle and high school.[3] The impact is significant: Black children who experience excessive punishment in school are increasingly enmeshed within the criminal justice system as they grow older.

Black children don't have the privilege of showing that they are operating with low capacity or that they have unmet needs. Their entire life trajectory can be altered if they slip up and express anger or act disrespectfully. White children are not under the same pressure to suppress their emotions and be perceived as well-behaved and respectful. Part of building an emotionally intelligent future involves educators, caregivers, and systems recognizing the biases that exist and actively working to create environments where all children, especially Black children, are given the grace, understanding, and tools to express their emotions safely. Only by addressing these disparities can we support every child in developing healthy emotional regulation.

Chapter 6

Sneaking and Lying

If we overreact to every misstep that our children
make (cue the yelling, crying, or generally unhinged
behavior that comes naturally to some of us . . .),
it makes it even harder for them to come to us with
the truth. If we can be easy enough to talk to, if we
can listen, understand, and help, we can encourage
our children to tell the truth next time.

—DR. ALIZA PRESSMAN, BESTSELLING AUTHOR
OF *The 5 Principles of Parenting*[1]

Gabe and his younger sister, Nina, are building a fort in the living room. Their mom, Alicia, hears them starting to argue about how the fort should be structured. She walks into the living room and sees Gabe hit Nina. Nina starts crying. "Gabe, did you just hit your sister?" Alicia asks him.

"I barely tapped her! She's such a baby!" he replies defensively.

"Gabe, I just watched the whole thing from the door. I know you hit her. Now you're lying too. You can go to your room and you've lost screen time for tonight."

"This is so unfair! She ruins the fort, yells at me, and I barely touch her and I get in trouble?!" Gabe shouts as he walks to his room.

This isn't the first time Alicia has caught Gabe in a lie. She's been noticing it more and more recently. She asks him if his teeth are brushed, and he says they are, even when Alicia knows they aren't. In the evenings, she asks him if he has any homework, and he says he doesn't, only for her to find him the next morning frantically trying to finish a worksheet before it's time to leave for school. She's frustrated, of course, but more so—she's worried. It's becoming a pattern and she doesn't know how to stop it.

Lying can be incredibly triggering. Many of us were conditioned to believe that lying was disrespectful and that disrespect needs punishment. With that in mind, it makes sense that Alicia turned to punishment when she caught Gabe lying. The tricky part about responding to lying with punishment is that punishments breeds fear and fear can create a cycle of more lying. Think back to the last time you lied. Why did you do it? What feelings drove the behavior? Fear? Embarrassment? Guilt? If you knew that your honesty would be met with empathy and emotional safety, would you have felt the need to lie? When Gabe lied about hitting his sister, he did so to avoid getting in trouble. He knew that whether he admitted to the hitting or he got caught in a lie, he was going to get in trouble. Attempting a lie was worth it because if he got away with lying, he could avoid punishment. When we respond to lying with punishment, we are inadvertently encouraging more lying.

Creating a Culture of Honesty

The first step in creating a culture of honesty is understanding that lying is developmentally normal. In younger children experimenting with lying is a cognitive milestone. The processes happening in a child's brain that are increasing their ability to focus, plan, and problem-solve are the very same processes that prompt them to try lying on for size. Some researchers have even called lying "executive function in action."[2] What that research tells us is that *lying in childhood is not an issue of morality, but rather a function of cognitive development.* As a child's understanding of the world around them grows in complexity, so can their lying. They may lie to avoid punishment, to avoid social stress, because of a lack of impulse control, or to preserve self-interests. Knowing that lying is a normal part of cognitive and social development, we can release the fear and moral judgments that may pop up for us around lying. When we aren't reacting to lying from a

Reasons Kids Might Lie

- Task Avoidance: A child lies about brushing their teeth in the morning.

- Embarrassment: A child lies when their friends ask if they passed gas.

- Guilt: A child lies when their parent asks who broke the picture frame.

- Control: A child lies about being first in line so they can pick their prize first.

place of judgment, fear, and punishment, it allows us to focus our energy on how we can create a culture of honesty in our families.

Alicia is at the end of her rope with Gabe's lying, and nothing she's tried is working. She's not sure she buys into the idea of not using punishment, but she's willing to try anything to change this pattern of lying.

Gabe and Nina are playing outside in their backyard. Alicia watches them out the window while she washes dishes. She sees them starting to argue over the rules of their game. Nina shouts at Gabe and he runs over to her and pushes her down. Alicia steps outside. "Gabe, I see you pushed Nina—what's going on?" she asks him.

"No! I barely touched her! She's being dramatic to get me in trouble!" he replies.

"I'm not being dramatic! He pushed me!" Nina shouts.

"Gabe, you're not in trouble. Nina, I believe you. I'm going to help both of you work through this. Before I saw the pushing, I noticed the two of you arguing. Did something happen?" Alicia asks.

"Yes!" Gabe shouts. "She won't let me decide any of the rules. She was yelling in my face because I tried to change the game. She's so rude."

Nina starts to interject, and Alicia responds, "Nina, pause, I'm going to listen to you too. Right now, I'm trying to respond to Gabe. Gabe, it makes sense that you felt frustrated if you couldn't make any rules of the game," Alicia offers.

"Yeah, it was so unfair! And then she was yelling at me. I couldn't take it anymore and I pushed her," Gabe says.

"It never feels good to lose control of your body. That's happened to me before too. Thank you for being honest with me. I'm going to chat with Nina for a bit, and then you and I can chat about what you can do next time you're feeling out of control. I can help you make a different choice in the future."

Alicia made a small but significant shift at the beginning of this inter-action: she didn't ask Gabe if he had pushed Nina. She saw him push her, so rather than give him an opportunity to lie, she just went straight into stating what she had seen. Recently, I saw that my son had written on his sister's bedroom wall. The first thing out of my mouth was, "Did you write on your sister's wall?" He looked at the floor and shook his head no. I paused for a moment and tried again. "Buddy, I see your writing on Nora's wall. Were you nervous I would be upset so you didn't want to tell me?" He nodded. Sometimes we unknowingly prime the pump for lying when we ask kids questions that we already know the answer to.

There's another important difference to note in this version of the scenario. Alicia helps turn off the alarms in Gabe's nervous system by saying, "Gabe, you're not in trouble." This doesn't mean "pushing is fine, go ahead and keep doing it"; it means that Gabe is safe to be honest with her. The more we help kids understand that they are safe to tell the truth, the more empowered they will be to be honest with us, even when it's hard. Alicia lets Gabe know that his feelings make sense and that she can support him in making a different choice next time.

You may have noticed that Alicia responded to Gabe first, rather than to Nina, even though Nina was the child who got pushed down. When we are responding to multiple children at one time, think of it like tri-age. Alicia took in the scene, noted that Nina was upset but unhurt, and shifted her focus to Gabe, who was dysregulated and had lost control. It can be hard to accept that the child who is perpetrating is the one who actually needs help first. You might have narratives about punishment

When a Child Lies, You Might Say . . .

- "I'm not mad at you. I feel upset about what happened because I want you to be safe. Let's chat about what could happen differently."

- "I will love you even when you make mistakes. It's safe to tell me."

- "Are you scared to tell me because you're afraid I'll be mad? [*pause*] It's okay for me to have a hard feeling. I can calm my body to help you."

- "I want you to feel safe telling me the truth. I will listen and we can always figure out problems together."

pop up. *How is he going to learn if he's rewarded for his behavior with attention? He doesn't deserve my help or attention right now.* Responding with safety and empathy requires us to shift our perspective. We have to believe that all behavior is communication of an unmet need. Kids do well when they can—so when they can't, we get to investigate and support them.

Lying Is a Stress Behavior

Eva, twelve years old, has an old iPhone that she's allowed to use for FaceTime and podcasts. The rule for the phone is that she can use it for one hour after school and then it's put away. She uses it for an hour and then her mom, Jane, stores it in the cabinet, as is their routine. Her mom goes to take a shower and start dinner. Eva is in her room with the door shut, which isn't unusual. She's been spending more and more time in her room as she approaches adolescence. Her mom knocks on the door. "Honey, what are you up to in there?" she asks.

"Just doing my homework," Eva replies.

A half hour goes by and it's time for dinner. Eva's mom opens Eva's bedroom door to let her know it's time to come to the table, and she sees Eva shoving something under her blanket.

"Eva, what did you just hide under your blanket?" her mom asks.

"Nothing, just my journal," Eva replies.

A few minutes later while they're sitting at the table, the ringtone for FaceTime starts going off, except it's not coming from the cabinet. It's coming from Eva's room.

"Eva, I can hear that the phone is in your bedroom. Why did you hide it from me?" her mom asks.

"I knew my time was up but I had to talk to Abby one more time! We're trying to coordinate our outfits for tomorrow and we didn't get a chance to finish. She was going to be mad at me if I didn't show up tomorrow in the right clothes."

Children in middle childhood are navigating choppy waters. They're dealing with increasingly complex social dynamics, waxing and waning friendships, and more pressure to look and act a certain way. When Eva used the phone outside of her allotted time and then hid it, she was responding to social stress. We can't respond to a child's stress with control—although the temptation is certainly there. It's hard to stay calm when faced with dishonesty; it tends to set off alarms in our nervous system. One way to turn down those alarms is to change the lens that we view lying through. Instead of seeing lying as a behavior that we need to stop, what if we saw it as a stress response that we needed to support our child through?

"Thanks for telling me the truth. I remember spending time on the phone with my friends when I was your age, trying to match outfits or plan what we were going to wear. The one-hour FaceTime rule still stands, but I also want you to know that if your time runs out and you need to finish a conversation, I can respect that. I'd rather you tell me and I can give you five more minutes than for you to feel like you need to sneak and hide the phone from me," Jane tells Eva.

"Thanks, Mom. Yeah, I really wanted to make sure Abby and I knew what our plan was for tomorrow."

"Okay, that makes sense. Next time something like that comes up, just let me know."

Eva's parents have created a culture of honesty in their home by responding with empathy and safety. While lying isn't an ongoing issue that they have with Eva, she still snuck and hid that phone. Creating an environment where kids are safe to tell the truth doesn't mean that they will never lie or be sneaky again. It's like other challenging behaviors: we address the underlying need and then work on different skills for the future. Jane recognized what was going on for Eva and validated that. She reiterated her expectation for phone use, but let Eva know that she was willing to be flexible. That connected and collaborative mindset allowed them to come to an agreement and create a plan for navigating something like that in the future.

Eva shows us that kids don't always lie because they're afraid of punishment—there's more to it. Kids might lie to try to fit in or to avoid embarrassment. They might lie when their task demand has exceeded their capacity in an attempt to lessen their load (remember Zeke from Chapter 3?). They might lie to try to escape or delay a tough conversation. The more we can respond with safety, and reduce their stress, the more likely they will feel like they can open up to us.

Relinquishing Control

What drives us to want to control our children? What makes us react so strongly to lying and sneaky behavior? We want them to be safe. We want them to make the right choices. We want them to be successful. Those are all important things for children. The truth is that control isn't going to help our children be safe, make good choices, and be successful.

I think back to when my oldest child was learning how to walk. She was eleven months old. I didn't want her to fall so I stayed close by. I would try to hold her hand or predict when she was going to fall and be there to catch her or help her up. She started to push my hands away. I kept trying to help her. Soon when I moved toward her, she would try to speed-walk away, which often led to falls and crying. I had to back off. She needed the space to figure it out without the pressure of my overbearing presence. She needed to try and stumble and then get up and try again. I was there to make sure she didn't get seriously hurt, but aside from that, I had to get out of her way so she could learn.

It's the same process in middle childhood except it's allowing for your child's emotional and social skills instead of their physical ones. They still need our boundaries and guidance to keep them safe, but they also need us to get out of the way. They need the space to stumble, make mistakes, get up, and try again. If we try to prevent them from taking risks or making mistakes, all we are doing is taking away their chance to learn how to think for themselves and make sound decisions. They have to be allowed to make mistakes. They're going to lie. They're going to sneak around. The key is making sure they know that when they do mess up, they can come to us.

Right now it's pushing a sibling or sneaking onto FaceTime with a friend. It's lying about homework, teeth brushing, or a social conflict. In adolescence the stakes get higher. If we respond to lying with control and punishment now, we set the stage for a teen who doesn't feel safe to come to us when they're unsure what to do, or they've messed up. I think back to my own adolescence and all the mistakes I made. The risky behaviors I took part in. I tried to hide them from my parents. I didn't want to disappoint them. I didn't want them to think less of me. Now I think about what my children will be like when they are teens. I imagine them at a party and they decide to try a few drinks. It's almost curfew and they're feeling the pressure to get home on time but they're drunk. Do they feel safe enough to call me? Or are they so afraid of my reaction to the drinking that they take the risk of trying to drive? I want my kids to call me. I want them to know that I can handle it when they make a mistake and I can help them make different choices in the future. I want them to know that nothing they do will change the way I feel about them. I know you want that for your child too.

We're setting the stage for those big moments of adolescence with these smaller moments in middle childhood. Every time we respond to lying with safety and empathy, we drive home a message that our kids need to hear: "You can tell me anything. I'm here to help."

Chapter 7

Navigating Peer Pressure

Humans are social creatures. We are born ready to connect with others. We have a biological propensity to care for and about one another. In early childhood, this manifests in our child's relationship with us. They meet their need for connection, belonging, and inclusion with their primary caregivers. In middle childhood, we see a big shift from our children meeting that need almost exclusively with us to suddenly becoming much more invested in their peers and social groups. As children become more interested in their peer groups, they also become acutely aware of what their peers are thinking, doing, and saying. They recognize that appearance, behavior, and adherence to social norms impact their place within their social group. For these reasons, this is the age when kids start to encounter peer pressure.

Peer pressure gets a bad rap. It's most often associated with kids influencing one another to take part in risky behaviors—drugs, alcohol, etc. That narrow view doesn't give us the full picture. Peer pressure is how peers influence one another, for better and worse. While negative peer pressure is what parents tend to be most aware of and concerned about, positive peer influence can be a force for good. It can be an opportunity for kids to become more self-aware, practice self-regulation skills, cultivate self-advocacy skills, and develop empathy.

In this chapter we're going to break down how peer pressure manifests in middle childhood, how to recognize if your child is struggling with peer pressure, how to help kids build self-advocacy skills, and how to meet their need for belonging in a way that supports their overall well-being.

Why Social Conflict Is Necessary

Social conflict can take many forms at this age. Disputing games at recess, having trouble getting along with peers, feeling left out, or navigating ever-changing friendship dynamics are all par for the course. Many of us view social conflict in children as a sort of necessary evil, something that just has to be accepted as part of childhood. While social conflict is necessary, it's *not* evil. Hear me out—I know how hard it is to see your child experiencing hard things. There's a part of me that wants to protect my children from conflict at all costs. That part of me never wants them to experience the negative side of peer pressure. The truth is that kids *will* be pressured by their peers. They *will* be influenced by them. Those experiences teach them valuable lessons that they will need in this life.

Picture your child as an adult, starting a new job. When they were interviewed, they specified the hours they could work. Now a colleague is pressuring them to swap shifts, even though they were clear about their availability during the hiring process. They recognize the need to assert themselves and maintain boundaries by sticking to the agreed-upon hours. It might be uncomfortable, but they communicate firmly yet kindly with their colleague about their availability going forward. Their communication aligns with their values and the workplace culture. The conversation may be tense, but they navigate it successfully and maintain a good working relationship with their colleague.

This is the dream, right? For our children to be self-aware, to be able to self-regulate and self-advocate so they can move through the world successfully. Peer relationships in middle childhood are a fertile ground for social pressure and conflict, providing countless opportunities to develop self-regulation, self-advocacy, and conflict resolution skills.

Penelope came home from school and suddenly she was desperate to have a pair of Crocs. A few weeks before, she had mentioned that a couple of her friends had Crocs and she was thinking she might want some. Crocs had never fit her feet well—her feet are too slender. She does better in an off-brand version that runs a bit more narrow. Her dad, Greg, explained to her that he wasn't going to buy her a pair of shoes that he knew wouldn't fit her well but that he was happy to help her find something similar that would fit, especially since she needed sandals for summer anyway.

"Okay, what if I spent my own money on the Crocs?" she asked her dad.

"Are you sure that you want to spend your money on shoes that won't even fit you?"

She rolled her eyes and sighed loudly. "Dad, everyone has the real Crocs. I earned that money. I want to have the Crocs. Nobody is wearing the fake ones."

"Fine, go ahead and spend your money on them, but you're not gonna like them and you're gonna waste your money."

Penelope walks away not feeling seen or understood by her dad and disconnects from him. Later, Greg revisited the conversation:

"You really want to fit in with your friends, huh?"

Another eye roll. "Well, yeah. Of course I do."

"I'm wondering if you'll be able to really play in those shoes because they won't fit. Do you think maybe your friends are more interested in being able to play with you than what shoes you have on?"

"Well . . . probably," she replied.

"Yeah, I think so too. I'm curious if it would be better to get the kind that fit properly. That way you can run and play with your friends."

"But what if they notice that they're the fake kind when we're at recess?"

"Hm, yeah. They might notice. I wonder what you could say if that happened?"

"Well . . . I could tell them that the real Crocs are too big for me and I can't run or play games in them."

"Yeah, what do you think would happen if you did that?" Greg asked.

"I think that they'd probably just want to play tag or basketball like we usually do at recess."

"Yeah, I'm thinking they're more interested in you being able to play with them than which shoes you have on. What do you think?"

"Yeah, I think so too, but I still want the Crocs," Penelope replied.

"That makes sense to me, hun. When I was little everyone had Jordans and we couldn't afford them, but I remember wanting them so badly, and if I'd had the money I would've spent it on Jordans to feel included too. I'll love you no matter what you choose to do."

Recently, I had a similar situation happen with my daughter. She came home and insisted that she needed a Stanley tumbler. I felt under-resourced that day and immediately jumped to control. I wasn't going to let her waste her money on a water bottle when we have plenty of them. Plus, it's just a passing trend and really doesn't matter. She didn't need to buy something like that just to fit in—she's worth so much more than a brand. While it's true that children should know their value is so much more than adhering to the latest trend, kids need to feel safe and seen to us in order to hear those messages. I had defaulted to control and, in turn, my daughter shut down and walked away from the conversation.

Greg's approach with Penelope was totally different. It was rooted in connection and collaboration. In order to navigate peer influence, kids rely on three skills that we've discussed as keys for emotional intelligence: self-awareness, self-regulation, and self-advocacy. We can help them develop and practice these skills at home. To do this, we must resist the urge to control or micromanage, and instead focus on building connections and solving problems together. While my controlling approach prevented me from helping my daughter build those skills in the moment, Greg's approach was much more effective. He helped Penelope notice that her desire for the Crocs was really a desire to fit in with her friends—allowing her to build awareness of what emotions might drive her behavior. He helped her feel safe by remaining collaborative, rather than taking control—and in turn she was regulated enough to think through what might happen with her friends if she didn't have the Crocs. When she expressed worry about what they might think if she had the off-brand shoes, he invited her to think about how she could advocate for herself. In that one short conversation he connected with her and helped her practice self-awareness, self-regulation, and self-advocacy. When they left the conversation, Penelope knew that her dad was someone she could turn to who would be there to support her. She was given guidance to dive into those conversations with her peers, knowing that her value as a person and a friend was so much more than having a pair of name-brand shoes if she chose the ones that fit her. She also knew that her dad's love was not contingent on what decision she would make, but rather, that it is unconditional.

It's not our job to make decisions *for* our children but instead to walk alongside them as they make their own decisions, allowing them the grace to grow without perfection. It's through making choices, mistakes, and failures that they'll learn the most. It can be triggering to watch them live a life outside of yours, where parts of you from your past remember certain experiences. It's hard not to project our experiences onto them or try and protect them from mistakes and challenges along the way. Pause and notice: What comes up for you now? What thoughts or feelings are you experiencing as you read this?

Handling Hurtful Behaviors

Hurtful behaviors like name-calling, purposeful exclusion, and teasing are maladaptive. They go against our biological drive to connect with one another. A child who is being unkind is communicating that they have an unmet need or an underdeveloped social skill set. Stuart Shanker, a distinguished research professor of philosophy and physchology, identifies the root of a child's unkind behaviors as "a pattern of poor arousal regulation, in particular regulation of their emotions."[1] In other words, the hurtful child doesn't know what to do with their hard feelings, so they subconsciously lash out or act mean in order to try to feel safe. On the other side of the coin, we know that unkind behaviors have implications for the child on the receiving end. So the approach to unkind behaviors has to be twofold: helping the perpetrating child get their needs met or helping them build a new skill, and helping the child on the receiving end to self-advocate and set boundaries with their peers. We add another layer of complexity to these situations when we acknowledge that most hurtful behaviors fly under the radar. So you have to strike the balance of helping equip your child to navigate these situations independently and recognizing when adult intervention may be necessary.

Simon's mom, Anita, had gotten an upsetting phone call from the school. One of Simon's fifth-grade classmates had accused him of calling her fat at recess that day. After looking into the situation, Simon's teacher and principal had concluded that it was true. Anita was shocked. She couldn't believe that her son would say something like that. The school asked her to pick him up early, so she drove there. Simon got into the car and looked down at his lap.

"Buddy, what's going on?" Anita asked. "Why would you say something so hurtful to your classmate? You know it's not okay to comment on someone else's body."

"I know, Mom. I was playing basketball with the boys and we were supposed to be taking turns being point guards. They kept skipping my turn and I was getting frustrated. The teacher noticed and said something to them and that made them mad. Then they started saying that I couldn't be a point guard because I'm too weak to handle the ball. They called me Scrawny Simon. I didn't know what to do, so when Brianna walked by, I just blurted out, 'At least I'm not fat like her!,' and that made the boys laugh and they stopped calling me Scrawny Simon."

Simon's hurtful behaviors are rooted in a lack of self-regulation and self-advocacy skills. He didn't know what to do when the boys started calling him names, so he tried to shift their attention away from him, and in the meantime caused harm to Brianna. Parenting the child who is perpetrating can be triggering. Nobody wants their child to be hurting others or to be seen as a troublemaker or, worse, a bully.

As bullying awareness and prevention strategies have been implemented in the United States over the last two decades, we've seen a pendulum swing in the definition of bullying. We've moved from a "kids will be kids" approach, where almost nothing was considered bullying, to the current climate in which almost every childhood conflict is swept under the umbrella of bullying. Elizabeth Englander, a professor of psychology and founder and director of the Massachusetts Aggression Reduction Center at Bridgewater State University, emphasizes the harm caused by the misuse of the word: "By calling everything bullying, we're actually failing to recognize the seriousness of the problem."[2] We know that bullying is real and must be addressed, but on the flip side we have the research to show that zero-tolerance policies implemented in schools aren't working.[3] Zero-tolerance policies for bullying enforce strict, predetermined consequences for students who engage in bullying behaviors, often without looking critically at the context or severity of the situation. Part of the challenge with zero-tolerance policies is our distorted definition of bullying, which has come to include any social conflict. The result? Kids lose the opportunity to understand the root of their own behaviors and the behaviors of others. They lose the opportunity to cultivate empathy and work through problems together. Part of the solution to bullying is recognizing normal childhood conflict and using it as an opportunity to support kids in building the skills they need to navigate it.

While Simon and Brianna both experienced unkindness at the hands of a classmate, neither child was a victim of bullying. Signe Whitson, author and national educator on bullying prevention, crisis intervention, and child and adolescent emotional and behavioral health, helps parents and educators define bullying by distinguishing it from rude or mean behaviors.

Rude = Inadvertently saying or doing something that hurts someone else.

Mean = Purposefully saying or doing something to hurt someone once (or maybe twice).

Bullying = Intentionally aggressive behavior, repeated over time, that involves an imbalance of power.[4]

If we continue to water down the definition of bullying, we risk over-responding to normal childhood behavior and underresponding to children who are experiencing true bullying. Children engaging in rude or mean behaviors, but who are not bullying, do not necessarily need an adult to step in and put a stop to the conflict. They *do* need an adult to help them cultivate skills for behaving in a prosocial way in the future. What could this look like for a child like Simon?

Anita wants Simon to be able to handle hard feelings at school without getting mean. It had always been a challenge for her to give Simon space to feel. As a baby, when he cried from frustration trying to reach a toy, she moved it into his reach. When he was a toddler, she quickly learned the things that would set off a tantrum and did everything in her power to avoid them. Simon did preschool at home because of the pandemic. Anita had always been able to control his environment and experiences and felt it was part of her job to keep him happy and shield him from adversity. Except now Simon needs a toolbox for navigating adversity. Anita starts by circling back to the situation with Simon and the boys at recess.

"Simon, I've been thinking about what happened at school with the boys. It made me think about a time my friends teased me. I had prominent front teeth and they said something about them and I felt so embarrassed."

Simon listened but didn't respond.

"Embarrassment is a really uncomfortable feeling. I can see why you wanted to shift the attention to someone else."

"Why did they have to call me Scrawny Simon?! It makes me sound like a loser."

"When someone makes fun of your body it can feel really crummy. . . . I wonder if that's how Brianna felt today too."

Simon got quiet for a moment and hung his head. "I wish I never said that about her."

"Yeah, it makes sense to feel guilty about hurting someone's feelings. I've felt that too. I wonder what would help you next time you're embarrassed? What could you do so that you don't lash out at someone else?"

"I'm not sure, Mom."

"Yeah . . . let's think on it together. I know for myself when I feel like someone is being unkind to me, I try to set a boundary and let them know I won't continue talking until we can both speak kindly to each other. I wonder how it would feel for you to do that."

"Maybe? What would I say though? If I tell the boys to be kind to me, they'd probably laugh. I'd sound like a teacher, not a kid."

"Hm . . . what about: 'Hey, guys, I don't want to talk about my body. I'm going to play somewhere else if you don't stop.'"

"Yeah, I could try that. I'm not sure who else I'd play with though. We play basketball almost every recess."

"Well, if you play every day, do you think that the boys would want you to keep playing with them?"

"Yeah, I think so."

"Hm, I'm thinking they'll probably stop talking about your body so that you'll continue to play with them. What do you think?"

"Yeah, I think so too. But what if they don't?"

"I wonder what else you could do at recess if that happens?"

"I think I could probably play kickball. That usually happens every recess. Plus, some kids play over on the soccer field too. So maybe one of those."

"That sounds like a good idea. Do you feel like you have options for if this happens again? I want you to have a game plan for next time so you don't lash out at anyone."

Simon nodded.

Self-Advocacy Scripts

- "I'm not okay with that game. Let's try something else."

- "It hurts my feelings when you say that. Please don't say that."

- "I need some space right now. I'll come back when I'm ready."

- "I don't think that's fair. Can we come up with a different plan?"

- "It makes me uncomfortable when you do that. Please stop."

Anita didn't want Simon to experience frustration, disappointment, or emotional pain and for the most part she'd been able to protect him from hardship. Enter elementary school social dynamics, and suddenly Simon is exposed to experiences that Anita can't control. Simon now needs a new set of skills for navigating social challenges. Public embarrassment, feeling rejected, feeling like he's been singled out—these are all new to Simon. It's hard to accept that our children will experience pain we cannot prevent. It's hard to come to terms with the idea that they'll experience hard things that we may not even know about. That desire to shelter them is so natural—we have a biological drive to want to keep our children safe. The truth is that we can't shelter them and the best way for us to foster their emotional safety is to empower them with the tools to deal with the inevitable social trials they will face. Anita is able to shift from sheltering Simon to empowering Simon—that's where the magic happens. If the root of unkind behavior is poor emotional regulation, the best thing we can do for our children is to give them the tools to regulate their emotions.

Simon lashed out because he didn't know what else to do. With Anita's help, he now knows he has other options and he has a plan for how to access those options in the moment.

Addressing Bullying Behaviors

So, what happens when it really is bullying? As discussed on page 110, many schools have zero-tolerance policies, but what do we do when these policies aren't effective? Zero tolerance might sound effective and straightforward, but in practice, it often doesn't solve the problem. Instead, it can lead to unintended consequences, like ostracizing both the child labeled as the bully and the victim of the bullying without addressing the underlying issues. It's like hitting the snooze button on the behavior: punishing the child might provide temporary relief, but without teaching the necessary skills to address the root causes, the behavior is likely to persist or pop up in different ways.

Understanding what's really behind bullying behaviors is important for both kids and adults because it helps build self-awareness and empathy on all sides. Bullying comes from unmet needs, unprocessed feelings, or insecurities, not from inherent malice. When we can recognize these underlying reasons, kids can learn better ways to express themselves, and adults can offer more helpful support.

Research shows that the most effective approaches to bullying are those that focus on understanding and addressing the emotional needs of all the children involved rather than simply assigning punishment.[5] Current brain science highlights that children need to feel secure and emotionally regulated to learn social skills and develop empathy, which are crucial for resolving conflicts and building positive relationships. Dr. Stuart Shanker tells us in his book *Self-Reg*: "The most important element in helping any child or teen shift from survival brain to learning is that he feels safe and secure: physically, emotionally, and as a learner."[6] In order to effectively stop bullying, kids need to learn empathy, social skills, and conflict resolution. Punitive zero-tolerance policies promote a stress response for both victim and bully, pulling kids out of their learning brains and into survival mode. A collaborative, empathetic approach aligns with modern neuroscience, which supports fostering emotional safety and connection as key elements in reducing bullying and promoting healthy social development.

Perhaps you've heard of restorative practice as an approach to bullying. Restorative practice is a strategy for conflict resolution that focuses on repairing the harm done. It's gaining traction as a new alternative to zero-tolerance policies. Restorative practices are emotionally literate and *can* work well, but the way they are currently framed and outlined for schools is cumbersome. This is a significant barrier for teachers and school admin who are already overworked and experiencing burnout. For both parents and teachers it can feel as though there is no clear-cut answer for how to mitigate bullying. Here is what we know is helpful:

Parents
- Warm, supportive relationships reduce the likelihood of a child bullying or becoming a victim of bullying.[7]
- Children who feel secure and connected are more likely to develop empathy and strong social skills.[8]
- Children with emotional regulation skills are less likely to engage in bullying behavior.
- Children with the emotional literacy necessary to feel empathy toward their peers contribute to a safer climate in schools.

Teachers and School Admin

- Reject zero-tolerance policies and punitive responses to bullying.
- Use the Five Phases of Emotion Processing, described in Chapter 2, and FACTS, from Chapter 3, and focus on creating a classroom culture that encourages self-awareness, self-regulation, and empathy.
- Facilitate conversations between the students involved in conflict to help them understand the impact of their actions, build connection, and collaboratively develop solutions to prevent future incidents.

Ultimately, addressing bullying requires a shift in perspective, from punishing behaviors to understanding the emotions and needs driving them. If you were raised in a culture where you learned that people are good or bad, this shift in perspective will involve acknowledging your bias about the child labeled as a bully. There can be a fear that if you connect with or provide empathy to the child who is bullying, you are condoning that behavior. Two things can be true at the same time: the behavior is not okay and the person is deserving of love and compassion. In order to be curious about what is driving the behavior, you will have to self-regulate in order to see beyond what's happening on the surface. While no approach is one-size-fits-all, prioritizing connection and collaboration over punishment offers a path toward meaningful and lasting change. Together, parents, teachers, and schools can build communities where every child feels seen, supported, and safe.

When Peer Pressure Isn't All Bad

Lydia came home from school in a mood. She walked in from the bus and slammed the front door. She sat down at the kitchen table, huffed loudly, and put her head down.

"Honey, is something wrong?" her mom, Janet, asked.

"Yeah, I got in a huge fight with Olivia today. She made me cry on the playground."

"Hm. Do you want to tell me what happened?"

"Well, we were playing Lava Monster in the jungle gym. It was my idea, and I had made the rules. It was me, Olivia, and Kiana. The rule was that if you fall into the lava you're out until the next round. Well, Olivia and Kiana decided they wanted to change the rules and make it so that if you fell, you became a lava monster too. But there was only supposed to be one lava monster!"

"So they changed the rules on you?"

"Yeah, so I told them I wouldn't play with them. Then Olivia said I was bossy and I always had to get my way. Then I ran away because I was starting to cry."

"Hm, it sounds like you really wanted to be in charge of the game, but they wanted to have a say in the rules too."

"Yeah, they did. But it was my game."

"Ah, so since you made up the game, you wanted to make the rules."

"Yes!" Lydia replied emphatically.

Janet made Lydia a snack and gave her some time to eat and decompress. After she finished her snack, Janet returned to the table.

"Lyd, I was just thinking about what happened today with Olivia and Kiana. I was curious if maybe they were also feeling frustrated. I wonder how it might feel to play in a game and not get to be a part of making the rules."

"Well, I was frustrated too."

"Totally. It makes sense to want to have a say in what you're playing. I'm wondering if that was happening for Olivia and Kiana today."

Lydia was quiet for a minute. She looked down at her hands and gave it some thought. She nodded at her mom, acknowledging that maybe her insights were correct.

When asked to describe her daughter, Janet shared that Lydia had always struggled with allowing other children to influence her play. She is the eldest in her family and controls play with her younger siblings. She is one of the oldest cousins in her extended family, and calls the shots in her cousin group as well. This situation with her peers is the first time Lydia has truly been challenged to include others in the creation and rules of her play.

Since Lydia was a toddler, Janet had been trying to get her to be more flexible in her play with others, without much success. Now that Lydia is invested in what her peers think and is motivated by a desire to be liked and accepted by them, she has the opportunity to cultivate and practice these skills. Being able and willing to collaborate with others is a life skill. Lydia will need it to be successful as she navigates school, and eventually when she is navigating a job and adult relationships. While it's never easy to see our children experience conflict or social pain, social dynamics can be an incredible motivator for kids to think about how others might be feeling and to begin to make choices from a place of empathy and understanding.

As an adult, it can be tempting to insert yourself to try and solve these social dynamics for your kids, sometimes by connecting with the other child's parents. Try to resist that. Kids get to practice problem-solving skills by navigating them with their peers. We can play a scaffolding or reflective role, like Janet did, to help our child build skills for perspective taking. We can be a safe space for them to turn to process experiences, but ultimately, allowing them the freedom with what happens next is crucial for their social development. This means sometimes they will fall, feel left out, feel embarrassed, or lose friendships. The lessons learned through those experiences will help shape them as people.

Chapter 8

Tackling Taboos

Body Changes, Sex, Substances, and Differences

We are inundated with stories about how hard teens are, how difficult their behaviors are, and how off the wall their emotions can be—so we expect them to be challenging. What we don't hear much about are the kids who are just beginning puberty. For girls this is typically between ages eight and thirteen, and for boys it's typically between ages nine and fourteen. This means that for many families, "teenage behaviors" emerge much earlier than expected—as early as eight or nine years old.

A prevailing myth about kids' behavior during this developmental time is the idea that kids just *become harder*. It's almost framed as if kids are making the choice to be difficult and emotionally volatile. We are irritated by their attitudes, we might feel annoyed with their sudden focus on appearance, and we can't understand how a simple conversation can turn into a total blowout in a matter of minutes. "She's only nine!" my friend groaned as she shared about her daughter's latest emotional outburst. Their days recently had become a pattern of extreme emotions, angry outbursts followed by crying and storming off. "I can't believe this is already happening! How am I going to survive her teen years?!"

The brain science on puberty is fascinating. Several studies have shown that the brain regions responsible for emotion, self-awareness, and self-regulation undergo a huge reorganization at the onset of puberty. The transformation is so significant that the changes in gray matter can be seen on an MRI.[1] No wonder my friend's daughter was emotional—her brain was overhauling itself. I think about the last time I reorganized my kitchen. I pulled everything out of the cabinets. Spices, pots and pans, cups, tumblers, all over the place. I emptied the pantry so I could clean it. Stale chips, crumbs, and empty wrappers littered the table. It looked like a tornado had ripped through the house. I couldn't get to my end goal of a neatly organized kitchen if I didn't first make the mess worse by pulling everything out to take inventory, get rid of what we didn't need, and reorganize what we did need.

The pubescent brain is my kitchen. Things get messy, chaotic, and overwhelming before kids get to the other side of it. These kids aren't choosing to be difficult or trying to get under our skin. There's a tornado ripping through them and they're just trying to ride it out. As their brain is remodeling itself, they're also experiencing stirring hormones, body changes, sexual curiosity, and exposure to more complex and difficult topics. If we want them to come to us when a classmate is talking to them about sex, or they're noticing things about their body or a peer's body, we have to be a safe place for them. We have the opportunity to be with them in the storm, to be the place they turn to ask their questions, share their feelings, and manage risk. To do so effectively, we must reject the prevailing cultural notions about pubescent kids.

Demystifying Body Changes

My daughter was five years old and I was breastfeeding her baby brother at a birthday party. "Mom, why are yours so much bigger than mine?" she asked. "To make room for the milk?" There was a part of me that wanted to shut down the conversation because I was worried someone might overhear. I remember in middle school getting in trouble when I needed a tampon and asked my friends in the hallway. The teacher had heard me say, "Hey, does anyone have a tampon?," and pulled me aside to let me know that my behavior was inappropriate. It was one of many experiences in my young life that created shame and secrecy around body changes and puberty. I knew I didn't ever want my children to feel that way, but there was also part of me that was like, *Really? She's asking now when we're at this party? Why hasn't she asked during the hundreds of times I've been nursing him at home with nobody around?*

"Yes, exactly. Mine are different because my adult body knows how to make milk. Someday, your body will be grown up and look similar to mine. If you have more questions about body changes, I'll answer them later today when we're home," I replied, hoping the public questions would cease until I had the capacity and regulation to answer with intention. Thank goodness these conversations are not one and done, that we get to come back and reopen them, because my first attempt is rarely the full picture or the way I want to answer once I'm regulated, especially when kids ask these questions unprompted or in places that aren't ideal for the conversation.

While sometimes the timing is inconvenient or even embarrassing, when kids ask questions about bodies, which curious kids will do, it's a great opportunity to talk about and demystify body changes and puberty. How we respond to them sends them messages about whether or not they can bring their questions to us in the future. The embarrassed part of me wanted to shush my daughter and tell her not to talk about my breasts in public. There was another part of me fighting to get through though— the part that remembers feeling ashamed as a kid and doesn't want my children to experience that, the part of *me* that had been curious as a kid and was made to be quiet. While I wasn't willing to have a full puberty talk at a birthday party, I did want to send the message that her questions were welcome, and that body changes are normal. I want her to know that although not every space is a safe space for these discussions, *I* am a safe person for her to have them with.

Although puberty and its associated brain changes can begin as early as age eight or nine, researchers have discovered a hormonal surge that happens even earlier. A measurable increase in adrenal androgens can occur as early as age six.[2] This developmental phase is now identified as "adrenarche." Adrenarche is believed to contribute to the emotional and behavioral changes observed in children before puberty. So while you may find yourself shying away from puberty talks with your child on the younger end of middle childhood, know that they are likely already experiencing some biological changes, and now is a great time to start opening the doors of communication. But what does that look like? *How do we have these conversations?*

Research shows that using anatomically correct terms for body parts is really important in decreasing shame.[3] This might sound awkward, but try practicing these terms without your child there first. Notice how it feels for you to say the words *penis, vulva, nipple, vagina, testicle, anus, clitoris,* and *scrotum.* Many of us did not grow up hearing those words from adults, which made them seem like they were too shameful to even be spoken. Imagine feeling as uncomfortable with the word *arm* or *nose.* It seems bonkers, right? But the truth is, they are all body parts, some of them have just been deemed more taboo to talk about than others. Melissa Pintor Carnagey shares sample scripts and ways to talk to kids about their bodies based on their age and development in her book *Sex Positive Talks to Have with Kids: A Guide to Raising Sexually Healthy, Informed, Empowered Young People.*[4] Here are some examples:

Ages 5–8

"All of our body parts do different things to help us stay healthy and strong. Some of your body parts are usually kept private behind clothes. It's important to know how to keep them clean. If you ever have questions about any of your body parts you can ask me."

Ages 9–12

"You may start to feel and see changes in parts of your body or hear friends talk about it. What do you know about puberty?"

"It's common to wonder, Is my body normal? Remember that bodies are uniquely designed and all bodies are good bodies. If you ever have questions about your body, let me know so I can help you answer them."

I was in fifth grade when I spent my precious dial-up internet time asking Jeeves how to make my body stop sweating. I wrote a note saying, "I want to get an endoscopic thoracic sympathectomy. It's surgery to make my armpits stop sweating. —Alyssa," and left it on my mom's pillow. My shirts were soaked with pit stains and, with no place to turn to talk about my body, I was left searching the internet for answers and feeling convinced surgery was the only option. My mom told me there were antiperspirant deodorants that I could try and got me one from the store, leaving it on my nightstand. The bottle said one to two swipes on the armpit, but knowing that I was the world's sweatiest human, surely I needed fifteen swipes. Three hours later I found myself wide awake, scrubbing my armpits with a wet washcloth because I was so itchy I couldn't sleep. It turns out fifteen swipes is too many. Again, with no person to talk to about my body, I was left to my own twelve-year-old devices. And as I continued to sweat through shirts at school, I was left feeling like no one understood what I was experiencing and that my body was so gross and weird.

With bodily changes happening for kids, so too come the feelings of being in (or not being in) a new body.

We can model body acceptance and neutrality at home and our kids will still be exposed to messaging in the world that is beyond our control. Perhaps the hardest part of parenthood is recognizing and accepting how little control we have. It can be grounding and helpful to ask, "What *can* I do?" You can cultivate a safe relationship with your child in which they know they are safe, loved, and valued always. The goal isn't for them to avoid hard, or even traumatic, experiences, but rather to know that they do not have to navigate them alone.

Our children are going to notice other people's bodies, Shira growing breasts before them, or Justine getting her period first in the friend group. It makes sense that they will wonder what their body should be doing or should look like. We have two options: we can either try to convince them that they're perfect and don't need to compare themselves, even when they feel imperfect and are already comparing themselves, or we can validate their experience and connect with them.

Sharing stories from your own experience with puberty can help foster open communication: "When I was in fifth grade, my best friend Jamie got her period and I remember feeling embarrassed that I didn't have mine yet. I thought my body was broken and didn't know if I'd ever get it. Actually, when I was thirty, my best friend got pregnant and had a baby when I wanted to be pregnant too. I didn't know if I'd ever get pregnant. Sometimes noticing what's happening with other people's bodies makes me compare myself to them and it can feel like my body is weird or broken. [*Pause.*] If you're ever noticing that, I'm here if you want to share about it. It's really common and you don't have to be alone with those thoughts if you don't want to."

Would it be rad for kids to stop comparing themselves to others? Absolutely! Telling them to stop comparing or not to pay attention to it doesn't make it go away; instead, it can make them feel like you don't understand what they're experiencing. Some helpful ways to support them in these conversations are to validate and open the space. Check the box that follows for some examples.

Sample Scripts for Talking About Body Comparison

- "You're noticing that his body looks different from yours. Yeah, he's definitely taller. What would it be like if you were as tall as he is? Can you imagine? Let's take a look around today—are other people taller, shorter, or somewhere in between? It's interesting to see how everyone's body is unique. Bodies come in all sizes, and that's just part of what makes us us."

- "You're comparing your body to her body. You're noticing a part of your body that makes you uncomfortable. You know what? Even if they don't act like it, everyone has a part of their body that makes them feel uncomfortable too."

- "My hair is straight, and Tia's hair is curly. I always thought, 'I wish my hair was curly like my sister's.' And you know what? I found out that Tia always thought, 'I wish my hair was straight like my sister's.' While I thought nobody liked my straight hair, it turns out my sister loved it all along. Everyone compares their body to other people's, and that's okay. And still, our bodies don't have to change to be lovable."

Puberty

We were at a graduation party for a family friend when my pseudo-aunt pulled me aside to say, "Can you talk to Janine about her period? She is refusing to use tampons, which means she is also refusing to swim or do any physical activity when she's on her period for fear of jostling blood out of the pad." I was six years older than Janine and she'd been like a little sister to me when we were growing up. We'd both been raised in households where the word *period* was whispered, if said at all. Our dads were repulsed by the mention of a uterus and there was not a chance in hell they'd be adding tampons or pads to their grocery list. We were raised to believe that there was shame in puberty, so questions and curiosities were not welcome.

At the ripe age of seventeen, I got Janine into a bedroom and said, "I heard you got your period. Man, that sucks, huh? It's so annoying, but I can teach you how to use a tampon." She was silent. I went on to describe how to use one, slaying the explanation and totally keeping my cool while I talked about it. When I finished, her silence broke as she said, "Yeah, that makes total sense. The thing is, I don't have that hole." After a moment of my utter confusion, she went on to say, "Ya know, the hole where the tampon goes? I don't have that hole." I'm not sure where she thought the blood was magically appearing from, but this poor girl had been living with her period for months without understanding her own anatomy. How terrifying that must have been for her, yet I completely got it. It's the same reason that, even though I had a well-meaning mom, it was a peer who taught me how to use a tampon: the culture around us was one of shame and secrecy. Think about the ways we behave or behaved around having a period. We hide our tampons as we walk to the bathroom, or sneak the box of tampons or pads onto the conveyor belt at the grocery and don't make eye contact with the cashier when they ring it up.

The culture of shame and secrecy doesn't just affect those who experience menstruation; it also extends to the male experience of puberty. Boys too are often taught to feel embarrassed about the natural changes in their bodies. Messages of shame can come in subtle ways—teasing about voice cracks, awkward jokes about body hair, or the pressure to "man up" as their emotions become more intense. We can help remove stigma and shame by normalizing puberty and the changes and experiences that come with it.

Sex

I was putting my three-year-old to bed when he asked if there was a baby in my belly. "No, remember? The baby that was in there was your sister and now she's out." "How did she get in there?" he asked. . . . Damn. This came out of nowhere. I yearned to just go back to reading *The Rabbit Listened* or moonwalk my way out of this conversation. *We are already doing this at three? How much do I share? What do I say?*

My brain scrambled and I answered something like, "When a sperm and an egg come together they can make a baby and then the baby grows bigger and bigger until it's ready to come out." Was it perfect? No. Was it the worst I could do? No. Was it over? Absolutely not. My goal here was to let him know that I am a safe person to turn to with these questions. My answers might be fumbled or imperfect. I will likely have to revisit conversations and revise information. But my ultimate goal is to send the message with my voice, tone, and words that there isn't shame in this conversation, and that I can handle it . . . honestly, even when I'm not sure how to handle it.

Good news, bad news. Bad news first: We are not here to tell you what to say to your child about sex. Every culture has different ideas of how to do this and there are incredible resources out there for doing so. A favorite of ours on this topic is *Sex Positive Talks to Have with Kids: A Guide to Raising Sexually Healthy, Informed, and Empowered Young People,* by Melissa Pintor Carnagey, LBSW. Ready for the good news? We are going to empower you with the tools to have a relationship with your child in which they can turn to you with questions, concerns, and curiosities about sex so they aren't looking to peers, porn, or the World Wide Web for answers.

How you feel about having conversations with your child about sex has a lot to do with how sex was communicated about to you. What did your parents or caregivers tell you about sex? What did it feel like when they told you? Maybe they said you could come to them with questions about sex, but when you did, they shushed you or said it was inappropriate, adding secrecy and shame to the topic. Sometimes when we encounter things in parenthood that we weren't allowed to express as children ourselves, we try to push away or ignore the discomfort. Feelings are contagious though. Your child will notice your discomfort and that's okay. We get to model how to be in discomfort and name it without wishing it away. The other day I was feeling sad and my son said, "Mom, don't feel sad. I don't like that." "It's uncomfortable to be around someone who is feeling sad, isn't it? I get that. You're safe and I can take care of you even when I'm feeling sad," I responded. It'll be key to get cozy with uncomfortable topics and conversations, as well as the ability to acknowledge that feeling of being uncomfortable as you move through it together.

Name the discomfort, connect, and get curious. "Sometimes it feels uncomfortable to talk about sex because a lot of people grow up learning that they aren't supposed to talk about it. You can always ask me if you have questions, concerns, or curiosities. What do you know about sex?"

The discussion of sex shouldn't be limited to one "big talk." Ongoing, age-appropriate conversations about bodies, relationships, and respect can help normalize the topic. While your child may bring questions to you to help spark the conversation, they might not. They might feel uncomfortable or nervous and keep their questions to themselves or go to their peers for information. If your child isn't coming to you with questions by age nine or ten, you can open the doors to communication by bringing it up with them. I know that for many of us that feels early, but the truth is that they will be hearing about sex and sexuality at school and may be getting misinformation from peers. Letting them know you are a safe space for accurate information can help foster a relationship in which they will come to you later when the stakes are higher.

Content Warning: Sexual Assault

When we are the safe space for kids to ask questions about sex, it's important that we are honest in response to their questions. This provides a foundation for them to understand consent. If all they hear from us is that sex makes babies, but from peers and out in the world they hear about sex as something people do for enjoyment, they can either recognize that we are not being honest with them and/or feel like we cannot relate to the current landscape they are experiencing and start to close doors for communication with us on the topic. Like how my mom told me I couldn't wear mascara until I was sixteen and assured me that putting Vaseline on my eyelashes would have the same effect. Spoiler alert: It does not. And in response, I learned that she didn't know or maybe didn't care about my experience, which led to my not asking anymore and instead keeping my mascara-wearing habits secretive by applying it at Kellie's house before hanging with friends.

When kids learn that there is pleasurable touch, they can also learn that there is unpleasurable touch, and when to turn to you for support. This is a foundation for reporting sexual abuse. There is a very powerful message you can pass on to your kids starting as young as the preschool years: "If you ever need to share that something unsafe has happened, I will believe you. You will not be in trouble." It's never too early or too late to tell them that.

Substances

I grew up in the age of the D.A.R.E. program's "Just say no" campaign, witnessing media advertisements such as an egg being held up with a woman saying, "This is your brain," and then cracking the egg into a sizzling pan while stating, "This is your brain on drugs." Everything I was officially told about drugs by authority figures had the same underlying message: drugs are bad, don't try them. Contrast that with the film and television portrayals of drugs and alcohol at the time, as seen in *Dazed and Confused*, where it seemed everyone was stoned and drugs were not just interesting but seemed essential for social connection. Or take the wildly successful film *The Hangover*, a fun and funny story of a group of friends who get so blackout drunk, they don't remember anything that transpired the night before.

In other words, the influential messaging kids of the eighties and nineties received was how cool and fun drinking and drugs could be, paired with the school messaging "But don't try it." This often came through an authoritarian lens of "because I said so" without room for questions and without explanation. This dichotomy led to many millennials drinking, smoking, and taking drugs. Years of binge-drinking games like flip cup and beer pong hit the scene, marijuana became mainstream and even legalized in some places, and kids found themselves needing an excuse if they chose not to participate. As the millennials of the "just say no" years came into adulthood, a spike in sober-curious and nondrinkers emerged, with mental and physical health cited as top reasons for not drinking. According to data from NCSolutions, "Alcohol consumption trends show millennials specifically had a major shift in their drinking behavior, decreasing by 40%" from 2023 to 2024.[5]

Recognizing the effects drinking has on one's health, and with the ever-rising lethal substances added to drugs, many parents today want to teach kids about drugs and alcohol differently than with the "abstinence or else your brain will be a fried egg" scare-tactic approach. But what does that look like? How can we support kids with tools for what to do when they encounter substances, and cultivate a relationship of trust with them so they feel safe to turn to us with questions, curiosities, and mistakes? And when do these conversations begin? Jessica Lahey's book *The Addiction Inoculation* is a fantastic, data-driven resource if you want to deep-dive into this.[6] Let's cover some things we know are key.

1. Children need to have at least one safe adult they can turn to without fear of punishment, shame, or harm with questions, curiosities, and mistakes.

As Jessica Lahey states in *The Addiction Inoculation*, "Authoritative parents explain the reasoning behind expectations, because rules enforced without reason tend to be ineffective,"[7] illustrating the need for conversation to be present instead of the top-down, authoritarian "because I said so" approach.

Above all else, begin by letting your child know they will not be in trouble with you for telling the truth, even if they have done something they know they weren't supposed to. Then, get curious—ask what they know about drugs and alcohol. You can tell them a story about a time you remember as a kid when you learned about drugs or alcohol and that you were curious but didn't have someone to talk to about it.

They will only come to you when they do something they weren't supposed to if they do not fear punishment, shame, or harm. Phrases like "I told you . . ." or "Well, what did you think would happen?" or reactions like grounding them, taking things away from them, or yelling at them will only teach them *not* to come to you. I was chatting with a nine-year-old who has been raised with parents who set and enforce clear boundaries and also have a policy that she is not in trouble if she tells them the truth. Their family refrain on repeat is "You're allowed to make mistakes, and honesty won't get you in trouble. We will always try to help you figure out the next steps." She has heard this since she was a preschooler, and her parents have followed through with it. They have added things like, "It's okay for us to feel disappointed or frustrated by your behavior. We still love you and want you to be safe."

When I asked her what she thought her parents would say or do if she ever tried alcohol or drugs when she was older, even though she knew she wasn't supposed to, she replied, "They would help me figure out the next steps. They would say I still wasn't allowed to do those things, but I wouldn't be in trouble. They always help me figure out what to do when I don't know." If we want our kids to come to us with the big stuff, we have to have first created a relationship in which they are able to come to us with the small things.

2. Children need to have coping strategies for navigating hard emotions.

"Woof, what a long day. I could really use a glass of wine."

"You drive me to drink."

"I just need some liquid courage."

It's been culturally accepted to use substances to numb emotions or stop feeling. When substances are used in an attempt to regulate your insides, we call them coping mechanisms. Coping mechanisms can provide temporary relief from hard feelings by reducing activity in your amygdala (reactive, emotional brain), but research shows that over time using alcohol to dull emotional pain leads to increased emotional pain. It's like putting a Band-Aid on a bullet hole. Rather than tapping into tools to regulate the nervous system and engage in processing experiences and emotions, using substances can help with the here and now, putting off the coping and processing until later, like hitting the snooze button on your alarm clock. When you keep turning to substances to dull the pain without engaging in coping strategies and emotion processing, things start to pile up, creating a mountain of pain to navigate. So what's the antidote? Fostering coping strategies and helping children learn how to experience emotional pain rather than trying to avoid it.

When you practice the CEP method as laid out in Chapter 2, kids get to learn that it's okay to feel hard things and they build coping strategies for moving through those emotions. Coping strategies can look like movement or exercise, art, music, therapy, connecting with a friend or someone you trust, a hug, creating something, or being in nature. When kids are having a hard feeling and we allow them to be in it, letting them know about coping strategies that exist when they're ready, they learn that they don't have to numb their pain or run away from it temporarily.

They build a feeling of safety and familiarity with difficult feelings by practicing being in them.

3. Children need to develop an understanding of the risks of substance use and have clear expectations.

We start reading to babies not so they will read back to us tomorrow, but to foster literacy skills that will be built upon for years. Talking to kids about substances isn't something we start when they ask to go to a party when they're sixteen years old, but rather a foundation we lay that leads up to that moment. You can tell them the science behind what substances do in their bodies.

"Drugs and alcohol can change the way your body and brain work in ways that hurt you."

"Drugs can confuse the messages that your brain sends to your body, like telling your heart to beat or your lungs to breathe. This can make people sick or hurt them."

"Alcohol changes how your brain works. It can make it hard to think clearly or stay in control of your body."

You can create family rules and expectations together and be clear about them. Jessica Lahey explains, "Children raised in families with permissive drug and alcohol expectations, who allow for sips or experimentation in the home, drink earlier, drink significantly more, and experience more negative consequences from their drinking than kids who are raised by parents who consistently communicate clear expectations for drug and alcohol abstinence."[8]

Some expectations from Lahey's book that you can begin to lay out include:

- We don't take illegal drugs.
- We don't take medicines we don't need or that are not prescribed to us. You can practice having your child read the first letter and eventually the name on prescriptions. We used letter stickers to put my children's names on their multivitamin bottle in preschool to start practicing having them find their letter and then read their name to make sure they only took their vitamin.
- We don't drink alcohol until we are twenty-one (or we don't drink alcohol, or we drink responsibly). Jessica notes that this is up to you, but acknowledges that kids who are raised under the clear expectation that they will not drink until twenty-one are far less likely to develop substance use disorder during their lifetime.

4. What is modeled for children matters—in real life and in the media.

Kids are more likely to repeat what they see than what we tell them to do or not do. If you say alcohol is bad for them and then they witness you drinking, it's confusing. You can acknowledge to them that many people choose to drink alcohol or use substances and break down why. Sometimes people don't know what else to do when they're having a hard feeling, so they use a substance to try and stop feeling their emotions. Some people like the taste of certain drinks and choose to have one sometimes. Some people are addicted to substances, which means their body keeps wanting more and more, and if they have any of it, they will keep going and have a lot.

If there is someone in their life who abuses substances, you can physically and emotionally be cautious around them and shield your children from them. As children get older, you can be clear that we are mindful when we are with Aunt Sarah because sometimes she drinks too much alcohol and isn't safe to be around when she does.

Call out media depictions. When you watch a show together and someone gets blackout drunk, ask your children why they think that person drank so much they couldn't remember anything. Acknowledge the ways substances are shown in the media and encourage them to get curious. It takes just milliseconds of being exposed to images and advertisements for messaging to start imprinting on children's brains. Help bring awareness to what they're seeing so they can be conscious of the underlying messaging they're being fed.

The lifetime risk of substance use dependence is just 11 percent if kids wait until they're twenty-one to drink. For kids who wait until they're eighteen, it's 17 percent, but for kids who start drinking in middle school, their risk of substance use dependence skyrockets to 41 percent. Having family expectations of no illegal drug use and no alcohol use until at least eighteen, coupled with a safe relationship and healthy coping strategies for emotions doesn't mean your child won't drink until they're eighteen, but it does mean they're less likely to do so than if it's made out to be no big deal, or worse, permissible. If they do try drugs or alcohol, having that safe relationship with you can provide them with an avenue to make a different choice in the future.

Sleepovers

When we chose to add this section to the book, we carefully considered where it would fit best. Ultimately, we placed it in this chapter because many of the top concerns parents have about sleepovers—such as the fear of sexual abuse, exposure to inappropriate content like pornography, or encounters with alcohol or drugs—are key reasons why some parents say no to sleepovers altogether. This is a shift from past generations. When I was growing up, and for generations before, sleepovers were a quintessential childhood experience, a rite of passage for many kids. But today, with the rise of technology and the constant flood of information, parental concerns about children's physical safety have surged. A quick Google search for "Are sleepovers safe?" yields countless blog posts from families who have made the decision to ban them altogether.

The constant access to alarming news, whether it's stories of predators, accidents, or the harmful influence of media, has heightened the anxiety many parents feel about letting their children outside of their supervision. This has led to a growing number of families deciding that sleepovers are not worth the risk. While this reaction is understandable, it raises an important question: What is the long-term impact of these decisions on our children's development?

In *The Anxious Generation*, Jonathan Haidt talks about the dangers of parents becoming overly protective of their child's physical safety. He explains that while it's natural for parents to want to keep their kids safe, too much caution can actually harm a child's mental health in the long run. By shielding them from risks and challenges, parents may unintentionally prevent their children from developing important traits like resilience, independence, and confidence. Children who are never given the opportunity to test their limits, navigate complex social situations, or make independent decisions may grow up feeling less capable when they eventually have to face tough situations on their own.

Sleepovers can offer significant benefits for children, helping them build independence, strengthen social skills, and support their emotional development. These experiences teach them how to handle new environments, engage in peer relationships without their parents present, and problem-solve in real time. For many children, sleepovers are their first experience with extended time away from home, and with it comes the opportunity to develop autonomy and self-confidence. Under the right conditions—like when they're with trusted friends and families—these experiences can be a valuable part of growing up. The relationships built during these times often provide children with important social anchors, and navigating the ups and downs of peer dynamics, even without parental involvement, can promote emotional growth.

There are valid reasons to say no to a sleepover if you don't know or feel comfortable with the family involved. If you have concerns about the values of the household, the supervision your child will receive, or the overall safety of the environment, then it's completely reasonable to decline. However, if you find yourself hesitating to allow a sleepover with a family you know and trust, it may be helpful to reflect on whether fear or anxiety is influencing your decision. While it's natural to worry, especially in a world filled with constant reminders of the dangers children can face, it's equally important to weigh the potential positive impact that sleepovers can have on your child's ability to navigate new environments, build resilience, and manage emotions in social settings.

Full disclosure: For many years, we had a strict no-sleepover rule for our kids. With the exception of family, it was an absolute no. I made that decision when our oldest was just a toddler, and until she turned eight, I hadn't really stopped to question why. All I knew was that I wanted to be in control and keep her safe. The idea of sleepovers made me feel like she was beyond my reach and outside of the safety net I'd built around her. A lot of her friends also weren't allowed to have sleepovers, which had reinforced the idea that this was the right decision.

Fast-forward to a mother-daughter movie night I was having with a couple of my friends and their daughters, who are two of Nora's closest pals. My friend, who was hosting, had offered for Nora to sleep over, and I had politely declined. We finished the movie, and the girls went to play while I chatted with my friends over coffee. I realized that of the three girls, Nora was the only one not participating in the sleepover. Moments later, Nora came downstairs to ask me if she could stay. My knee-jerk reaction was to repeat my usual no, but instead, I took a minute to think about it. These were two of Nora's best friends. I knew them well, and I knew their families well. Both of the moms were my good friends. *What is my fear?* I asked myself. As I thought about it, I wasn't actually fearing for her safety. I knew that my friend would care for her and keep her safe. My fear was that she would experience something emotionally or socially hard when I wasn't there. What would happen if she was homesick, or there was conflict between the girls? I didn't want her to experience something hard without me there to help her.

But the reality is that our kids will experience hard things outside of our presence throughout their lives. The goal isn't to prevent those experiences, but to allow them so that our kids have opportunities to navigate them. In fact, learning how to manage conflict, deal with homesickness, or handle a tough social situation at a sleepover can be incredibly empowering for a child. It builds problem-solving skills, fosters self-reliance, and teaches them that they can handle challenges, even without a parent by their side. These are crucial life skills that will serve them well long after childhood.

Here are some questions to consider when opting to allow sleepovers:

Does the family own firearms? Are they stored safely?

Will the kids have internet access during the sleepover? Does the family use parental controls?

How is alcohol stored in the home?

Does your child have a way to reach you if they need to? Do you have a safe relationship with your child in which they can communicate with you if anything uncomfortable or inappropriate occurs, knowing they won't be in trouble?

Depending on your cultural and family values, there may be other questions you ask prior to allowing a sleepover. There is no one-size-fits-all approach to making your decision. Each child and situation are different. Ask yourself, *What is my fear?* Reflecting on that will help you make an intentional decision about what is best for your child in that specific scenario. It's also important to communicate with your child and prepare them for potential challenges they may face during a sleepover, equipping them with tools to manage emotions or conflicts. That way, even if the sleepover doesn't go perfectly, they know that they are capable of handling it—and they know that you'll be there to support them afterward.

Chapter 9

Tech Boundaries
in a Connected World

M om, can I play Roblox?" my daughter asked me over lunch, "Jackson plays it." At the time I hadn't heard of Roblox and I had no idea what it was. I could answer her I was going to have to figure out what Roblox was, decide if the content was appropriate for her, figure out what device she would play it on, decide how much time we would allow her to play it, and then communicate the boundaries with her and uphold them. I was tired just thinking of all the mental footwork required to answer her seemingly simple question.

Our kids are growing up with tablets, smartphones, and media sources that weren't around when many of us were their age. With their increasing desire for independence and social connection, kids in middle childhood want to play games, create videos, game with peers, text each other, and video-chat, and may even ask for social media accounts. In this chapter, we won't provide a prescriptive outline for what screen time "should" look like in middle childhood. Instead, we'll review the current research on technology and social media use during this stage. We'll offer practical tips for managing this tech-heavy landscape, aiming to help you find the approach that feels right to you. You'll gain tools to set technology boundaries that suit your child and family, and strategies for navigating the emotions that may arise as you maintain those boundaries.

What Does the Research Say?

For years the American Academy of Pediatrics recommended a maximum of two hours of screen time a day for kids from ages six through ten[1] (it now takes a more nuanced stance and doesn't have a specific time limit recommendation—more on that in a bit). All you have to do is Google "kids and screen time" and you'll find dozens of articles on the negative impact of screen time in childhood. You may have received handouts at your child's pediatrician's office warning about the risks of excessive screen time. Our pediatrician asked about screen time at every well-child visit from the time my kids were one year old onward. The message for parents is clear: if you want to do a good job, you'll strictly limit screens. On the flip side, take a video game study from 2022 involving nine- and ten-year-old kids.[2] In it, kids played video games for three hours per day— well above the previously recommended upper limit for that age group. MRI imaging of the gamers' brains, compared to those of kids who didn't play, showed better working memory and impulse control. The kicker? The gamers *did not* have worse behavioral or mental health outcomes than the non-gamers.

What does this mean for families who are trying to make decisions about screen use? It means that the research isn't cut-and-dried, and we don't have a concrete answer about how much and what kind of screen use is ideal for children. It calls into question the umbrella statements about strictly limiting screens and prompts us to look at the quality of screen use, rather than just the quantity. As we learn more about technology and young brains, we are seeing that not all screens are created equally. This understanding of the nuance of tech use was likely what drove the AAP to revise its guidelines. It no longer recommends a specific time cut off, rather encouraging families to create habits that balance screen time with physical activity and to be mindful of the quality of their children's screen use.

Think back to the last time you found yourself doomscrolling Insta-gram. Think about how it felt in your body and brain. Now think about a time you spent video-chatting with a friend or family member. How did that feel in your brain and body? There's a stark contrast, right? It's the same for kids. Some technology use is stressful (some can even be harmful) and some can be cup-filling. Remember Mateo from Chapter 2? FaceTime with his nana was one of his coping strategies when he needed connection. While the lack of concrete, comprehensive research on kids and tech can feel frustrating—what parent needs more mental gymnastics added to their plate?!—it is also empowering. We get to take the research and information available to us and find a way to make technology a positive addition to the lives of our kids. Let's begin by looking at the different ways kids use technology (this is a starting point, not an exhaustive list; as tech continues to evolve, more categories of use are emerging):

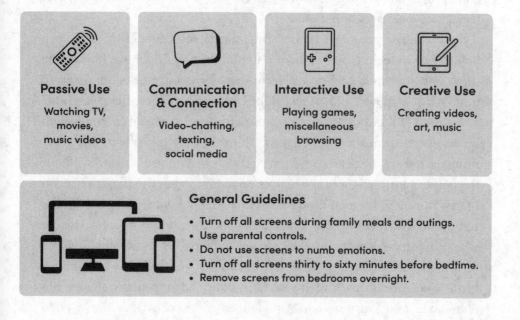

Passive Use

Watching TV,
movies,
music videos

Communication & Connection

Video-chatting,
texting,
social media

Interactive Use

Playing games,
miscellaneous
browsing

Creative Use

Creating videos,
art, music

General Guidelines

- Turn off all screens during family meals and outings.
- Use parental controls.
- Do not use screens to numb emotions.
- Turn off all screens thirty to sixty minutes before bedtime.
- Remove screens from bedrooms overnight.

Even when we break screen time into different categories, there isn't research that clearly labels any category of screen use as inherently good or bad. Remember the study about video games improving cognitive skills? There are also studies showing that interactive screen use can lead to less sleep for kids.[3] The point of looking at different types of screen use isn't to say one is better than the other, but to use this information as a starting point for making decisions. Take Mateo, for example. When he uses FaceTime, he's using tech, but he's communicating and connecting with his nana. His needs are being met. If he were just watching a show by himself, that need wouldn't be fulfilled. That doesn't mean vegging out in front of the TV is off-limits, and if Mateo's mom had decided to just put on a show for him so she could cook dinner, that would have been fine. Yes, he would still be needing connection, but we can't always access the ideal scenario in the moment. Sometimes we are surviving, not thriving. When I'm in the surviving-not-thriving trenches, I don't use the categories to decide on screen time. I ask myself one question: *Do I need a break from parenting in order to continue to be a kind parent?* If the answer is yes, I let them use screens without guilt.

I used to have a saying when my high-needs, sensory-sensitive son was a toddler: If I'm feeling bitchy, we're watching *Blippi*. *Blippi* was his favorite show, and if I could feel myself teetering on the edge of being mean to him, we'd sit down and watch *Blippi*. Was *Blippi* beneficial for him? The jury is still out on that, but it was definitely beneficial for me (which by extension meant it was benefiting him). It gave me fifteen or twenty minutes to reset my nervous system so that I could move forward with our day without losing it on him when he cried for the ten thousandth time. If fifteen minutes of screen time meant he had a regulated caregiver for the rest of the day, I was in. All of this to say, the categories for screen use are a helpful jumping-off point, they are not the be-all and end-all.

If the research isn't going to tell us exactly what's best, where do we turn? The American Academy of Child and Adolescent Psychiatry has reasonable and commonsense guidelines for screens that are a good starting place.[4] It recommends turning off all screens during family meals and outings, using parental controls, not using screens to numb emotions, turning off all screens thirty to sixty minutes before bedtime, and removing screens from bedrooms overnight. Combining these guidelines with using the categories in the figure above, you have a good rubric for creating screen time boundaries in your family.

Social Media: A Category of Its Own

While the research on overall screen time is ambiguous and contradictory, the research on social media is pretty clear: it's not good for kids' development and it can harm their mental health. The best-case scenario for children is to stay off social media until age eighteen. It's not an easy ask; I get that. My nine-year-old is already asking for access to social media because some of her peers are on TikTok and Instagram. Jonathan Haidt's book *The Anxious Generation* is an excellent resource for those looking to explore this topic further. In this section we'll outline some key takeaways.

Most social media companies have *unenforced* age limits that are supposed to require kids to be thirteen years and older to access their platforms (and many experts say kids should be much older). Despite these age restrictions, the US Surgeon General reported in 2022 that nearly 40 percent of children eight to twelve years old are on social media.[5] This means that kids are bypassing the age requirements and entering the bumpy landscape of these apps well before their brains are ready. What is the impact of this? Haidt shares: "The first generation of Americans who went through puberty with smartphones (and the entire internet) in their hands became more anxious, depressed, self-harming, and suicidal." He also notes that while mental health declined across genders, girls were impacted more significantly than boys, and preteen girls were harmed most of all.[6]

The brain changes happening in puberty make kids especially vulnerable to the pitfalls of social media. Human brain development requires in-person connection across all ages, but puberty is an especially sensitive period of development when face-to-face peer interactions are critical for the development of the skills kids will need in adulthood, like problem-solving, risk assessment, sound decision-making, and the ability to navigate social interactions. Haidt posits that a play-based childhood has been replaced by a phone-based childhood, and while exposure to explicit sexual content, online shaming or bullying, and completely unrealistic beauty standards are certainly harming our kids, it goes much deeper than that. The time that kids spend on social media each day pulls them away from the play that their brains are wired to experience. It's a double whammy—social media exposes them to harm *and* it prevents them from engaging in critical, skill-building, in-person relationships.

What is perhaps most alarming about social media is the way it takes over the human brain. Its addictive nature is intentional; it is designed to make us crave more and more. Every like, comment, and notification lights up the dopamine pathways in our brains. Without even realizing it, we begin to reach for our phones more and more. At some point, our phones start to pull us from things that we know are so much more important—our relationships with our children and our partners. I was recently sitting on the couch with my husband after getting the kids to bed. We'd been looking forward to watching the Olympics together and yet I found myself repeatedly picking up my phone. I was tired—summer parenting can be tough—and my brain was looking for a dopamine hit. What I really needed was to spend that quality time with my husband, having a shared experience and talking about what we were watching. That craving for the phone was so real though, I had to consciously stop myself from picking it up and scrolling to find my next hit. If adults with fully developed brains are struggling to limit their social media use, think about how hard it is for children. This is an area where they really need us to step up and set and enforce boundaries.

One of the things that I find helpful when setting boundaries that feel hard is to ask myself, *Is this a health or safety issue?* If the answer is yes, it's much easier for me to put in the time and effort of setting and enforcing the boundary. When it comes to social media, it is absolutely a health and safety issue. With that in mind, setting boundaries becomes easier. The best thing we can do for children in middle childhood is keep them off social media entirely. In the absence of attention-monopolizing apps, kids will find ways to engage in the real world.

Why Can They Have It and I Can't?

I ended up deciding not to allow my daughter to use Roblox. I just didn't feel ready to navigate learning the game myself, deciding what I was okay with her experiencing through it, and figuring out how to manage that through parental controls. Naturally, she was upset. She was frustrated because Jackson was playing Roblox and constantly talking about how much fun it was, and she felt left out, unable to share that same experience. My daughter is my ultra-social child, so my saying no to Roblox didn't just feel like a game denial; to her, it felt like I was saying no to a connection with her friends.

"But why can't I have it? I'm the same age as Jackson, and he gets to. Even his younger sister gets to use it and she's a whole year younger than me!" She crossed her arms tightly and slumped back in her chair, her frustration palpable.

I took a breath and said, "Yeah, I totally get why that would feel unfair. I'm open to learning more about Roblox, but until I do, it's just not something we're doing."

"But why do you need to do research? Why can't I just have it?"

"Well, Roblox isn't just a game, it's a whole platform. There are lots of things that could happen on the platform, and some of those things might not be safe for a kid's brain. I need to learn more about the game and how I can keep you safe if you play it. That's going to take some time for me to do."

Her response was immediate: "Ugh, this is so unfair!" She stood up quickly, her chair scraping loudly across the floor, and stomped down the hallway to her room. The door slammed.

In that moment, I reminded myself: Kids will be disappointed and frustrated when we set boundaries they don't like. Let them feel it. From my daughter's perspective, the only fair outcome was for me to say yes—especially since her peers were allowed to play. Even though I validated her feelings, even though I explained my reasoning, she was still angry. And that's okay. She gets to be angry, and I get to hold the boundaries that protect her safety. The following box provides some sample language for navigating these conversations with your child.

Boundaries Around Screens Might Sound Like . . .

- "I'm not going to let you use TikTok right now. There's a lot of content there that isn't made for kids, and it's my job to make sure you only see things that are safe and helpful for you."

- "Screens before bed can make it harder for your brain to calm down and get a good night's sleep. We'll use this time to read or relax so you can sleep well."

- "We're only using tablets or phones in the living room or kitchen where I can see. That way, I can help if something confusing or inappropriate pops up."

- "Mealtimes are screen-free times. There's so much to focus on outside of our family, but mealtimes are when we focus on our family."

- "We'll revisit social media when you're older. It's my job to help keep your mind safe and balanced. For now, I'm doing that by helping you focus on connecting with friends and families in ways that don't involve screens."

Screens and Dysregulation

Think back to the FACTS described in Chapter 3 that we use to help kids regulate their nervous systems. Tech use can impact four of the five components of FACTS; activity, connection, sleep, and tune-out. That's a significant portion of their overall nervous system regulation.

Screen use becomes dysregulating when it prevents kids from accessing regulating activity, having downtime, connecting in person, and getting enough sleep. For a child who needs a lot of movement to be regulated, spending several hours sitting still while playing a video game can really drain their battery. For a child who craves connection, FaceTime or texting a friend can be regulating, but watching a TV show solo might be dysregulating. A child may not show any behavioral impact from watching a morning cartoon, but may struggle to fall asleep if they watch something after dinner. If you're noticing that your child has a hard time transitioning off of screens when their time is up, or that they have behavioral changes after using screens, refer back to FACTS to support their nervous system. A note on sleep: We know how important sleep is for children's growth and development. The blue light from screens can inhibit melatonin production and make falling asleep harder. If screens are a part of your evening routine as a family, consider using blue-light-blocking glasses to mitigate its effect.

I'll share a personal example of how FACTS impact our screen use as a family. My daughter has very high movement needs. If she uses screens in excess, we see it in her regulation levels. She gets snarky and irritable. She doesn't yet recognize when this starts to happen; we have to recognize it, set the boundary, and hold it. "Okay, I'm setting the timer for ten minutes, and then it's time to turn off screens and go outside to swing or climb on the pergola." One of our personal screen time boundaries for her focuses on the quantity of movement she's had that day. I am more inclined to say yes to screen time if I know she's moved her body enough. My son, on the other hand, has lower movement needs but higher connection needs. He also seems to recognize when he's reached his limit of screen time, because he'll simply get up, turn it off, and come find me to connect.

You know your child best, and you can observe their behaviors and adjust your screen boundaries as needed. You might notice that your child needs really clear, firm, and predictable boundaries. They might need to know exactly how much time they're going to have before they even start. You might have a kid who plays a game for twenty minutes and then moves on to something else of their own accord. For the child who craves the screen time and wants to know exactly how much time they'll have, they may need concrete, predictable rules so they know what to expect. For a child who uses screens and then moves on independently, you may be able to take a more flexible approach.

Do as I Say, Not as I Do

Technology is here to stay. We live in a world where our kids will be exposed to screens on a regular basis. Many of our children will likely end up with jobs in media or technology. While screens have their place in this world, it's also crucial for children to engage in activities beyond technology. Reading books, creating art, playing together, and real-life problem-solving are essential for their well-being and growth. As adults, we play a crucial role in this process. We need to lead by example— reading, creating, and being active ourselves. It's important for them to see us setting aside our phones during meals or when spending time with friends. While research on kids and screens is rather murky, there is some compelling evidence about parental phone use. Parents using a smartphone are less sensitive and responsive to their children[7] and more likely to be irritable and impatient while using devices[8]—because when you're focused on your device, your child's needs feel like an interruption or an inconvenience.

The algorithms are designed to steal our attention. Every time we click, like, or comment we tell the app's algorithm what we should see next in order to keep us hooked. It makes sense then that parents get irritated when they're interrupted. We have advanced technology working around the clock to keep us addicted to our apps, which are designed to capture our attention in a way that makes it incredibly difficult to shift gears back into real life. Big Tech has learned how to hijack the dopamine pathways in our brains, making us feel like we need to stay focused on that screen to get our next hit. Meanwhile, our kids are standing right next to us trying to get our attention about something. The system is rigged, but it's a system that our kids will have to learn to navigate too. We can use our own screen time challenges as a teaching opportunity. "Ugh, these apps work hard to make my brain want to keep scrolling! Thanks for getting my attention and reminding me it's time to put my phone away."

As you create screen time boundaries, consider including your own boundaries in addition to the ones outlined above. Keep smartphones away from the dinner table, family outings, and bedtime. Carve out time when you and your kids are in one another's company sans screens. Prioritize your own nervous system regulation alongside your child's. We can tell kids all day long about why their screen time needs to be balanced and why we have boundaries, but those words will fall short if we don't model balance and boundaries for ourselves too.

Chapter 10

School Transitions and Refusal

Calliope was five years old and had just entered kindergarten. Up to this point she had been at home with her mom, Iris. Iris had been really intentional about prepping Calliope for what to expect at school. She'd made her a visual calendar outlining which days were school days, she'd read her stories about what school would be like, and they'd done a meet and greet with her teacher. Iris was expecting drop-off to be tough the first week and was pleasantly surprised when it went without a hitch. Going into week two of school, Iris was optimistic. But Monday morning came around and Calliope was teary-eyed getting ready for school. They got there and she started to cling to Iris and was now fully sobbing. Drop-off was a disaster that ended with Calliope's teacher peeling her off of Iris's body, and Iris crying while walking out the door to the sound of Calliope's sobs. What was going on? What had changed?

Adjusting to Back to School

The entrance into kindergarten is not a small thing for kids. Whether they've been home with a parent throughout early childhood or have been in childcare or preschool, kindergarten is a whole different ball game. Kindergarten tends to have higher student-teacher ratios, less opportunity for play, more academic and behavioral pressures, and less realistic expectations than what children have previously experienced. Calliope's story highlights two important school transition phenomena: the honeymoon period and the way that intentional prep and hard emotions can and do coexist.

The back-to-school honeymoon period is a tease. You drop your kid off, all is going well, and you think, *Wow, is this actually going to be easy?!* Only for the honeymoon to end and all the hard emotions and big behaviors to surface. Know that this is normal. The excitement and novelty of entering school sometimes make the initial transition really smooth, only for things to totally change when that novelty wears off.

The other part of Calliope's story that is really important to understand and internalize is that even with all of Iris's intentional prep work, Calliope still had hard feelings about school. That doesn't mean that the prep was a waste of time. Kids feel secure when they know what to expect, and for kids in younger middle childhood, visual aids like the calendar that Iris used can help them understand their new schedule in a tangible way.

Imagine that you're starting a new job, and your boss has sent you the employee handbook and your schedule. It outlines what you can expect and what is expected of you. You're still really nervous about starting, because it's all new, but you feel secure knowing what to expect. It's the same for kids. Helping them prep for school doesn't mean that they won't have hard emotions, but it does mean that their brains have more space to process those emotions, rather than trying to absorb and remember the new logistics of their day. This doesn't just apply to kindergarten either. Each school year brings new challenges logistically, academically, and socially. Let's outline a few strategies you can utilize for the back-to-school transition.

Visit the school. If this is a new school, set up a time to visit it with your child. Even better if you can do a meet and greet with their teacher. The school may already have this scheduled prior to the start of the school year. If your child is entering kindergarten, a kindergarten screening (an assessment of your child's kindergarten readiness) may be required, and your child will meet their teacher at that time.

Talk about lunch. Where will your child eat lunch? Will it be in a cafeteria or in their classroom? Lunch is a big social time and can be overwhelming for kids. Let them know what they can expect.

Will they get a hot lunch? How will that work? If you're packing a lunch and your child is on the younger side, they may need to practice opening and closing their lunch box independently.

Adjust bedtime in advance. If your child's been living young, wild, and free all summer, start adjusting bedtime ahead of back to school. As I write this, my kids are exactly two weeks away from returning to classes. I know how painful it is to think about shifting away from summer freedoms and into more structure. The pain is worth it though—a cranky, sleep-deprived kid will struggle even more to adapt to back to school.

Validate their feelings. Feeling nervous or anxious about going back to school is normal. You might worry that if you validate your child's nervousness, you'll make them more nervous. The opposite is true: kids feel safe when they know that their feelings are normal and expected. You might be tempted to say something like, "Hey, don't worry about school! You'll see all your friends and have so much fun!" The message that sends isn't going to help your child not worry, but it might make them feel that you're not a safe place to bring their concerns. Try this instead: "Change is hard. I remember feeling nervous going back to school too. It's so normal to feel that."

Discuss regulation. The school environment is full of stimuli and can be exhausting for a child's brain and body. On top of the sheer sensory input from school, they're also tapping into their cognitive brain, stretching it like a rubber band trying to learn new content and social skills each day. Help them understand how their brain and body process the information of the school day and create a plan together for what to do to support their nervous system for regulation. Scan the following QR code to take a quiz to understand their unique nervous system as well as ways they can regulate throughout the day. Planning this outside of the moment helps them be able to access the information in the moment.

Model confidence. When you think about your child's emotional climate during transitions, picture yourself as their thermostat. You get to set the emotional "temperature." If you become dysregulated by their feelings of nervousness or apprehension, you'll turn the thermostat up, and in turn, their stress response will intensify. Our job isn't to stop their hard feelings, but we do need to be aware of regulating our own emotions so that they are getting messages of safety from us.

School Refusal

Every child occasionally complains about school or asks to stay home. School refusal is different, more consistent and more intense. School refusal includes *extreme* reluctance to go to school, or even absences from school. It can be incredibly challenging for both kids and parents.

School refusal is a symptom, not a diagnosis. It is often related to anxiety and stress, academic challenges, peer conflict, or family dynamics. School refusal can include meltdowns or tantrums related to school, but it can also manifest as more subtle somatic symptoms. Kids may complain of stomach pain, nausea, head pain, or fatigue. While the stress response is emotional in origin, the somatic symptoms can be and often are real. The key to responding to school refusal is to identify the cause and collaborate with the school to help your child cope with the stressors.

There are three main causes for school refusal: separation anxiety and attachment, stimuli and dysregulation, and inclusion and belonging.

Separation Anxiety and Attachment

Across the board but particularly in lower elementary school, a driving force behind school refusal is separation anxiety. When my son started kindergarten, drop-off was a disaster. It would start during the car ride to school and escalate. By the time we reached his classroom he would be fully crying. There was a part of me that wanted to scoop him up and bring him home and never, ever let him experience that heart-wrenching feeling. There was another part of me that recognized that adversity is required to build resilience, and that this was just one of many moments when I would have to witness him experiencing something difficult.

Separation anxiety is developmentally normal for young children, especially during school drop-offs. How you respond in the moment will influence your child's emotional experience. When parents or caregivers show uncertainty or hesitation during goodbyes, it can inadvertently heighten the child's anxiety. Children are remarkably attuned to the emotional cues of their parents; if they sense doubt or worry, they might feel that there's something to be fearful about. A predictable, quick goodbye routine can serve as an anchor in this moment of uncertainty, providing reassurance and stability. When your child knows exactly what to expect each morning, it reduces the anxiety that comes with the unknown. A routine might include a warm, confident expression of love, such as, "I know it's hard to say goodbye. I can't wait to see you this afternoon. I love you." This assures your child that they are loved and that you will return, which can help them feel secure even in your absence. Lingering or hesitating, on the other hand, can create a mixed message. It may suggest to your child that you are not sure about leaving them, which can make them more anxious and reluctant to let go. They might start to worry that something is wrong or that there's a reason to be afraid of the separation, making future drop-offs even more challenging. Maintaining a confident, positive demeanor and sticking to a brief, consistent goodbye routine can help ease your child's transition and, over time, can reduce separation anxiety and help your child develop the resilience to manage other transitions and separations in their life.

School separation anxiety can also be a great opportunity to connect with your child's teacher. I knew a second-grade teacher who had created a coping strategy for separation anxiety that she offered to any of her students who might need it. If separation anxiety struck during the school day, she had special paper that she would give to the student. That student was given time to write a note to their parents about the anxiety they were experiencing. The act of writing helped to calm the child's nervous system, and became a coping strategy they could use again and again. Separation anxiety can be as hard on teachers as it is on parents and children. Collaborate with your child's teacher to see if a coping strategy like this can be offered to your child.

Stimuli and Dysregulation

Jada was in first grade when she started to exhibit physiological stress symptoms of anxiety: "My belly hurts," "I have a headache," "I'm too sick to go to school." Her moms kept her home some days, wanting to send the message that it's okay to take a day off if you're sick. But it continued and the complaints of pain and sickness grew in frequency. They brought her in sobbing, communicated with her teacher, and felt like they were trying everything, but nothing was changing. Then her teacher and the guidance counselor met with Jada's moms and asked if one of them wanted to accompany Jada for a full school day to help her feel safe at school. Then they would follow a slow schedule to gradually decrease the time Jada's mom was there as Jada grew more comfortable.

On the first day, Jada's mom Shaina walked into the classroom and noticed the signs and artwork filling the walls. She heard the sounds of kids chatting as they got their things ready to start the day, chairs squeaking when they sat down at their desks, and the hustle and bustle of everyone in the hallway getting to their classrooms. The bell rang to signal the day beginning and the teacher quieted the class for everyone to focus their attention on the morning announcements. Jada was as small as she could be, retreating into her seat, holding Shaina's hand next to her, trembling with overwhelm. "My head hurts, Mom. Can we just go home?"

A lightbulb went off for Shaina: Jada was clearly overstimulated. Her nervous system was clocking all the information around her, noticing every movement, sound, smell, and texture. She was in a reactive fear state, scanning the room as her brain asked, *Am I safe? Do I have to pay attention to that?* As the day went on, Shaina experienced the controlled chaos of the lunchroom while Jada refused all food. She watched Jada flinch at the sound of the bell each time it rang and saw her zone out when it was small group time and each group filled the classroom with its own discussion.

Jada *was* feeling sick, she *did* have headaches, but now it was clear to Shaina why it was happening. Jada's body was pumping adrenaline and cortisol, living in a stress state as it felt the overwhelm of the stimulation flood her, causing real, physical symptoms of distress. Jada's school refusal wasn't misbehavior; it was stress behavior.

Self-awareness and self-regulation skills are essential for kids to develop resilience to stressors at school. When children are self-aware, they can identify and understand their emotions, recognizing the physical and mental cues that signal when they are feeling overwhelmed, anxious, or upset. This awareness is the first step in managing their emotional responses, helping them to avoid becoming overwhelmed by their feelings.

Kids with strong self-regulation skills are better equipped to pause, assess the situation, and choose a response that supports their emotional wellness. This ability prevents them from getting stuck in negative emotional cycles and reduces the likelihood of anxiety spiraling into patterns like school refusal or other avoidant behaviors.

The goal is not to shield kids from difficult emotions or to just fix them when they arise. Instead, it's about empowering children to recognize what's happening in their bodies and minds. By doing so, they can use tools and strategies from their regulation toolbox to navigate these emotions in healthy, constructive ways.

Shaina met with the school team and shared what she knew about her daughter and how her body responded when she was overstimulated. Together, they created a plan for Jada to start the day with the behavior specialist for some quiet one-on-one time. Jada was offered sensory breaks every two hours to allow her nervous system to recover from the stimuli. She was given earplugs that helped drown out the noise around her a little, giving her nervous system some relief.

As the other kids noticed Jada's earplugs, the teacher held a morning

Advocating for Your Child's Sensory Needs

- Ask to meet with teachers/admin, presenting them with information on your child's sensory needs.

- Request sensory breaks in the classroom.

- Utilize accommodations in the classroom (fidgets, a wobble chair, noise-canceling headphones, etc.).

- Practice self-advocacy phrases with your child.

Classroom Scripts Around Sensory Needs

- "When my body feels wiggly, I try to listen to what it's telling me. 'Oh, what, body? I need to do some big body movements? Okay!' And I go do them. What does your body tell you?"

- "Sometimes, when I'm feeling really annoyed or grumpy, I pause and think, 'Hmm, I think my body needs something.' What do you think my body needs when it's annoyed and grumpy?"

- "Have you ever noticed what the classroom is like when you first come in for the day? What about right after lunch? What's it like before we go outside? What about after? Let's brainstorm why we show up differently at different times of the day."

meeting to chat about how our brains and bodies notice details around us. The kids got to discuss what drained their batteries and what recharged them. As some other kids noted the sound of the classroom or the bell feeling hard for them, the teacher offered them earplugs too, to help them feel safe and focused during the day. Some kids said it was hard to sit still for work time and were offered different seating options, the choice to stand, or a resistance band on their chair they could push their feet against. Jada led the way to a rich opportunity for the children to learn how their unique nervous systems work so they could have access to as much regulation, and thus capacity for learning, as possible.

Inclusion and Belonging

Chelsea, nine years old, had been struggling with school refusal for a long time. So much so that it was creating tension between her parents because they were stressed by their days of missed work and couldn't see eye to eye on how to tackle the issue. Chelsea's school refusal was multifaceted. She felt overwhelmed by the stimulation of the classroom. The noises, the bright lights, and the multitude of transitions throughout the day drained her battery. At baseline, a normal school day was tiring for Chelsea. Add social dynamics and things got even harder for her.

Chelsea had one classmate in particular by whom she felt challenged. This classmate could be antagonistic. Likely she was looking for a way to connect, but without the skills to do so with Chelsea in a prosocial way, she provoked her instead. There were many times when Chelsea would have massive meltdowns on school mornings, and after chatting with her mom, it would come to light that she was worried that her peer was going to say something mean or tease her. Chelsea was experiencing a lot of social discomfort at school.

As children focus less on life at home and more on friendships, peers, and social dynamics, they begin to experience new emotional challenges. Feelings of shame, embarrassment, and exclusion are common factors contributing to school refusal during the upper elementary-school years. The bad news is that there is no quick fix. I get it, I hate seeing my kids experiencing social pain, which brings up my own embarrassing and painful memories from childhood. The good news is that you have the tools and strategies necessary to help your child cope. Let's outline the key strategies for helping kids cope with emotional turmoil at school.

Help your child identify and communicate what they're experiencing

When your child comes home upset about something that happened at school, your first instinct might be to jump in and fix the problem (relatable). But before you do, take a step back and help your child identify and communicate what they're *actually experiencing*. Start by asking open-ended questions: What really took place? Who was involved? How did it make you feel? Encourage your child to express their thoughts and feelings openly, without jumping to conclusions or labeling the situation right away. Model for them that it's important to get the full picture before deciding on the next steps.

Once you have a clearer understanding, try to determine whether the issue is just garden-variety peer conflict—something all kids go through as they learn to navigate social relationships—or if it's something more. Is your child feeling left out or struggling to fit in with their peers? These feelings are common but can be very painful for a child. Or could it be something more than that, something that requires adult intervention?

This is where Signe Whitson's framework from page 110 can be incredibly helpful. She offers a clear way to distinguish between rude behaviors, mean behaviors, and bullying. Rude behavior might be unintentional and thoughtless, like a kid cutting in line. Mean behavior is more deliberate and hurtful, like name-calling or excluding someone on purpose. Bullying, however, is a repeated, intentional attack, whether it's physical, verbal, or social.

Teaching your child to recognize these differences is a valuable skill. It not only helps them understand their own experiences better but also empowers them to respond appropriately. If it's just rude behavior or a one-time mean remark, they might be able to brush it off or respond with assertiveness. If it's bullying, they'll need your support in taking further action.

By helping your child navigate these nuances, you're equipping them with the tools they need to handle social challenges now and in the future. And as a parent, you'll feel more confident in knowing when to step in and when to let your child work things out on their own.

Normalize conflict

Conflict is a natural part of life, and it's important for kids to understand that it's something everyone faces when interacting with others. When we normalize conflict, we help children see it not as something to be feared or avoided, but as an opportunity to learn and grow. Remind your child that experiencing disagreements or challenges with friends is just part of being in a relationship with another person. The goal isn't to avoid conflict altogether, but to develop the skills needed to navigate it successfully.

If your child is struggling with school refusal due to social issues, and you've ruled out bullying, this may be a sign that they're still working on building their confidence in conflict resolution. It's okay for them to feel unsure or uncomfortable in these situations—it's a skill that takes time to develop. Encourage them to keep practicing, and reassure them that it's normal to find this challenging.

You might find it helpful to revisit the "Handling Hurtful Behaviors" section of Chapter 7. It provides practical advice on how to support your child through these tough moments. It offers scripts and strategies for self-advocacy that you can share with your child. These tools can help them feel more prepared and confident when they encounter conflict, knowing they have the words and the approach to handle it effectively. Over time, this will boost their self-assurance and help them become more comfortable facing and resolving conflicts on their own.

Help them know when to ask for help

The goal of teaching kids self-regulation and conflict resolution skills isn't to make them completely independent of adults. Children still need to know they have a trusted adult to rely on when they face situations they can't handle on their own. It's important that they feel safe turning to us, knowing we won't automatically take over but instead will support them in navigating the situation. I remember having a conversation with my daughter about a social conflict she was experiencing and, as she was telling me, I offered to contact her teacher. She paused, looked at me, and said, "No, Mom, I'm just trying to tell you about this. If you talk to my teacher, you'll make it worse." I had to pause, take a breath, and go through the "Handling Hurtful Behaviors" strategies to figure out exactly what was going on for her. If you identify that your child is experiencing rude or mean behaviors, you can give them strategies for navigating it, without stepping in yourself. If you're concerned that bullying is behind your child's school refusal, that's an indicator it's time to connect with their teacher and/or school administration. You can find resources for navigating that conversation in Chapter 7.

To recap: There is a difference between your child having an off day when they need to rest and chill and your child experiencing consistent, ongoing school refusal. When it is school refusal, there are often three main causes: separation anxiety and attachment, stimulation and dysregulation, and inclusion and belonging. As you help create a feeling of safety with your child at school, their nervous system can calm and school engagement can change.

Navigating Extracurriculars

Talia's dad, Asa, had signed her up for soccer and was so looking forward to watching her play. The setup was perfect too. Soccer practice was at her school, directly after school. It didn't add any stress or additional back and forth for her family. Plus, Asa had been worried about Talia. After school she went right to her room to draw or read. She didn't show much interest in playing with the neighborhood kids or seeing her friends outside of school. Asa thought soccer would help Talia branch out and grow socially.

A few weeks into the season, Asa got an email from Talia's coach. She was refusing to participate in practices. She spent practice lying in the grass or perched in a tree next to the field. The coach said that she was welcome to be on the team, but only if she participated. Asa was frustrated. When he'd pick up Talia from soccer practice, she'd act normally and even say that practice "went well." Now he comes to find out she hadn't even been participating!

Asa decided he would start attending practices to monitor Talia. When he arrived at the field, he found her sitting next to it, picking at the grass as her teammates went through their warm-up drills.

"Talia, go join your teammates."

Talia looked at the ground, shook her head no, and crossed her arms.

"Talia, this isn't optional, get up and go run drills with your team."

"Dad, I can't! I'm tired!" She started to cry. Asa began to feel manipulated.

"You have all the energy in the world to read, draw, and create things in your room at home. This is no different—get up and go. I'm going to count to five and if you're not on the field by five, there will be a punishment."

Talia continued to cry, but walked reluctantly onto the field. She forced herself to move through the steps of practice. At the end of practice, Asa praised her. "Talia, I am so proud of you for getting out there!" He expected Talia to feel pride in herself too. Instead, she slumped into the back seat of the car, looked down at her feet, and didn't respond to her dad. Frustrated, Asa got in the car and drove home silently.

Parents often hear about the importance of extracurricular activities in helping kids develop social skills, build confidence, and explore new interests. It makes sense that Asa wanted Talia to join soccer; he wanted her to be fulfilled and successful. He wanted her to spend her after-school time with her friends rather than alone in her room. There's no question that sports and other extracurriculars can be highly beneficial for some children. However, if we look at extracurriculars through the lens of a child's nervous system needs, not all extracurriculars will be a good fit. Some children may thrive in environments with lots of stimulation, while others may find noisy, chaotic settings overwhelming and draining. This was the case with Talia.

If you have a child who recharges with downtime, you might have found Talia's story relatable. When a child needs alone time to reset, it's easy for us to start creating narratives that aren't particularly helpful. We might wonder, *Why are they so antisocial? Why do they prefer to play alone?* Or perhaps, *Why does she go to her room to draw for hours instead of running around outside with her friends?* These questions often lead us to see their behavior as something that needs "fixing." That's why Asa pushed so hard for Talia to join the soccer team, trying to correct what he saw as a problem rather than honoring her natural way of recharging.

Asa decides to have a meeting with Talia's teacher to get a better grip on what might be going on at school. He's worried he's going to hear that she's withdrawn in class. He doesn't want his child to be a loner. How will she succeed as an adult if she can't interact socially? He's relieved when Talia's teacher describes her as cheerful and well-adjusted socially. She has friends at school and interacts well with all her classmates. She engages in group work without an issue and participates with others at recess. Her teacher has no concerns about her social skills.

Talia is thriving at school—she's socially skilled and feels at ease with her peers. So what's behind her resistance to soccer? When we look at what Talia enjoys doing after school, we start to get some answers. Before soccer came into the picture, she would head to her room for quiet activities like reading, drawing, and creating art. This routine aligned with what her nervous system needed. She was likely using up most of her social energy at school, and afterward, her body craved calm and a break from stimulation to recharge. Soccer, with its noise and chaos, was pushing her past her limits, doing the exact opposite of what her body was asking for.

It's easy to believe that our kids are missing out on essential experiences for their development when they choose to opt out of certain activities. The truth is that there is no one-size-fits-all approach to what is best for a child. Opting out of extracurricular activities can be perfectly fine, especially for children who need reduced stimulation to help regulate their nervous systems. Many kids, particularly those who are sensitive to sensory input or have neurodivergent traits, can become overwhelmed by too much stimulation. Allowing them to skip certain activities provides the space to recharge, process their emotions, and return to a more balanced state. Instead of packing their schedules with numerous activities, focusing on a few that truly resonate can lead to deeper engagement and fulfillment. This approach encourages kids to explore their interests without the pressure of constant participation.

When families opt out of extracurriculars, children gain valuable time for unstructured play, which fosters creativity and problem-solving skills. They benefit from the freedom to explore their environments and engage in imaginative play without adult interference. Additionally, learning to say no to activities teaches children self-advocacy and helps them understand their own needs—an essential skill for managing stress and anxiety throughout life.

Ultimately, choosing to opt out of extracurriculars isn't a sign of missing out; rather, it's an opportunity to prioritize mental health and well-being, supporting each child's unique needs and fostering their overall development in a balanced way. On the flip side, you may have a child who is fulfilled by extracurriculars. My daughter is one of those children. Her social cup never seems to be full. She also has very high movement needs. Putting her in sports helps to meet both of those needs. She gets to move her body and spend more time with her friends. It's a win-win.

The key for making decisions about extracurriculars is to block out the messaging about how important they are and look at the child in front of you. What makes the most sense for your child's unique needs? What will foster safety and emotional wellness? If it's more time at home for rest and recharging, that's perfectly okay.

Chapter 11

Navigating Heavy Topics

had just arrived at a girls' night and was chatting and snacking with my friends when my friend Ashley picked up her phone and looked over at me. "Hey, Rach, Cody just texted me and asked if you could give him a call right away." *I've only been gone from home for thirty minutes, what could he possibly need?!* I thought to myself. I found my phone in my purse and saw three missed calls from him and a text message. My husband is a first responder and whenever I have multiple missed calls, it usually means he's been called out and I need to get home to be with the kids. I clicked open the text message and my stomach dropped. "Active shooter Lewiston" was all it said. I called him back and told him I was on my way.

When I arrived home, he was in the driveway ready to go. "I've got to go now, this is bad," he said. "The kids are still awake waiting for you to lie down with them." He kissed me and hopped in the truck. I walked inside to the sound of his siren screaming down the street and away from me. My kids were used to him getting called out at all hours, so bedtime went normally. I still didn't know the gravity of the situation. It wasn't unusual for Cody to get calls involving shootings or violence, and they often turned out to be misunderstandings or situations in which things could be defused and nobody was hurt. This wasn't going to be one of those scenarios.

When the kids fell asleep, I snuck out to the couch to scroll my phone and wait for Cody to get home. When I opened Facebook, I started to realize the reality of the situation. My entire feed was about the shooting. I turned on the news, and it was everywhere. Mass shooting, several fatalities, shooter on the run. Outside our house I heard the sound of sirens over and over. Police from across the state were arriving in our town. I started to feel really scared. I texted my friends, updating them about the situation—they were still at our girls' night, unaware of what was happening. Two of them decided to come over to my house so I didn't have to be alone while waiting to hear from Cody. Soon after they arrived, Cody called me.

"Are you alone?" he asked.

"No, the girls just got here, why?"

"They found his car down the road from our house. Lock all the doors, turn off the lights, and stay away from the windows," he said. "Several of us are headed that way."

We ran around the house, locking doors and turning out the lights. Then we sat in my dark living room and tried to stay calm. The sound of a chopper outside drew our attention. We peaked out the window and saw a helicopter with a spotlight flying circles around my neighborhood. Police cruisers drove back and forth past my house, spotlights on—searching.

Cody was there, searching on foot. I felt so grateful that my children were asleep and unaware of what was happening right outside our door. The girls and I hardly slept that night as the search continued. The sound of the chopper would lull me into a light sleep on and off, but I'd find myself jolting awake, checking my phone, texting Cody "Are you safe?" and waiting to hear from him. When morning came, my kids woke up and the questions began. "Why did Miss Stacie and Miss Ashley stay over? Where is Dad? What's wrong, Mama?" I wasn't sure where to begin. They still hadn't found the shooter. He could be anywhere, and he was armed. Days later, when he was located, I felt grief and gratitude simultaneously. Grief for all the people who had lost their lives, and gratitude that it was finally over and we were okay.

The shooting in our community was one of over six hundred mass shootings in the United States in 2023. Active shooter drills have been normalized in our schools. As much as we want to protect our children from exposure to death, war, and gun violence, they have become commonplace in our country and around the world. The question isn't *if* we will have to have these conversations with our kids, the question is *when*.

Death Permanence

Between the ages of five and seven, children's understanding of death begins to evolve. They come to realize that death is permanent and irreversible. While younger kids might discuss death with a casual attitude, elementary-school-age children grasp its reality. This explains why we often see an increase in questions and fears about death during this stage of development.

"Mom, why are you crying? What happened to Grandpa?" Fiona, age six, asked. She had just overheard her mom talking on the phone.

"We lost Grandpa last night, honey," her mom responded.

"Lost him? Where did he go?"

"Oh. He's not lost. He died, sweetie."

"So he's gone? How?"

"Well, he was old and his body was getting tired. Last night, his body wasn't able to keep going, and his heart stopped working."

"What will happen to his body?"

"He wanted to be cremated, which means he wanted his body to be turned into ashes by a special machine that gets really, really hot. After he's cremated, your aunt and uncle and I will keep some of his ashes."

"So he's going to turn to ashes? I'll never see him again?"

"Yes. He's not in his body anymore. He's gone. His body will turn to ashes in the machine."

As adults, we often use euphemisms to soften the impact of death because discussing it in straightforward terms can be uncomfortable. This can be confusing for children, especially children between the ages of five and seven. Talking about death directly and clearly, while uncomfortable for us, is important for children. The goal is for them to know that their feelings are welcome and normal, and that we are there to answer their questions and help them navigate their emotions. It can be helpful for us to share our own feelings in a way that shows it's normal to be affected by loss.

Just like adults need time to process death, kids do too. Helping your child understand and cope with death won't happen in one conversation.

Talking with Children About Death

- "Nonna died. Do you know what it means when we say that?"

- "When somebody dies, their body stops working. Feel your heart beating in your chest? Feel your breath coming in and out? When somebody dies, their heart doesn't beat anymore. They don't breathe anymore."

- "When somebody dies, we don't see them anymore. That can feel really sad. You might see the adults around you crying because they feel really sad."

- "It's uncomfortable to feel sad or see others feeling sad. We don't have to make those hard feelings go away though. It's okay to feel them."

Scripts adapted from those in Ali Waltien's Voices of Your Village *podcast, episode 241, "How to Talk to Kids About Death with Child Life Specialist, Ali Waltien."*

They may have a lot of questions, many of which feel repetitive. They may seem like they've grasped the concept and then days later return to the same conversation, needing more clarity. Emotional responses to death can vary widely too. Some kids will want to talk and express their emotions right away, and some kids may seem unaffected or even cavalier about it. It's okay if your child needs time before they're ready to talk and process. Make yourself available to chat with them, but don't pressure them into talking before they're ready.

School Shootings

I was teaching in my classroom the day of the Sandy Hook school shooting on December 14, 2012. I remember seeing the news midday and a panic setting in at my New York City school. Parents started showing up, taking their kids home, holding them closer and longer than usual. There wasn't a blueprint for how to be a teacher or parent in a world where your children's lives were in jeopardy every time they went to school. At the time, parents and teachers weren't talking to us about school shootings regularly, because the most recent had been the Columbine High School massacre in 1999, the deadliest K–12 school shooting until the Parkland high school shooting, which wouldn't take place until 2018. Now we live in a world where there have been 413 school shootings since Columbine. There were forty-six school shootings in 2022, more than one per school week throughout the year. Over 378,000 kids have experienced gun violence at school in the last twenty-five years, with hundreds of thousands more traumatized by the news and drills meant to prepare them for the possibility at their school.[1]

The rapid increase in school shootings came with active shooter drills and bomb threat drills in schools. During these drills, kids are meant to be quiet and still, getting as small as possible as they wait out a potential shooter in the building. These drills are not accompanied by emotion processing or spaces for children to share their feelings or learn why gun violence is so rampant in schools. They are treated like a school fire drill, something we do every month just in case a fire breaks out in the building.

I don't share this to scare you, but instead to show the reality of what our kids are experiencing versus what we experienced in childhood. There are some things we can do to support children as they experience these drills and absorb the news.

1. Be their safe space to discuss and process. Start by asking what they already know and how they feel, allowing them to lead the conversation. It's important to listen actively, validate their feelings, and reassure them that it's okay to feel scared or confused. Avoid projecting your own anxieties; instead, focus on providing a sense of security and calm. Let them know that it's your job to keep them safe, and you're there to support them in understanding and processing what's happening in a way that feels manageable for them.

2. Advocate for your child's school to stop active shooter drills and instead focus on proven school safety strategies like threat assessment

programs, access to mental health professionals and social support for students, nonpunitive disciplinary processes, and commonsense gun laws and practices in the community like secure storage to ensure that guns are not easily accessible. Active shooter drills in schools are associated with increases in students' depression (39 percent), stress and anxiety (42 percent), and physiological health problems (23 percent) overall, including in children from as young as five years old up to high schoolers, their parents, and teachers.[2]

Racial Disparities

I was sitting with a white nine-year-old and asked, "What do you think about when you think about Black people?" "Oh! They used to be slaves and now they are free. I learned that." For many kids, this is the extent of their understanding of racism—a story of the past, something that was wrong but is now "fixed." They are taught that Black people were once enslaved and are now free, without a deeper look at how racism persists in everyday life. But the reality is far more complex.

Racism is not just history—it is woven into the present, shaping access to education and opportunities for children of color through systemic barriers like the preschool-to-prison pipeline. According to the US Department of Education, "in the 2013–2014 academic year, researchers estimated 2.6 million public school students received one or more out-of-school suspensions. . . . Although Black students made up only 15% of the student population, they received as many as 39.3% of all out-of-school suspensions. . . . Despite the significantly higher rates of out-of-school suspension for Black students, they are less likely than their . . . peers to carry weapons to school. They are equally or less likely to have access to illegal drugs at school."[3]

The unfair treatment of Black children in schools is not an issue of the past—it is happening now. Helping our children understand this reality allows them to become aware, engaged, and, ultimately, grow into advocates and allies in the fight for equity.

As white women writing this book, we believe it's imperative for white folks to be on the front line in advocating for fairness and equity for all humans. A few years ago, my husband was sharing a story about a work discussion with a female colleague of his in his male-dominated field. She was curious about pay and benefits, no doubt wondering if what she was receiving included the female tax, aka less pay and decreased odds of promotions. "Not only does she need to know what you're making and have access to, but she needs you to fight *for* her. It's not on her to change the systemic issues of patriarchy in the workforce. Be in her corner. Use your male voice," I told him. People with power and control are responsible for advocating for the disenfranchised. It's incumbent upon white folks to be not just allies, but advocates for BIPOC.

In *Raising Antiracist Children*, Britt Hawthorne emphasizes practical steps that can help white children ages five through twelve develop empathy, critical awareness, and a commitment to fairness. Here are three key takeaways:

1. Promotion of Empathy and Self-Awareness: Hawthorne advocates for teaching children empathy by helping them understand their own emotions and biases. She suggests that parents model self-reflection and encourage children to be curious about differences in others' experiences and perspectives. This can help children identify and understand bias in themselves and their surroundings, building a foundation for compassionate allyship.

2. Active Inclusion and Anti-Bias Actions: Encouraging kids to take active steps to include and stand up for others is another central theme. Hawthorne advises involving children in small acts of inclusion, such as making sure everyone is involved in play and encouraging them to speak up when they witness unfair treatment. This approach aims to make inclusion part of daily life, empowering children to act when they see others excluded or treated unfairly.

3. Community Engagement and Conscientious Choices: Hawthorne also encourages families to be mindful of the impact of their

community activities, whether that's choosing to shop at local businesses owned by people of color or participating in community events that support inclusivity. By integrating these practices into everyday family life, parents help children connect their values to real-world actions and understand their role in fostering a fairer world.[4]

These takeaways illustrate Hawthorne's approach to guiding parents in creating environments where children can grow as thoughtful, fair-minded allies. For more insights, see the book's breakdown of exercises, reflection questions, and activities tailored to different age groups, which can be especially helpful in engaging children in meaningful, age-appropriate ways.

Some incredible resources to dive deeper into racial disparities include:

Social Justice Parenting by Traci Baxley
Raising Antiracist Children by Britt Hawthorne
Why Are All the Black Kids Sitting Together in the Cafeteria?
     by Beverly Daniel Tatum
So You Want to Talk About Race by Ijeoma Oluo

Heavy, hard topics will continue to surface for years to come. There will be new movements and challenges bringing different issues to light. You might notice your own triggers and biases become apparent as things you believed to be true from your childhood or through your social lens are called into question. You might feel a pull to defend what you experienced growing up. Before diving into heavy topics with children, pause and notice your internal reactions. Ask yourself these three questions:

1. What is happening to me physiologically? Is my heart racing? Are my shoulders tense? Do I feel panicky?
2. What thoughts are coming up for me?
3. What fears are surfacing about what this means for my child?

Then, lower your shoulders, open your palms, and breathe in through your nose and out through your mouth. As your heart rate and thoughts slow down, ground yourself with this thought: *It isn't a threat to my identity to listen to learn rather than to defend.*

If we want kids to talk to us about heavy topics, we have to be able to regulate our reactions to create a safe space for them to share. This starts with regulating our own emotional reactions. When a child shares something difficult, they are often testing the waters to see how we will respond. If we react with shock or distress, they may feel emotionally unsafe, which can cause them to shut down or avoid discussing difficult matters in the future.

By maintaining calm, showing empathy, and validating their feelings, we can demonstrate that we are a stable presence they can rely on. It's important to listen without interrupting or immediately jumping in with advice or solutions. Instead, create space for them to express their thoughts fully, and let them know that whatever they are feeling is okay. This gives children the confidence to approach us again when they are dealing with tough emotions or complex situations.

Our role is not just to hear their words but to model how to process emotions, navigate discomfort, and engage in respectful, open communication. By regulating our own reactions, we create a consistent, trusting environment where children feel secure enough to be vulnerable. This foundation of trust is key for fostering honest and meaningful conversations about the tough stuff of life.

Chapter 12

Anxiety

A nxiety has been on the rise in children since the early 2000s.[1] I used to describe anxiety as being stuck in fear, but more accurately, and thanks to Jonathan Haidt's book *The Anxious Generation*, I can clarify that fear is being scared of something in the present, while anxiety is being scared of something in the future.[2] You might be afraid of getting hit by a car while in a busy parking lot. You might have anxiety about trying out for the dance team next week. Anxiety is when we are saying, "I'm afraid of what could happen." Anxiety is an emotion, but the physiological experience of it can spiral into feeling stuck in that state, with symptoms such as a racing heart, feeling clammy or sweaty, an inability to slow down or pause, dizziness, restlessness, upset stomach or bowels, headaches, teeth grinding, shaking, and pins and needles. It shows up in our bodies to warn us about future dangers, but we are not able to distinguish a perceived danger from actual danger when we are anxious.

Anxiety is great at getting you to try to avoid hard experiences. It remembers that time when you saw your friend be made fun of at lunch for what was in her lunch box and will be damned if you experience that same embarrassment. It partners up with other emotions like anger to fight for you to escape physical or emotional peril. They show up together to yell at your mom not to pack that gross lunch, saying it's disgusting and I hate it. Anxiety can get fiery and fierce but can also be found silent, disconnected, or trembling in fear. What if we could empower children with the tools to identify anxiety when it pops up and know how to be with it without being controlled by it?

• • •

> Parents have a profound impact on the health of our children and the health of society. Yet parents and caregivers today face tremendous pressures, from familiar stressors such as worrying about their kids' health and safety and financial concerns, to new challenges like navigating technology and social media, a youth mental health crisis, an epidemic of loneliness that has hit young people the hardest.
>
> —US SURGEON GENERAL DR. VIVEK MURTHY[3]

There is a deep feeling for parents of needing to do this parenting thing right—to say the right thing, to make the right choice for our children—and we are exposed to a never-ending deluge of information about it. From social media posts telling us exactly how we *should* respond to our child to what we definitely *should not* say to our child, it feels like we are playing a game of "You Can't Win."

On the way home from school the other day, my friend's child said to her, "Mom, I want to talk about differences in people. Did you know that Orah in my classroom has brown skin?" Immediately, my friend's stomach dropped. *This is my shot or she's going to be racist,* ran through my friend's mind, the pressure mounting for her to say the right thing in the moment and an immediate desire to comb the internet for the way she was supposed to respond. We've moved people so far from their intuition, so far from their knowing that you aren't going to screw up your kid by saying "good job" or telling them you're proud of them, that, instead, we have parents riddled with anxiety about how to be in relationship with their child the right way. In the way that Jonathon Haidt explains how teens are anxious due in large part to social media, parents today can find themselves in much the same situation. We've become so used to looking outside of ourselves for answers, and we're terrified that we will talk too much or not enough or that we won't do the exact right thing all of the time and it will screw up our relationship with our child. Of course parents are living with such high levels of anxiety; it's exhausting to feel like there is one right way to do everything and you are trying to figure it out without a manual.

With parental anxiety at a high, it's imperative that we address the parental toolbox in order to support parents, caregivers, and teachers with the tools to respond to children's anxiety with intention. Just as we address the FACTS with kids, we need to start there with ourselves as adults.

Food
When was the last time you ate food that nourished your body? Is your blood sugar low, causing the physiological experience of anxiety?

Activity
Has it been more than two hours since you moved your body in a way that fills your cup? Not sure what type of movement is regulating for you? Head to www.seedquiz.com to learn more about how your unique nervous system works.

Connection
Is it time to send a friend or partner a message to share something that's coming up for you today? You are not alone in this journey, and no one is meant to go it alone.

Tune-out
Are you anxious, or is your child asking seven thousand questions while hanging on to your body? Are you feeling overstimulated? If so, can you step away for one, three, or five minutes? Is it possible to pop in earplugs or headphones, close your eyes, be in a room (the bathroom counts!) solo, turn off the lights, and take deep breaths? I know it sounds so simple, but it is *so* impactful. It's like plugging your phone in to charge when the battery is dying.

Sleep
One of the greatest factors in mental health is sleep.[4] When we are able to practice good sleep hygiene, like going screen free before bedtime, getting into bed at a consistent time, and sleeping seven to

nine hours a night, our nervous system can have more capacity for navigating all that comes with being awake during the day.

It's key to pay attention to what makes the anxious feelings stronger versus what lessens them. If you call Kaitlin to share with her and leave the call feeling more anxious than when you started, Kaitlin is not your pal to call when things start to spiral. If you call Francesca and notice that you feel calmer after talking to her, Francesca is your anxiety outreach pal. The same goes for the food we consume (including alcohol and substances), different types of activity and movement, what precedes sleep, and different types of stimuli or environments.

Here are five ways to take care of yourself when anxiety pops up in the moment after addressing the FACTS.

1. Identify one thing you see, one thing you smell, one thing you hear, one thing your body is touching.
2. Relax your jaw. Drop your shoulders. Breathe in to fill your belly and release a deep exhale to let it go.
3. Remind yourself, "I have survived every scary thing before this one."
4. Notice what message is circulating inside of you. What does this anxious part of you need you to know? *My daughter is a stealing and lying thief. This is going to escalate to shoplifting or stealing from her friends. How do I stop this problem now before it gets worse?* In the moment you might even feel like it's irrational and simultaneously feel like it isn't.
5. Write down your thoughts or reach out to someone whom you feel safe with. Start by letting them know, "I'm feeling anxious about this and need to vent about it." You might add, "I'm not ready to solve it, yet," because often what we need is to have a friend listen instead of going into problem-solving mode.

Anxiety is not something you need to escape. It's something you can notice and experience without letting it consume you when you have the tools for physiological regulation. In the same way that you can have a good cry about something when you're sad and still feel sad without continuing to cry after that release. When anxiety is running your life, it is exhausting and demanding. My favorite book for adults to better understand anxiety is Ellen Vora's *The Anatomy of Anxiety*.

As you are building your toolbox for being with and moving through anxiety, your children will be watching you model how to navigate it. They will get to learn more skills through observation than we often realize. They're constantly scanning their environment and observing us to learn what to do, what's expected, and how to handle things. When we talk to kids about our experience and tools, it can help them build context and understanding for what they're seeing. It's key that we are mindful of not making them responsible for our regulation. Avoid saying things like:

"I need you to be quiet, I can't handle your noise right now. You're giving me a headache."
"It stresses me out when you're constantly fighting with your brother. I can't make your dinner or help you with your homework if you won't stop it."
"Your attitude is going to ruin this family outing. I'm about to lose it."

Instead, we can communicate about our experience while owning our responsibility for regulation. Here are some ways to put it that may be helpful:

"Those sounds are too loud for this part of the house. You can go outside or downstairs if you want to play loudly."
"I'm in the middle of getting dinner on the table, so I can't help you right now. The two of you need to play separately until I'm done cooking and then we can chat about what's going on."
"I'm going to step away for a few minutes to take some deep breaths. I can feel my body getting worked up. I'll be back in a moment to help you with whatever is making you frustrated right now."

Responding to Anxiety in Children

We opened this chapter with information about adult anxiety because research has demonstrated the importance of the parental response to their children's anxiety. A study in 2019, led by Dr. Eli Lebowitz at the Yale Child Study Center, showed that parents play a significant role in managing childhood anxiety, and their behavior can either help alleviate or worsen it.[5] The study focused on an intervention called Supportive Parenting for Anxious Childhood Emotions (SPACE), which centers on changing the parents' behavior rather than directly treating the child.

Anxious parents who accommodated their child's anxiety by adjusting the environment or daily routines to minimize anxiety-provoking situations were inadvertently reinforcing the anxiety. For example, parents might allow their child to avoid certain activities, provide excessive reassurance, or even help them avoid things that trigger their anxiety (like not going to school or not attending social events). While these accommodations are well-intentioned, the study found that they can actually maintain the child's anxiety over time.

Damien's dad, Jeremy, feels overwhelmed by his son's emotions. Damien is eleven years old, and for the past two years he's been in charge of switching over the laundry in the basement from the washer to the dryer and then bringing the dry clothes upstairs for his parents. But recently, Damien has been refusing to go downstairs alone. He says that he's scared, and while Jeremy doesn't fully understand what's changed, he doesn't want to deal with it. When Damien gets worked up, it's so much effort to get him calm again. Jeremy feels tired just thinking about it.

I asked Jeremy to walk me through what it looks like when he tries to get Damien to take care of the laundry.

"Damien, you've been doing the laundry for two years. I don't get why all of a sudden you're saying you can't. Come on, buddy, it's just laundry. You know where everything is."

Damien starts to fidget and looks at the ground. "I just . . . I don't want to. I don't want to go down there."

Jeremy sighs and rubs his temples, already feeling his frustration rise.

"Why? You've been doing this forever, and now suddenly you're scared? Seems like you just don't want to do it."

"I just . . . I don't like it down there anymore. I can't go down there."

Jeremy's irritation grows, but there's also a feeling of helplessness bubbling up. He doesn't know how to handle Damien's emotions right now—he just wants the laundry done without turning it into a big deal. "Damien, you've done this a hundred times. Why now? This is ridiculous."

Damien starts to cry. "No, Dad, I swear! It's . . . it's different now. I get this feeling, like my chest gets tight, and I just . . . I can't breathe right."

"Fine, if you can't do it, I'll find something else for you to help with. Go tidy up your room for now."

Later, Jeremy reflects on Damien's personality. "He's hard on himself," he admits. "He worries about everything—grades, sports, his friends. If he thinks he did something wrong at school, he'll ruminate on it for days. If he makes a mistake in a soccer game, he tells me he should just quit because he's so bad. And heaven forbid he gets in a fight with a friend. The last time he got in an argument with his best friend, he came home and told me he hated his friend and then tried to get out of going back to school for the rest of the week. It's like everything is all or nothing with him. The second something challenging happens, he's spiraling into worst-case scenarios. It can feel like a lot sometimes. He'll get worked up over something, and it just snowballs. Honestly, I don't always know what to do when he gets like that, so I figure it's better to just change things before it turns into a whole situation."

Perfectionism and anxiety are closely intertwined, as we see in Damien. When kids set unrealistically high standards for themselves, even the slightest deviation from those expectations can trigger feelings of inadequacy and fear. Anything that feels outside of a child's perceived control can be an anxiety trigger. They can also fear disappointing others, especially if they are neuroceptive-sensitive humans who read the energy of the room and are nervous to influence it negatively. One of my favorite phrases for kids who struggle with perfectionism is to let them know, "Nothing you do will ever make me love you more or less. You aren't lovable because of what you do or don't do. You're lovable because you're you." Take a closer look at how Damien copes when he's dealing with something stressful. He messes up at soccer and wants to quit the team. He gets in a fight with a friend and doesn't want to return to school to see that friend again. His go-to response to stress is to avoid, to flee. So it makes sense that when he started to feel anxiety in the basement, he immediately jumped to avoidance.

While Damien hadn't been allowed to quit the team, or stop going to school, his dad did accommodate his basement fear. It makes so much sense too. As a parent of an anxious child, I really feel for Jeremy—it can be mentally exhausting. Keeping yourself calm and steady so you can be the confident anchor your child needs isn't always easy. Anxiety doesn't just go away. It's not something that you can talk your child out of. When a child is in the thick of that physiological experience, they need a steady, calm adult to teach them how to calm their body. The fear may not go away, but they can calm their nervous system so that the fear is easier to handle.

As a child, I experienced intense separation anxiety. While my peers were happily having slumber parties, I struggled with sleep even at home—often creeping into my parents' room at night and sleeping on their floor. I remember one particular instance when I was probably eight or nine years old. My parents were going on a weekend trip together and my aunt was going to take care of me. When my parents told me about their plans, I immediately felt a knot form in my stomach. As the days led up to their departure, I couldn't stop crying, the fear growing larger each day. I didn't know why I was so upset. I loved my aunt, I always had fun with my cousins, and my parents assured me everything would be fine. But no matter what they said, I couldn't shake the dread.

One evening, as I sobbed into my pillow, my mom sat on the edge of my bed, trying to comfort me.

"Sweetheart," she began softly, "I know this is hard for you. But your aunt loves you so much, and you're going to have such a great time with your cousins. You'll be safe, I promise."

I wanted so badly for her words to calm me, but they didn't. I nodded, trying to believe her, but the tightness in my chest wouldn't loosen.

"But what if I miss you?" I whispered.

"You probably will," she replied gently. "And that's okay. It's normal to miss people we love. But your dad and I will only be gone for a little while, and before you know it, we'll be right back home with you."

"Promise?" I asked, needing reassurance and hoping that somehow hearing her say it again would make the anxiety disappear.

"Promise," she said, kissing my forehead.

My dad came in then, sitting beside my mom. He wrapped his arm around her shoulders and smiled at me.

"Kiddo, I know this is tough, but you're a lot stronger than you think. You're going to have so much fun, you'll hardly notice we're gone. And guess what? We'll call you every day to check in. How does that sound?"

I forced a smile, but inside, my heart was still racing. The reassurance in their words was what I longed to hold on to, but something deeper was gripping me. I knew my aunt would keep me safe. I knew I'd have fun. I knew my parents were coming back. But I didn't know how to stop the swirling thoughts in my mind. I didn't know how to quiet the pounding in my chest or calm the rolling in my stomach. Every time I thought about them leaving, it felt like the world was tilting under my feet.

I look back on that experience now as a parent of an anxious child myself and I'm so grateful for how patient and kind my parents were. They didn't accommodate my anxiety. They pushed me to move through it. The more repetitions our brains receive of experiencing something safely, the easier it is to tell our brain that we are safe, which can help calm future anxiety. It turns the unknown into a known. They did their best to help me. I needed more though, and many children do. Some anxious kids need additional support for calming the intense and scary nervous system response they're experiencing.

Anxiety can trigger the fight-or-flight response in a child. Their brain has perceived a threat (whether it's real or not doesn't matter to the nervous system) and activates this powerful physical reaction called fight or flight. What does that mean for your kid? When your child is anxious, their brain is responding as if *a tiger is chasing them down*. Sure, it's just the basement, it's no big deal to us.

But to your child's brain and body, it's an emergency. During a flight-or-fight reaction, heart rate increases and the body is flooded with stress hormones. It's a primal survival response and as the body works to make sure it stays safe, it diverts energy away from anything nonessential and puts it all into muscle activation and heightening of the senses.

If your child is experiencing fight or flight, here are some strategies that can be helpful.

In a Calm Moment, Talk to Them About What's Happening in Their Body

"Sometimes, our bodies get confused. They think we are in real danger when we aren't. Like when you're nervous because you got in an argument with your friend, and suddenly your heart is racing, and your hands are shaking. This happens because our bodies have a special alarm system that helps keep us safe. When we feel scared or stressed, our brain sends signals to our body telling it to get ready to fight or run away, just like it would if there was a real danger, like a loud noise or a big dog.

"But sometimes, that alarm goes off even when we are just feeling upset or worried. It's like when a smoke alarm goes off when there's no fire! When your heart races or your hands shake, it's your body's way of saying, 'I'm ready to handle something!' But we can remind our bodies that we're okay and that there's no real danger right now."

Help Them Build a Calming Toolbox

Every child is different and there is no single strategy that will work for everyone. Part of helping your child learn to calm their body is to offer several strategies and let them experiment with what helps.

Breathing Techniques: "When you feel that panic, it can help to take a few deep breaths. Breathe in slowly through your nose, hold it for a moment, and then breathe out gently through your mouth. This can help calm your body and reassure it that you're safe, even if your mind is feeling a little worried. While you're breathing, you can remind yourself, 'I'm safe.'"

Grounding Techniques: "Let's play a game to help bring your focus back to the present. It's called the 5–4–3–2–1 game. I want you to look around and name five things you can see. Now, can you feel four things around you, like the chair you're sitting on or your favorite blanket? Next, listen closely for three things you can hear—maybe a bird outside or the hum of the fridge. Then, let's find two things you can smell. And finally, think of one thing you can taste, like your favorite snack. This will help remind your brain that you're safe."

Movement: "Sometimes, moving our bodies can help shake off those anxious feelings. You could go outside for a short walk, jump on the trampoline, or even dance to your favorite song. Let's move together!"

Visualizing a Safe Place: "Close your eyes for a moment and think about a place where you feel really safe and happy. It could be the beach, a cozy room, or anywhere you love. Picture what you see, hear, and feel there."

Perfectionism may convince your child that they need to "get rid" of their anxiety, and when they can't do that, they may feel discouraged or want to give up. Remind your child that the goal isn't for the anxiety to never happen again, but for them to have the tools to remind their body that they are safe.

Process with Them

When children start to regulate their sensory systems, then we can dive into emotion processing with them. Often kids' emotions live on the surface—"I don't want to go to dance"—but granularity is helpful for processing what is really driving those surface feelings and subsequent behaviors. Help them get specific with nonjudgmental curiosity.

"Okay. Are you feeling nervous to go to dance or do you not feel like doing anything, even if it wasn't dance—like going to Target?"

"I want to go to Target. I don't want to go to dance."

"Did something happen at dance class? I'm curious why you don't want to go."

"No, I just don't want to."

"I recently joined a group called the PTA and it's a group of parents who help the teachers with things at school. When I first went to a PTA meeting I was nervous, but also excited to meet new people and help. When it was time for the second meeting, I didn't want to go. The first time I went, people were in groups and talking to one another, but I didn't know anyone, so I was by myself. I wished I could crawl inside of a space and hide. I felt embarrassed to be myself, like I didn't have any friends.

[*Pause.*]

"When you first started dance you seemed excited and now you don't want to go. Sometimes after we do something where we have a hard feeling, like when I felt embarrassed, a part of us pops up inside that tries to keep us from feeling that hard thing again. It's a protector part that says, 'Don't do that or you'll have a hard feeling!' I'm wondering what the part of you that doesn't want you to go to dance is worried might happen if you go."

"Everyone knows what to do and I don't know what to do. Miss Johanna moves too fast and I can't follow her like everyone else does."

"What might happen if you aren't doing what other kids are doing?"

"They'll make fun of me and won't want to be my friend because I'm not a good dancer."

"Yeah, okay. You're nervous that if you aren't doing the right moves at the right time, then your friends in dance will notice and not want to hang out with you?"

"Yeah."

"This part of you is so good at trying to keep you safe from feeling left out or embarrassed, huh? That makes sense. Those are really hard things to feel. Hm, I wonder what would happen if you were left out and they didn't want to be your friend."

"I'd be sad and lonely."

"Yeah, that makes sense. What would happen if you felt sad and lonely?"

"I don't know."

"Have you felt sad or lonely before?"

"Yeah, it sucked."

"Yeah, it makes sense to want to avoid feeling sad and lonely. I also have parts of me that try to avoid those feelings. Would it feel helpful for this part of you to make a plan for what to do if you feel sad or lonely?"

"Yeah."

"Okay, let's make one together."

Our anxious parts are so good at trying to protect us. They observe things that have hurt us or others in the past and avoid them like the plague. When we can slow down and spend some time getting to know what they are trying to protect us from, we can show up for those parts instead of having them drive our decisions. We get to let those parts of us know that it's okay for us to have hard experiences and feelings; we can handle them. Parts work is a component of Internal Family Systems (IFS) developed by Dr. Richard Schwartz, author of *No Bad Parts*.[6] IFS is a psychotherapy approach that views the mind as a collection of sub-personalities, or "parts," that each have their own unique qualities and perspectives.

If your child is still struggling with anxiety even after implementing these strategies, it may be helpful to seek additional support. Consider talking to a pediatrician or a mental health professional who specializes in working with children. They can provide guidance tailored to your child's needs.

Chapter 13

ADHD, Dyslexia, and Learning Differences

How to Navigate the Emotions and Identity of Common Diagnoses

At Bodhi's end-of-season soccer party, we were playing a game in which each kid took a piece of paper from a bowl, read the word written on it, and acted out the word for their team to guess it. Bodhi hesitated when it was his turn, reluctant to participate. His mother, knowing he'd likely enjoy it once he got started, gave Bodhi a gentle nudge of encouragement. She watched as he laughed along with his friends, confident that when his moment came, he'd have fun too.

But when his turn arrived, Bodhi wanted to pass. His friends protested, insisting that everyone had to take part. As the pressure mounted, the next two minutes stretched endlessly for his mother—just like those car rides when he was a baby, screaming and gagging before they even left the driveway.

Bodhi struggled to read the word on the slip of paper, sounding it out with difficulty. His friends urged him on. "You have to do something!" one called out. "Just read the word and act it out! The timer's running!"

That was when it hit them both: he couldn't read the word, and everyone was watching him try.

Desperately, he made a guess and acted something out. When his friends failed to recognize what he was miming, he crumpled up the paper and mixed it back into the bowl, as if hiding it away could erase the moment. Relief flooded his face as his turn ended and the group's attention shifted to the next child.

Bodhi's mother had known he was behind his peers in reading, but she hadn't realized how much—or how deeply it was affecting him socially.

Not long after, Bodhi was diagnosed with dyslexia. The news felt like a breath of fresh air, finally explaining so many of the struggles they had witnessed academically and socially. But the relief was short-lived, lasting only about a day before the weight of new worries set in.

Should they tell him? How and when? Would he be teased? What would this mean for school, for college, for his future? What else might come with this diagnosis? And most important—what should they do next?

Being the parent of a child with disabilities, learning differences, and diagnoses can come with a slew of emotions and questions. Some parents report relief when they receive a diagnosis for their child, because so many things finally make sense and there will be folks to turn to for support and guidance. Some parents share fear and worry about what it will mean for their child. All feelings are welcome here. What you grew up exposed to has created implicit biases that will surface as you receive this informa- tion. Today, there's a new conversation happening about sensory-friendly classrooms and supporting all learners, yet there is still a long way to go for inclusive education. Our goal in this chapter is not to dive into specific diagnoses, but instead to support you with ways to connect with your child and let them know they are worthy, valued, and loved for exactly who they are, not what they can or cannot do.

The Adult

When Bodhi's mom finally received a diagnosis, she felt a wave of relief— there was now an explanation for why things at school had been hard for Bodhi, showing up in academia but bleeding into his social interactions as well. But after that relief, a flood of emotions followed: overwhelm, sadness, fear, and even guilt. As parents, we often wish for control over our children's experiences, and a diagnosis can feel like a loss of that control, triggering anxiety and uncertainty.

"What does this mean for their future?" It's natural to worry about the long-term impact. Will my child thrive in school? Will they find meaningful friendships? Know this: A diagnosis doesn't define your child. While there is no denying that diagnoses still carry stigmas in our culture, I encourage you to reframe what your child's diagnosis means to your family: it gives you a clearer understanding of their needs, and allows you to identify what supports will help them thrive.

"How am I supposed to handle this?" The weight of managing therapies, accommodations, and plans can feel overwhelming. It's okay to feel unsure, but you don't have to tackle everything at once. Take it one step at a time. Lean on professionals, reach out to support networks, and remember that you're not alone in this journey.

"Will others see my child differently now?" It's difficult to think that teachers, friends, or family might treat your child differently. This is where you can step in to advocate, ensuring that others understand the diagnosis as a tool for support, not a label of limitation. Your child's diagnosis doesn't change who they are; it offers insight into how they experience the world and how you can support them. Your most important role is to be their safe space, showing them they are valued, understood, and loved exactly as they are.

The Child

Diego is eight years old and in the third grade. Last year, in second grade, he was diagnosed with dyslexia and ADHD. His younger brother, Javier, is in kindergarten. Diego struggles every day at school with reading and writing. He isn't a fluent reader yet, and as his peers continue to grow in their literacy skills, he notices more and more that he's different.

This year, a new dynamic has emerged. Part of their family routine is for Diego to read aloud at bedtime to everyone. Diego really looks forward to this time when he gets to practice reading without the pressure of teachers or peers. He knows his mom can help him if he gets stuck too. The problem is that now when Javier sits next to Diego, he's noticing sight words that he knows and calling them out before Diego gets to them. At first Diego ignored it, but on the third night it happened, he lost it.

"Why am I so stupid?" he said. Tears filled his eyes. "How does Javier read better than me? He's only in kindergarten!"

Kids will internalize our society's ideas about what is good and normal, and what doesn't fit into that definition. Even if we try our hardest to reject ableism, in a culture that worships intelligence, ability, speed, and productivity, living with a learning difference can feel like you're outside of what is good and normal.

How your child feels about their diagnosis depends on their age and understanding, but most impactful of all is the way you present the diagnosis to them. If you approach it with confidence and acceptance, they will reflect that. If you approach it with shame, they will feel it too. Your unwavering confidence in them helps them feel safe as they navigate this new information. Some children may feel relieved to have an explanation for their struggles, while others might feel confused or worried about being different. Here are common feelings they may experience and ways to help them navigate:

Confusion: Your child may ask, "What does this mean?" It's important to explain things in an age-appropriate way. You might say, "This just means your brain works in a different way, and there are things we can do to make learning easier."

Frustration: Your child might wonder, *Why is everything harder for me?* Acknowledge their feelings and remind them that everyone has challenges, and that this diagnosis helps you and their teachers better support them.

Worry: They may fear being different from their peers. Reassure them that everyone is unique and that needing support is normal. You might say, "This doesn't make you less—it just means we understand how to help you better."

Relief: Some kids feel a sense of validation, knowing there's a reason for their struggles. Emphasize that their difficulties aren't their fault and that now you have tools to help.

Embarrassment: Especially as children get older, they may feel ashamed or worry about how others will see them. Create a safe space for them to talk about these feelings, reminding them that their diagnosis doesn't change who they are.

Hope: Some children may feel hopeful that things will get better now that they understand what's going on. Use this as a chance to remind them that you're on their team, ready to support them.

Our culture often labels learning differences negatively, but it's essential to shift the conversation from *what's wrong* to *what works* for each child's unique brain and body. Encourage your child to describe their needs in specific, constructive terms. For instance, instead of saying, "I'm not a good listener," they could express, "I learn best when I can listen and see at the same time. I need pictures, charts, and other visuals." Instead of saying, "I can't sit still," they might say, "I need to take movement breaks to stay focused." This shift can help your child view their diagnosis in an affirming and empowering way, rather than as something that places them outside the norm.

Fostering an affirmative family culture around learning differences is key as your child navigates peer relationships. When children feel confident discussing their learning needs, they can help others understand that having different needs is simply part of being human. This understanding can break down barriers and create a more inclusive environment. You can provide your child with specific language for navigating questions or interactions with their peers, such as, "Everyone's brain works differently, and we're just figuring out what my brain needs." When children recognize that their unique ways of learning are valid, they are more likely to self-advocate within their peer group. Research shows that the more children are exposed to difference and disability, the more positive and affirmative their attitude about it will be.[1] If your child has a difference or a disability and they are self-affirming and have the language to describe and normalize their needs to their peers, we can move the needle toward more inclusive environments for all children.

Your child's relationship with their diagnosis and how it impacts their sense of self will likely not be linear. When Diego was first diagnosed, he expressed relief and even excitement about accessing support. When he learned he would have an aid to help him every day with reading, he felt a weight lift off his shoulders. He became excited to go to school again. Initially, his diagnosis seemed to bolster his self-image. That shifted when Javier started to pick up reading. Suddenly, the differences in their learning needs became glaringly apparent to Diego. He's the big brother, shouldn't he know more? What does it mean if Javier becomes a better reader than he is? What does that say about him?

Diego didn't want to finish reading that night. He went to his room to take some space. After a little while, his mom went in to check on him. "Buddy, are you ready to talk?" she asked.

He looked up, with tears still in his eyes, and nodded. "I just feel so dumb. I'm never going to be smart like my friends."

"It's totally okay to feel frustrated and even sad about the ways reading can be extra challenging. What you're feeling is completely normal, and I'm so proud of you for sharing it with me. You aren't dumb, and I know that it's hard to feel like you're different from your peers or like you're somehow falling behind Javier."

"Yeah, I can't believe he already knows those sight words! How is it so easy for him? It's not fair."

"It doesn't feel fair, I know. Dyslexia means your brain works in a really unique way, which is why learning to read can take more time. It's like having a brain that's built for solving big puzzles in a new way—it might be different from how your friends' brains work, but that doesn't make it any less powerful or special. Some things that might feel harder for you now could actually help make you amazing at other things as you grow up."

"It doesn't feel very amazing right now."

"I know. I'm here with you. I want you to remember that everybody has something that makes them different and sometimes makes things harder. Javier has things he's working on too, even if it looks different than reading. We all have strengths and challenges—it's not just you."

It's natural to want to make things easier for our kids, but we don't need to talk them out of their feelings or minimize the challenges that come with a diagnosis. Frustration and discouragement are normal, especially as they face new obstacles. Building resilience involves allowing them to feel the hard stuff and supporting them through it.

Masking, Suppression, and Restraint Collapse

For children with learning differences, school can be a real challenge. To navigate the demands of the classroom, they often engage in "masking," a form of coping in which they suppress or hide behaviors, emotions, and natural responses in order to fit in or avoid drawing attention. Masking requires enormous energy, as it forces children to focus not only on learning but also on managing how they appear to others. While it helps them get through the day at school, masking often has consequences within and beyond the classroom.

What does masking look like? Well, unless you're looking for it, it doesn't look like anything. It looks like "normal" behavior. At first glance you may think the child with ADHD who needs constant movement is "doing a great job" sitting still. Looking more closely, you may see them sitting on their hands, or white-knuckling their desk to keep still. On the surface it looks like good behavior, but inside their body they are using huge amounts of energy and driving up stress levels. For a child who struggles with social cues, you might notice them echoing what they hear from their peers. This helps them blend in, but it requires intense focus to monitor and replicate what they see and hear from others. There are many ways that masking can manifest, but the important thing to understand about it is that it is hard to pick up on unless you are intentionally looking for it. Understanding masking and identifying if it's happening with your child is important because masking impacts learning and regulation in very real and significant ways.

It's also helpful to understand the difference between masking as a social skill and high masking, which is more of a survival skill. Neurotypical children often learn to mask to some degree as a social skill—knowing how to navigate different settings and relationships by moderating their responses or adjusting their behaviors appropriately. I think about a recent trip to the grocery store. It had been a hard day, I was sleep deprived, and I could feel that I was right on the edge of tears. The checkout clerk looked at me and said, "Hi, how are you tonight?" and that was all it took to release the floodgates I'd been holding back. I broke down into full sobs.

The grocery store isn't an appropriate place for me to break down. The checkout clerk, who is a stranger to me, isn't responsible for fielding my emotions. However, I was so depleted that day that I couldn't summon the energy required to mask—and nothing harmful happened to me as a result of dropping the mask. For neurodiverse children, however, masking often becomes a survival skill; they feel compelled to hide parts of themselves not only to blend in or adhere to social norms but to avoid judgment, rejection, or punishment. This kind of masking requires sustained focus, draining their energy reserves and often compromising their ability to engage with learning, process emotions, and regulate effectively. While neurotypical masking is adaptive and context-based, masking for neurodiverse children is a high-stakes attempt to make it through environments that feel unsafe, which can impede their overall well-being.

Sascha is a bright, active fifth grader with ADHD who seems like she has it all together at school. She's engaged, attentive, and rarely causes disruptions. Her teachers regularly report to her parents that she is a joy to have in class. In fact, Sascha has become a master at putting on her "calm and focused" face for the entire school day. But all that energy it takes to keep her ADHD symptoms under wraps is chipping away at her ability to focus on learning. She often ends up leaving class with gaps in her understanding and a feeling of dread at the thought of trying to do her homework later.

And when she gets home? As soon as she walks through the door, Sascha is a different kid: emotional, argumentative, and overwhelmed. The smallest things can set her off, and homework is a battle. Her family sees the side of Sascha that her teachers don't—and they just don't get it.

Why do her teachers get the best of her, and they get her messiest, hardest behaviors? It doesn't seem fair.

This can be one of the most challenging aspects of masking for families: parents often feel like they're getting the "worst" of their child, while everyone else experiences their "best" self. You might wonder why your child seems to save their big emotions, meltdowns, or stress for home. The truth is, kids mask when they don't feel safe, holding back parts of themselves to fit into environments where they worry about judgment or rejection. At home, they trust that they can let their guard down and express their true feelings. Understanding that your child's difficult behaviors stem from masking doesn't mean that all behaviors are fair game. This doesn't mean that boundaries and expectations go out the window, but rather that you can understand *why* they are so drained, and can access the empathy and compassion necessary to support them.

Learning Differences and the Central Nervous System

While the cause of learning differences is still not fully understood, there is research that indicates that differences in the central nervous system are implicated in the pathogenesis of learning challenges.[2] For example, studies have demonstrated that children with ADHD process auditory, tactile, and multisensory input differently than neurotypical children.[3] Unsurprisingly, there were also significant differences in emotional/social responses and behavior outcomes. Nervous system regulation and organization directly influence behavior. A diagnosis of a learning disability lets us know that a child's nervous system may work differently and that we need to be especially intentional about offering opportunities for regulation throughout that child's day.

In school, this may look like advocating for your child to have an IEP or 504 plan, which are specialized education plans that can help support your child at school. At home, it might look like creating an environment where opportunities for sensory regulation are built in: a cozy tent where they get to decompress from stimulation, or an office chair available for spinning, or a rope ladder for climbing. The more a child has ongoing access to regulation tools, the more they can proactively increase their bandwidth for learning. Scan the following QR code to access our free regulation quiz to identify the best way to support your child's regulation and learning.

Chapter 14

Respecting Diversity

Kai is at meet-the-teacher night at his school. He's entering first grade, but this is his first year at this particular school, so all his classmates are new to him. When he enters the classroom, his new teacher shows him where he can write his name on the sign-in sheet. Kai has a congenital limb difference and his new classmates notice immediately. He hears one of the kids ask his mom, "Hey, what's wrong with his hand?" and the mom shushes and chastises the boy.

For the rest of the time in the classroom, the other kids stare at Kai's hand, but they don't come over to talk. His mom encourages him to join the group of other kids, but Kai is nervous and discouraged that they only seem to see his hand, not his whole self. When they go out to the car, he cries. He doesn't want to go to school anymore.

Children are naturally skilled at noticing differences because their brains are wired to categorize. This ability to observe and categorize is not inherently problematic. In fact, recognizing differences is an essential first step toward respecting and embracing diversity. However, the issue arises when the dominant cultural narrative frames differences in an "us versus them" mindset. This mindset positions the dominant group (e.g., white, heteronormative, cisgender) as the norm and labels anything outside of that as "other."

This is exactly what we saw happen in Kai's story. It's not that Kai's peers are unkind or intentionally exclusive; rather, they needed help recognizing that everyone has unique qualities, not just Kai. The parent who shushed and chastised their child, though well-meaning, unintentionally reinforced the idea that being different is bad. We can't shame children for noticing differences and then expect them to embrace those differences.

I wonder how Kai's experience would have been different if a grownup had stepped in and said something like, "I heard you noticing Kai's hand. Bodies come in all shapes and sizes, including limb differences. There is so much more to Kai than what his hand looks like. I know that Kai loves soccer and playing monster trucks. What do you like to do for fun?" What would it have felt like for Kai to be seen as fully human? What would it have felt like for his peers to understand that Kai's limb difference was just one part of him, and have the scaffolding they needed to build a connection point with him?

Most parents work hard to teach their kids values like acceptance and inclusion, but the truth is, we're up against a world that often sends a very different message. Take the media, for example. TV shows, movies, and ads tend to feature able-bodied people as the standard for beauty, success, and capability. When players with disabilities do appear, they're often side characters, defined by their disability rather than portrayed as full, complex people. It's subtle, but this kind of representation reinforces the idea that being able-bodied is "normal," and anyone who isn't is on the outside looking in.

Schools can also unintentionally send the wrong message. Special education programs, while absolutely necessary, sometimes isolate kids with disabilities in ways that limit their interaction with other students. This separation can make it seem like children with disabilities are different in a way that keeps them from fully belonging, even though we know that inclusive classrooms benefit all students by exposing them to diversity.

Then there's the design of everyday spaces, like playgrounds. Many playgrounds are built with able-bodied kids in mind, which means children with mobility challenges are often left out. The very layout of these spaces sends a message: if you don't fit into the "norm," the world isn't always made for you.

Limb differences and physical disabilities are just one example. There are so many ways that our culture excludes and dehumanizes folks who are not part of the dominant group because of race, gender, sexuality, weight, religion, learning differences, neurodiversity, and so much more.

The purpose of this chapter isn't to review all of these categories like a checklist. The goal is to help your child build a foundation of inclusion that sees differences of any kind and welcomes them—and that starts with looking at ourselves.

I was sitting at a café with my two children eating lunch. My son was almost four at the time. He looked over at the table next to us and noticed a man who was overweight. "Mama! Why is that guy so huge?!" he practically shouted. I knew the man had heard him—there was no way he hadn't. I wanted to disappear into the floor. I wanted to chastise my son and tell him to never say something like that again. I felt flustered and embarrassed. "Time to go!" I told the kids. We wrapped up our sandwiches, and I turned to the man at the table. "I'm so sorry," I said as I hurried the kids toward the door.

We got out to the car and I had a second to breathe. "Mama, why did you say sorry to the big guy?" my son asked me.

"Buddy, I want to talk to you about bodies for a minute."

"Okay, Mama."

"Bodies come in all shapes and sizes. Some bodies store a lot of energy; those bodies are bigger. Some bodies store less energy; those bodies are smaller. It's okay if you have questions about size, I'm happy to answer them. I also want you to know that talking about someone's body can make them feel uncomfortable."

"How come?" he asked me.

"Well, there are some people who believe that bigger bodies can't be healthy or good. They believe that being smaller is always better. That's not true, but a lot of people believe it. So pointing out that someone is big can make them feel bad, even though there is nothing wrong with being bigger."

It was one of many conversations we would have going forward about bodies, food, energy, and health. The lunch encounter hadn't been an ideal learning situation—it was embarrassing and awkward for me—but it did give me important insight: my kids needed more exposure to different kinds of bodies. They needed to know that there isn't one type of "good" or "normal" body. Although I felt like that was the message I was sending to my kids, my son had a different understanding. He had categorized that man's body as something out of the norm. The goal is for kids to see a person's body and recognize it as one of many varieties of normal, not to see it and compare it to the dominant standard of thinness.

Explicit Attitudes Versus Implicit Bias

Creating a family culture that embraces diversity starts with recognizing biases. Implicit bias refers to the unconscious preferences or prejudices we hold without realizing it. These biases form as our brains make quick judgments influenced by social programming, cultural norms, and exposure to stereotypes over time. Here's the reality: everyone has implicit biases, and having them doesn't reflect negatively on your or your child's character. The important thing is to identify these biases so we can avoid modeling or tolerating unfair treatment of others, and ensure our children treat people fairly.

We know that children are not born with biases, but they are born ready to take in information. Even the youngest babies are incredibly observant. Studies have demonstrated that babies as young as six months old show preference for their own race. Does this mean that six-month-old babies are racist? Of course not. Babies are quick learners and they are taking in and mimicking the world around them. In a 2024 study out of MIT, researchers were working to figure out how children acquired bias so readily and so early in life:

"A crucial component of how children 'catch' racial biases comes from young children's ability for observational social learning and imitation. Although all animals learn, human children are unique in the animal kingdom in their tendency to learn mannerisms, skills, social practices, and values simply by observing the nonverbal behavioral patterns of other people."[1]

These babies are learning bias from *nonverbal behavioral patterns*. So much of what we teach kids isn't from the words we say to them, but from how they see us behave, and how the wider community and culture around them operates.

In our culture, weight stigma is rampant. Thin bodies are praised and fat bodies are criticized. Knowing this, I had made a conscious effort to expose my child to media and books and conversations that demonstrate that all bodies are good bodies and health isn't a number on the scale. However, there is one area that continues to be a challenge for me—dealing with my own body image issues. Having recovered from anorexia as a preteen, I have inner narratives around health and weight that continue to surface for me. While I made sure to reject diet culture and speak about bodies neutrally with my kids, I wasn't doing that for myself. I started to wonder: How many times had my son seen me try on clothes, look at myself in the mirror, and get frustrated or upset before changing my outfit? Had he overheard me talking to my husband about my increasing jean sizes during his early years and noticed the tone of my voice? Had he observed me tracking my food and taking notes while I ate? Of course he had. Kids are *so* observant. They're always watching—they're wired for it (as the researchers from MIT pointed out). How is my child supposed to buy into the idea that all bodies are good bodies if my behavior around my own body isn't modeling that for him? This is where uncovering our own implicit biases and inner narratives becomes crucial. Our explicit attitudes are often in conflict with our implicit biases, and the reality is that our kids will believe our behaviors, regardless of what our words tell them. Our values are only our values if we live them.

The good news is that culturally our explicit attitudes around diversity and inclusion are improving. This means that a lot of the explicit information your kids are taking in will support the goal of helping them affirm diversity. However, as seen in my story about body neutrality and weight stigma, even if kids are being told a narrative of acceptance and affirmation, they're still taking in the implicit information that is often in conflict with what they're learning explicitly. This means that in order to teach our children to welcome diversity, we have to uncover our own implicit biases. The Implicit Association Test (IAT) is a great tool for this.[2] By understanding these unconscious attitudes, we can be more mindful of how we might be unintentionally communicating with our children through our behaviors.

There was a child in my kid's preschool who was hurting peers every day. His body craved touch and proprioceptive (deep pressure) input and he was really social. He wanted to engage with those around him and was still building the skill set for entering into play. When we look at the FACTS, his needs for activity and connection were driving a lot of his behavior. Within a couple of months of his being at the school, a group of families with kids in the classroom banded together, using words like *bully* to describe him. He was two years old. Two. These same families are folks who explicitly advocate for inclusion, yet when faced with the opportunity to live those values, they combined forces to have this child removed from the program. Remember, our values are only our values if we live them. Living out our values requires us to understand our implicit biases. If the families valued inclusion, they could have banded together to fight for this child to have all the resources and support he needed to thrive in the classroom. Instead, they focused their efforts on getting him removed from the school. What would it look like to say to their children, "His body is learning what it needs to calm and ask how to play with you. We are all helping him learn those things. Hm, what is your body still learning?"

Kids are never too old or too young to have these conversations. We get to model what inclusion looks and sounds like in practice. Wanting to protect our children makes absolute sense both physically and emotionally. We are not responsible for our initial reaction. We *are* responsible for our secondary response. The question I ask myself is "What needs to happen in my child's classroom so that all of the children can learn successfully?," and that is where I place my energy.

I was picking my daughter up from school when I overheard two girls say, "Oh my god, I can't believe she is actually wearing that." When I realized they were talking about my daughter, even though she hadn't heard it, I wanted to fight these eight-year-old girls. I wanted to go and tell them how dumb their outfits were. I immediately felt defensive of my child and wanted to protect her.

The unfortunate reality is that I can't protect her from pain, from embarrassment, from other humans ostracizing her because they are still learning how to feel included and lack additional skills to do so. What I *can* do is chat with my daughter about how other people sometimes say and do hurtful things. We can discuss what it looks like to choose friends that fill our cups rather than drain them. I can create a safe space at home where she can turn when she needs to process the hard experiences that will come her way. In order to do that, I need to notice my initial reactions to build awareness of my implicit biases, like my bias that cliques and cattiness are threats that should be shut down. I was on the receiving end of these behaviors in my childhood, and there is a part of me that wants to protect my daughter from that same experience—but really wants to protect myself from that. I get to remind myself that my daughter isn't me and her experience will be her own. I get to ask myself what would've been helpful for the younger me when I navigated those challenges, and I get to provide that for my daughter. I get to imagine a world where I had tools to feel my hard feelings, a space to turn with them, and the ability to see another person's behavior as a reflection of them, not of me. Then, I get to co-create that with my daughter, equipping her with the tools to have resilience in the face of preteen (and teen) drama. This all starts with us noticing our internal reactions and biases that surface. That self-awareness can allow us to self-regulate to respond with intention. We cannot regulate what we are not aware of.

Chapter 15

Raising a Kind Human

My sister and her kids came to watch my daughter's soccer practice after school. While our younger children played together by the sidelines, my nephew, who's the same age as the kids on the team, stood nearby, clearly interested in joining. He watched the practice intently, but even with the coach's approval and my daughter waving him over, he hesitated. He didn't know these kids, and stepping in felt daunting. That's when one of the older boys on the team walked over. He's a standout player, well-liked, with a lot of influence at my daughter's school.

"Hey, we need an extra player—want to jump in?" he asked my nephew. In that simple, quiet moment, my nephew's uncertainty faded, and the two of them jogged onto the field together. It wasn't a grand gesture, but it was a meaningful one. That small act of kindness, inviting someone in, made all the difference. This is the type of kindness we want to nurture in our kids—not just in big, obvious ways, but in everyday moments when they choose to include, to reach out, and to show care for others. Acts of kindness like this don't just benefit the receiving child. Research demonstrates that *performing* acts of kindness boosts happiness and well-being.[1]

So what does this look like in practice? How do we raise kids who will notice a peer who feels left out and find a way to bring them into the fold? Throughout this book we've covered the importance of self-awareness, self-regulation, empathy, and social awareness. These skills all work together to help kids be thoughtful and caring in their interactions with others. Self-awareness helps them recognize their own emotions and understand how their behavior impacts those around them. Self-regulation teaches them how to manage those big feelings without reacting impulsively. Empathy helps them see things from another person's perspective, fostering connection and compassion. Social awareness gives them the tools to navigate relationships and read social situations with sensitivity. When kids have these skills, kindness naturally follows.

Not only is kindness lovely to witness and experience, it has also been shown to increase self-esteem, empathy, and compassion, and improve mood. It can decrease stress hormones and lower blood pressure. People who are kind to themselves and others tend to be healthier and live longer. Kindness has been shown to increase your sense of connection, decrease loneliness, combat low mood, and improve relationships, according to an article from the Mayo Clinic.[2]

Outside of building the skills we've outlined throughout this book, the most impactful thing we can do is to treat our children and others with kindness. Easier said than done sometimes, I know. It's not easy to respond with kindness when you're navigating oppositional behavior, impulsivity, meltdowns, sibling rivalry, lack of accountability, disorganization, lying, or anything else on the laundry list of parenting challenges. I know that sometimes our own children have a way of getting under our skin that nobody else does. It's okay to feel annoyed with your kids—in fact you definitely will somewhere along the way. The key is not to act on those feelings.

All throughout this book we've focused on helping kids foster and access self-awareness and self-regulation so that they can respond with kindness in the moment. If we're expecting our children to do it, we must expect it from ourselves too. We can't hold them to a higher standard than we hold ourselves.

We were leaving the grocery store when I observed a mom with a cart full of groceries and tantruming children. As her oldest screamed about how it isn't fair that he never gets to have anything and his sister always gets to pick something, the sister was teasing her brother with her new ChapStick, and the youngest was trying to bolt into the parking lot.

Pushing my own cart of groceries, with my child walking alongside me, I said, "Come on, buddy, let's help them." I walked over, looked right in the mom's eyes, and said, "I've been here. I can take your cart and snag your youngest." "It's okay. You don't have to," she said quickly. "I know I don't have to, and *you* don't have to do this alone." Relief flooded her face, and I asked my child to wait with the two carts while I caught up to the running five-year-old. After reaching her, I held her hands and said, "I'm so fast and I know I can beat you to my shopping cart over there, but guess what? A person loses if they touch the parking lot. We have to figure out other spots to run to win. Ready?" Her eyes lit up and I could tell I had her in that moment. "GO!" She started to run for the grassy patch by the parking lot as I chased behind her. When we made it to the cart, I asked if she wanted to play another game with us where she rides in the cart with the groceries and tells us where to go, but she can only do it while talking like she thinks a pig would talk. We made our way playfully to her car, joining her mom and siblings, who were still screaming at each other. I buckled her in and unloaded the groceries into the trunk with my child before telling the mom that she was killing it and that parenting can be so exhausting. She let out a deep exhale and asked, "It won't always be like this, right?" "I think it's always some version of this, or at least for a while, but not every moment in there is like this. If I find the magic wand to get rid of the hard parts, I'll let you know, but for now, we can all just lean on each other through them." She teared up and mouthed, "Thank you," as I smiled and walked to my car. My son didn't say anything until we were pulling out of the parking lot. Then he asked, "Mom, why did you do that?"

"Do what, buddy?"

"Play that game with that girl?"

"Sometimes we all need some help and for someone to be kind to us. People have been kind to me when I've needed it too. When we helped that mama get that girl and groceries to the car, she was able to just focus on the big kids who needed her help with their feelings too."

Our kids are watching us to see how we treat people around us—from how we talk about people who aren't in the room to how we engage with people we know and those we don't know. Every night at dinner we share one thing someone did that was kind to us that day and one thing we did for someone else that was kind. Research shows that what we talk about and focus on is what our brain looks for and practices. When we are looking for kindness, we will see it and spread it.

The rule in our household is that kindness is the way we show up, including kindness to yourself, kindness to others, and kindness to the environment.

I was tackling an evening work challenge while the kids were watching a show after dinner and said to myself, "Ugh, Alyssa, you're such an idiot." "Hey, be kind to my wife," my husband replied. "Thank you for the reminder," I said cheekily. About a week later, I was in the Starbucks drive-through trying to find a gift card I got for my birthday when I mumbled, "You're so scatterbrained. Why do you always lose these cards?" To which my son replied, "Hey, be kind to my mom."

Our kids notice how we talk to ourselves, about ourselves. They hear how we talk about our partners, co-parents, their siblings, and often about them. What would it look like to be kind to yourself? How does it feel to do so?

When the kids were young, kindness to the environment meant household rules about not drawing on walls or breaking objects around them with intention. Now it's taking care of our things so we can enjoy a shared space together. It's putting things away rather than putting them down so we know where to locate them next.

Kindness to others can be a tough one because it's easy to be kind to humans who are kind to you. It's so much harder to be kind and compassionate toward humans who are not, but they often need our kindness the most. This doesn't mean that people get to be rude to you and you become their doormat. We talk about how kindness to ourselves includes setting boundaries to support our physical and emotional well-being. Sometimes this sounds like: "Hey, what's going on? You aren't speaking kindly to me and I'm wondering what's up." "I noticed you were rude to your sister this afternoon, did something happen at school that's bothering you, bud?"

We can choose to be right or we can choose to be connected.

My daughter went through a phase of what I called "compulsive honesty." It was almost as though she needed to confess her thoughts to me. To give some background, this is a child who holds it together for everyone in her life except me and her dad. She is incredibly thoughtful when it comes to her peers, aware of how her actions might impact others, and is willing to go out of her way for the people she loves. When it comes to me, I am her safe space . . . and the way that often plays out is that I deal with all the crap she's held in for the sake of others.

Around the age of six, she started telling me things like:

"Why are your arms so jiggly?"

"Why are your teeth like that?"

"Your stomach looks funny when you sit down."

Not all her thoughts were appearance-based, but most of them were. At first I tried to respond nonchalantly, hoping that if I didn't give it much power, it would subside.

"Oh, that's just how my arms are."

"Oh, that's because I didn't wear my retainer after I had braces."

"Yeah, my stomach got stretched out when you and Abel were in my belly."

Unfortunately, my approach didn't work. She would continue to share every observation about me, kind or not. As kids start to develop a sense of right and wrong, they're learning that honesty is important, but they also get mixed messages about it. We tell them not to lie, but when they're brutally honest, like saying something awkward or pointing out a hard truth, we often tell them that's rude or unkind. It's confusing for kids who are trying to understand the balance between being honest and also being considerate of others' feelings. Research demonstrates that adults actually respond more harshly to children's blunt truth-telling than they do to a child lying in the name of being polite.[3] Our expectations for honesty and politeness are often in conflict with each other, and kids are trying to get a grip on the complex social terrain that sometimes encourages or requires lying.

There was another layer of complexity in this situation: Nora's tendency toward people-pleasing and perfectionism. While she was throwing rude thoughts at me left and right, she was actually almost the opposite with other people in her life. She would tiptoe around their feelings so as to not upset anyone. With all of this in mind, I felt torn between wanting to make sure she continued to feel safe talking to me and the reality that I wanted her to know that even with me, her safe person, there were certain thoughts that I didn't want to hear from her. Having recovered from an eating disorder in my youth, I found the comments about my body especially upsetting. I knew that I needed to communicate a boundary with her before my emotions got the best of me and I responded in a way that wasn't supportive of our relationship. I started the conversation with curiosity.

"Nora, I've noticed you've been sharing a lot of thoughts about my body. Do you know that it's unkind to point out negative things about someone else's body?"

"I know!" she replied emphatically. "It's just that I tell you everything, and so I feel like I have to tell you those things too."

"Totally, that makes sense. I'm curious if part of why you feel like you need to tell me is because you know the thoughts are unkind and you're feeling almost like you have to confess them to me?"

"Yes. I just feel like I have to say them to you. I feel bad if I don't but also bad when I do."

Nora's experience illustrates the inner conflict children face as they try to balance their developing sense of right and wrong with their understanding of social etiquette. What Nora was actually communicating to me at that moment was, "I'm having thoughts that make me uncomfortable and I'm not sure what to do with them."

"I want to tell you something. Everybody thinks unkind things sometimes. Not every thought you have is going to be kind and loving, and that is normal. The important thing is to pause between the thought and your action."

"What do you mean?"

"Well, when I'm frustrated with Dad, I might think to myself that he's so annoying. It's natural for a thought like that to pop up. If I say that to him, that's not kind. Instead, I might take a breath and say, 'I need to take some space and come back when I'm calm.'"

"But, Mom, these thoughts happen even if I'm not frustrated with you. They just come out of nowhere."

"Yeah, that's normal too. When I have a thought that I don't like, I picture it like a cloud in the sky and I let the wind blow it away. I remind myself that it's just a thought and I don't have to get stuck in it or worry about it."

"But I still feel like I need to tell you."

"Okay. I have two things you could try. You could try the cloud thing and see if that helps your thoughts pass. If it doesn't, and you still feel like you need to get it out, you can write it in a journal."

"Are you upset with me when I have those thoughts?" she asked.

"Not at all. I don't want to hear unkind things about my body, but that doesn't mean your thoughts are bad. Thoughts are normal, and I'm going to help you take a different action in the future."

It's completely normal for kids (and adults!) to have unkind thoughts from time to time. The key is helping children understand that having those thoughts doesn't make them bad or define who they are. What truly matters is how they choose to respond. We can teach kids that there's a difference between what they think and what they do—just because a thought pops into their mind doesn't mean they have to act on it.

By giving them space to pause and reflect, we empower them to make choices based on kindness, rather than just reacting to whatever they're feeling in the moment. This kind of emotional awareness helps them better manage their thoughts and emotions, and, over time, it helps them build stronger, more compassionate relationships with the people around them.

In a way, it's like giving them the tools to step back, notice how they're feeling, and decide if their actions are aligned with the kind of person they want to be. When kids understand that they have the power to choose how they respond, it can be incredibly freeing. It encourages self-compassion and the confidence to make decisions that contribute to a more positive social environment, even when their emotions feel big or overwhelming.

We also have the power to choose how we respond. We might find ourselves thinking unkind things or feeling annoyed with our kids. As you work on teaching your kids to create space between their thoughts and actions, maybe you're still teaching yourself that too. If that's the case, you're in good company. This work is an ongoing practice.

Chapter 16

Creating Connection with Your Child

When our children grow up, they also grow out.

—ELI HARWOOD[1]

Parents recently reached out to me, feeling completely burned-out and discouraged with their daughter, Autumn. Despite their best efforts, it seemed like nothing was working. They explained that they had been doing everything they thought was right, yet every attempt at enforcing a boundary, engaging in a conversation, or making a decision together turned into a battle. It felt like no matter what they did, the smallest things would spark an argument, and getting through even the simplest tasks of the day felt like pulling teeth. As their daughter's behaviors increased in frequency and intensity, they found themselves turning to control and punishment because they weren't sure what else to do. The more they tried to buckle down on control, the more their daughter pulled away. They were at a loss, unsure of how to break the cycle or get through to her without the constant resistance and conflict.

I asked them to tell me more about their child and the relationship they shared. "She has always been a bright, sweet, happy girl," her dad said. "This last year we've seen a change though. She wants more alone time to call her friends, she's highly emotional, and it feels like we're walking on eggshells with her feelings."

I asked him to walk me through a typical day. "She gets home from school, her backpack hanging halfway off her shoulder, and drops it on the floor with a thud. I remind her, as I do every day, to hang up her backpack and put her shoes where they belong. But instead of the usual 'Okay, Dad,' she snaps back, 'I never get to relax in this house!' She storms off to her room, and I feel that familiar frustration rising. I understand she's had a long day, but so have I.

"Later, I head to her room to let her know dinner's ready, hoping to catch a moment with her. Instead, I'm met with a shout about how I 'don't respect her privacy.' It's the same struggle in the morning too. I try to greet her with a smile and a hug when she comes out of her room, wanting to start her day on a good note. But she just shrugs me off and rolls her eyes like I'm a total annoyance. Honestly, it hurts my feelings.

"If I then go to spend time with her younger sister, she's quick to jump in and accuse me of playing favorites. I feel like I can't win. I want to reconnect with her, to bridge this growing divide, but every attempt seems to hit a wall. Lately, I've resorted to just responding to her behavior. If she's disrespectful, I send her to her room. If she won't listen, I take away screens. None of it seems to change a thing; the attitude just keeps coming back.

"I miss my kid—the one who used to run to me after school, who would curl up on the couch and share every little detail of her day. Now it feels like I'm navigating a minefield, unsure of where to go next."

As we've covered throughout this book, it's normal for children to begin pulling away from their parents as they negotiate the delicate balance between wanting independence and still needing a lot of guidance. This developmental phase, often referred to as "individuation," happens as kids begin to understand their place in the world beyond the family, as they explore friendships, hobbies, and their own sense of identity. There's an internal push-pull happening, because the prefrontal cortex, responsible for decision-making, planning, and self-control, is still developing during this time. As a result, children may want to make choices independently but still lack the executive-functioning skills to manage these decisions effectively. This is what the parents who reached out to me were dealing with—the push and pull of individuation and the emotions that accompany it. The challenge with children this age is that they may begin to dodge your attempts at connection. The child who once loved to hold hands or cuddle on the couch now rolls their eyes at the idea. You might wonder if maybe they just don't need you in that way anymore. Don't be fooled—they still crave and need connection with you, they just need it to look differently than before.

As I continued chatting with the parents who had contacted me, they realized that as their daughter had been asking for more independence, they'd felt hurt—rejected even. As her emotions became harder to navigate, they felt distant from her, unsure of how to move forward. As her behaviors got trickier, they turned to control and punishment—moving further and further away from connection and collaboration. As they talked this out, it really resonated for me. I was in a similar stage of development with my own daughter and had felt the emotional push-pull of her seeking more and more autonomy while trying to figure out how to stay connected with her. I shared the information about connection blueprints and FACTS with these parents. We chatted about brain development and the why behind the changes they were seeing and experiencing. I asked them to keep me in the loop as they moved forward with their daughter. A month later, I got a message from them:

> Things are so much better now! We honestly can't believe the difference it made once we figured out how to genuinely connect with her. At first, we didn't see any major changes in those first couple of weeks, but then, out of nowhere, something shifted last week. It feels like she trusts us again! Sure, she still has her mood swings and all the usual kid behaviors, but it's so much easier to handle them now that we're on the same team—not butting heads all the time!
>
> We realized we had inadvertently made her feel guilty for wanting more independence, which was breeding resentment and disconnection. When we took FACTS into account, we realized we were dealing with after-school restraint collapse, not just a rude and defiant kid. We decided to change up our after-school routine in order to build in time for her to

decompress, instead of having her jump right into her chores/ household expectations. We learned that acts of service made her feel seen, loved, and connected to us. Something as simple as saying, "Wow, it looks like you've had a long day. I put a snack at the table for you," when she walks through the door after school, rather than harping on her immediately about hanging up her backpack, totally changes the tone of the afternoon. She'll sit down to her snack and start sharing about her day.

As children go from relying on their parents for survival into becoming themselves and finding their own identity, it can be tricky for parents to evolve alongside them. Let's dive into how to create a lasting connection with your child through the ebbs and flows of their growing into who they are.

Independence, Autonomy, and Change

> To love someone long-term is to attend a thousand
> funerals of the people they used to be.
>
> —HEIDI PRIEBE[2]

Remember the family from the section above? As their daughter moved out of early childhood, they temporarily lost their ability to connect with her. They were in some ways holding on to a child who wasn't there anymore. They wanted to be able to soothe and connect with her like they had when she was a little girl—but her needs had changed. One of the most profound privileges of parenting is watching your child grow; it can also be one of the most painful and challenging parts too. When we encounter the eye rolls, or the need for privacy, or the shrugging away from affection, it's natural to feel hurt and miss the way you used to connect with your child. The thing is that your child still needs to connect with you, but you might inadvertently be preventing that connection by trying to cling to old patterns in your relationship.

My husband and I married young; I was twenty-one and he was twenty-three. Our prefrontal cortexes were not fully developed yet. Our worldviews, values, and belief systems were not fully developed yet. In the thirteen years we've been together, we've both changed immensely. We've grown up and into our full selves. Our needs within our marriage have shifted, as have the ways we connect with each other and nurture our relationship. Imagine your own relationship with your partner or spouse for a moment. Think about the ways you need each other and the way you need to connect. What shifts have you made over the time you've been together? Now think about how it would feel if your partner didn't allow you to grow and change over the years. What if they resented it and tried to cling to the relationship dynamics that you were trying to shift? How would you feel? Frustrated? Stifled? Misunderstood?

This is what we often unintentionally do in our relationships with our children. We want to hold on to old patterns, and when we can't, we start to feel like the relationship is spiraling out of our control. So we hold tight to our perceived control with punishments and dominating behaviors. We send them to their rooms, we ground them, we take away screens. Yet, the behaviors persist, because our children's needs have shifted, and we haven't made the shift necessary to meet them.

"So I just have to deal with my kid yelling at me or refusing to do what I ask?" you might ask. Not at all. Allowing our children to grow and need us less or in a different capacity doesn't mean that disrespect, defiance, or rude behaviors are permissible. Part of this process is helping kids learn the appropriate way to communicate their needs. If a child comes home from school, drops their stuff on the floor, and then shouts at you when you ask them to take care of it, addressing it is a two-factor process.

First, we deal with the dysregulation. The family from the section above did a great job of this. They noticed that their daughter was experiencing after-school restraint collapse, so they created a routine in which she could decompress and eat before having additional expectations placed on her.

Later, outside of the heat of the moment, we work on part two of this process: building skills for better communication. "Hey, remember earlier when you came through the door and I asked you to take care of your stuff and you shouted at me? [*Pause*]. It's okay to be too overwhelmed or tired to jump right into chores at home. I totally get that. I feel like that after work sometimes. Instead of shouting at me, you can just let me know, 'Hey, Dad, I'm exhausted. I need to rest and eat before I can think about taking care of my stuff.'"

The goal isn't for kids to never change or challenge us. It's to make sure they have the skills to communicate and self-advocate for their evolving needs in a way that is supportive of family relationships. Then it's our job to hear that self-advocacy and meet them where they are. Rather than holding on to who your child was, welcome who they are becoming. Let them know you see that they're changing, and you're willing to change alongside them. If they are worried about judgment or guilt, it will be hard for them to be open to connection. Every boundary we set, every expectation we place on them, every conversation we have happens within the context of our relationship with them. A child who feels seen, heard, and emotionally safe is much more likely to be collaborative and cooperative. So, as you reflect on your relationship with your children, ask yourself: How can you create a space in your home where both you and your children feel safe to express your needs and grow together?

Sensory Systems and Connection

"I feel bad even saying this, but it's easier for me to connect with my seven-year-old than it is with my ten-year-old," Mei shared with me. "My youngest, Lila, loves to snuggle, read together, and just be close. We can literally sit on the couch and watch a movie, and her cup is filled. My older daughter, Amani, is a different story. She's not into physical affection and can't sit still to read together. She wants me to play soccer or jump on the trampoline or watch her do tricks. If I can't do those things, she expects my undivided attention for conversation. She'll ask me questions and want Ph.D.-level answers! It's exhausting. I wish we could just hang out, but she always seems to need something more from me. Sometimes I find myself feeling resentful or pulling away because she demands so much."

I asked Mei to tell me more about how she likes to relate to others outside of her children. "I usually prefer to avoid large groups and chaotic environments because I often feel overstimulated and overwhelmed by excessive noise, especially when there are competing sounds. For example, if there's background noise—like a TV or multiple conversations happening at once—I struggle to focus. In those moments, I tend to retreat inward and just observe. That said, I really enjoy spending time with my friends, and I can be pretty social when I'm with them. I value those connections and the good times we have together. However, after being in a social setting, I often need some downtime to recharge."

In the same way that our connection blueprint plays a role in how we connect with others, our unique sensory profiles do too. Sometimes within a parent-child relationship there is a sensory mismatch. This is what is happening between Mei and her ten-year-old. What fills Amani's cup (near-constant movement and lots of conversation) is draining to Mei. Conversely, what is fulfilling to Mei seems to be draining for Amani. When her mom tries to snuggle or read to her, she doesn't want to. She doesn't love touch and she seeks stimulation. She wants to play, move, and chat with her mom. On the flip side, Mei connects easily with Lila because their sensory systems are more similar—they both love physical touch and quiet activities like reading. Sensory mismatch can leave parents feeling disconnected or frustrated, especially when their efforts to bond don't seem to land with their child. Often, we instinctively offer connection in the way that feels good to us, without realizing that what recharges us might drain our child. When we can shift our focus to what fuels our child's unique sensory system—whether that's more movement, less touch, or a different kind of interaction—we open the door to authentic connection. Scan the following QR code to access our free regulation quiz to learn more about the most effective way to connect with your unique child.

Emotional Suppression

Near the end of the day during a recent observation in a kindergarten classroom, the teacher stood up and said, "Okay, if you were good at this morning's meeting, you can come up and choose your prize. If you're not sure, look at your name on the board. If there's a green clip next to it, you get a prize today."

Later, when I debriefed with the teacher, I asked her, "What does being 'good' mean to you?"

She explained, "At morning meeting, we all sit on the carpet and go over the day, the date, the weather, and the schedule. I also choose the line leader. The kids know that they're expected to sit quietly, raise their hands instead of calling out, and keep their eyes on me."

I asked her what kinds of behaviors are challenging during the meeting.

"Sitting still is hard for several students," she replied. "They get one warning for being wiggly, and then they lose the prize. I also have a couple of kids who get really upset if they aren't picked as line leader. They'll say it's unfair, or they'll cry. I give one warning for talking out of turn or making a fuss as well."

This approach to behavior management—rewarding "good" behavior and punishing "bad" behavior—is common in both schools and homes. But how do we define "good"? Often, it's about being obedient or not showing inconvenient emotions. What are we really telling children when we ask them to ignore their needs to keep the adults around them happy?

The child who can't sit still at morning meeting or struggles to stay at the dinner table isn't thinking, "I'm going to do the opposite of what my adult wants." Kids want to do well. They want to feel seen and accepted for who they are. They're wired for connection. Their behaviors aren't malicious or manipulative—they're expressions of unmet needs. In the case of wiggly children, their nervous systems are seeking input. So we can either teach them to support themselves or we can teach them to suppress.

Our culture relies heavily on rewards and punishments to shape behavior, assuming that external incentives will motivate compliance or discourage unwanted actions. This approach, while widespread, focuses on short-term results rather than fostering emotional growth and self-regulation—it's a Band-Aid on a deeper issue.

Many parents ask, "If I don't use punishments, how will my child know they're not supposed to behave like that?" But here's the thing: they already know. Kids don't misbehave because they don't understand the rules—they misbehave because they can't stop themselves. When we tell them to sit still or face punishment (like losing a prize), the message they receive is: if you try to meet your body's needs, you'll be shamed and punished in front of your peers. Similarly, when we tell kids they can't cry when they're upset, they learn that adult convenience is more important than their feelings.

Children don't need constant reminders about acceptable behavior; they need support to find the regulation necessary to meet expectations. What they truly need is to feel our belief in their inherent goodness, even when they're struggling to be "good." Building a meaningful connection requires that children feel safe enough to express challenging or inconvenient emotions.

Consider the child who can't sit still at dinner. Instead of resorting to punishment, what if we said, "It looks like sitting still is really tough for you right now. Your body needs to move. Let's figure out a way to help—maybe we can add some movement before dinner, or you could try sitting on a yoga ball. It's important to me that we have this family time, and I want to support you. What do you think could help?"

Or think about the kindergartner who wasn't chosen as line leader. What if the teacher said, "I understand you're feeling disappointed, and that's okay. If you need to cry, that's totally fine. I cry when I'm disappointed sometimes too." How would this impact the connection in that moment? How could it impact the children observing this interaction in understanding that their emotions are welcome too? Imagine the shift from feeling shame for expressing emotions to feeling connected and supported when expressing emotions that's possible if teachers allow feelings to be expressed in a safe way rather than trying to make them go away.

When children are not safely expressing emotions, like when they are hurting themselves, others, or damaging the environment, we need to first support their nervous system to get them back to a feeling of safety. Then, when they are regulated, we can help them build skills for what to do when that feeling arises again. Teachers and parents of multiple children: We have the opportunity to promote empathy and compassion here. The children watching will witness you respond to a child's dysregulation as a sturdy leader with compassion. We also get to turn to them after the fact and let them know that that child is still learning what to do when they're feeling dysregulated, and that we can help them in this process. We can acknowledge that we are all still learning things and we get to work together to build these tools. By doing this, we are normalizing the hard emotions, letting the other children know we will keep them safe, and supporting them with empathy and compassion for the child who was having a hard time. Responding in this way will require us to pause what we were doing to attend to this child. It requires cognitive flexibility for us as adults to pivot from plan A to plan B and adjust our expectations. If we are planning out our days without any room for spontaneous response, we will constantly feel thrown off balance by children's dysregulation.

The behavior specialist team received the most support calls about Liam. He would go into fight mode, ripping things off the walls or throwing things in the classroom, often leaving his peers feeling scared of him. When he wasn't in fight mode, he was fleeing, running out of the classroom and through the halls. If on a scale of one to ten, where ten is a distressed nervous system living in survival mode and one is a regulated system with access to the prefrontal cortex, the rational-thinking, and problem-solving part of the brain, Liam was living at an eight or nine, easily getting to a ten and having a hard time dropping to a six or seven. Accessing academics seemed impossible for him, and the school was at a loss for what to do with him.

When I came in to work with the school and Liam, the school administrators shared their breakdown of his ACEs. ACEs, or adverse childhood experiences, are traumatic events like abuse, neglect, or household dysfunction that occur before age eighteen. They can negatively impact brain development, emotional regulation, and physical health, increasing the risk of chronic diseases, mental health issues, and difficulty in relationships later in life. Liam was living with an aunt and uncle whom he barely knew, after having been recently removed from the house of his mom and her boyfriend. While the school didn't have his entire history, they knew he'd been exposed to addiction and domestic violence. Considering this, it made complete sense for him to live in fight-or-flight mode.

When I got to his classroom, he wasn't there. The teacher already had made a behavior support call for him and he was with one of the support specialists, who had not been able to get him to go back to the classroom. I watched as Liam tore through the hallway, ripping signs off the walls. I followed behind him from a distance, but within view. He ran to a stairway where he found a corner and faced away from everyone. His eyes tracked the stimuli around him like an animal running from its predator, remaining quiet and hidden but on high alert, ready to bolt at any moment. I sat down about ten feet from him, dropping my shoulders back, relaxing into the wall behind me, and in the softest voice possible said, "Hi, buddy. You are not in trouble. I'm not mad at you. I'm here with you." Then I paused as his body softened, just a little, but was still on guard. "My name is Alyssa and I'm going to sit here with you. Take your time, bud. You're safe." Then I sat there in silence and allowed him to experience safety. After a couple of minutes, I softly told him, "I noticed something about you. I noticed that your body is so good at keeping you safe. When you felt nervous or overwhelmed to go back into the classroom, your body fought and found a place to go that felt safe."

His eyes looked over at me for the first time since I'd sat down. I smiled softly at him and he looked away. "I have a notebook here and a pen that I was writing some things down in. Would you like to write or color in it with me?"

He nodded his head, and before going toward him, I asked, "Do you want to come grab it or would you like me to bring it over?"

"You." He spoke for the first time to me. I slowly slid over and handed it to him.

"Sometimes when I feel scared I like to draw a picture of something that makes me feel safe or happy. You don't have to, though. You can do whatever feels right for you, bud. Can I stay here with you?"

He nodded his head and as he drew in the notebook his body slowly melted into mine. He leaned into me, allowing me to hold his weight in my lap. I gently rubbed his arm and said, "I'm glad I got to meet you. It's nice to spend time with you. In a few minutes, could you show me how to get to your classroom? I'm still learning about this school."

"I don't want to go," he said.

"Yeah, this school is new for you too, huh? Man, being in new places can be scary, especially if you don't know where you feel safe there yet." I paused.

"Can I stay with you in your classroom for a little bit?"

"Yeah." He nodded.

He held my hand on one side and the notebook on the other as we walked back to the classroom together. When we entered, he showed me his desk and we drew in the notebook for a little while before I asked him, "It looks like it says it's math centers on the schedule. Do you know what we are supposed to do now?" He shook his head and we went to ask his teacher together. I followed him through math centers, where we engaged in the activities, and Liam was in a relaxed state, able to learn and participate in academics. When we were in one of the centers, one of the kids said, "Liam, I didn't know if you were coming back after you freaked out." I saw his face tighten and popped in, "Did you see Liam's body trying hard to find a way to feel safe? I saw that too. He's still learning where and how he can feel safe here in the classroom. I wonder how we can help Liam know he's safe."

The classroom teacher and I had an opportunity to connect and chat about what it would look like to pivot when Liam was dysregulated and support his nervous system. We discussed her fears of not getting to teach academics as she spent time on social emotional learning. Her concerns were valid, considering all the expectations on teachers to hit performance measures in academia. We made a plan for Liam to feel connection and safety from the moment he came to school, throughout the day, and through dismissal. We discussed how she could talk about Liam's behaviors to the whole class, bringing them in as compassionate, empathetic peers. When we shun emotions and behavior, we shame them. When we can talk about them, addressing the root of them, we invite compassion.

When children are conditioned to expect rewards for "good" behavior or punishments for "bad" behavior, their focus shifts from understanding their emotions and actions to simply avoiding consequences or earning praise. This transactional approach erodes the trust and deeper connection we aim to build. Instead of learning how to regulate their emotions or problem-solve, children may suppress their feelings to gain external validation. In the long run, this hinders emotional development and weakens the bond between child and adult.

Teaching kids to suppress emotions is so ingrained in our culture that we often don't realize we're doing it. From an early age, children are told, "Stop crying," "Calm down," or "Be brave," especially when they're upset. These well-intentioned phrases are meant to comfort, but they send the message that certain emotions—like sadness, anger, or fear—aren't okay. Over time, kids may feel they need to hide their feelings, leading to difficulties in processing emotions in a healthy way.

This approach is often driven by a desire to avoid uncomfortable situations or make things easier in the moment. It can be hard for adults to handle big emotions, so it's tempting to rush children through them. But when we do that, we lose a valuable opportunity to teach them how to understand and manage their emotions. Instead of learning how to express their feelings, they learn to bury them, which can lead to anxiety and relationship struggles later on in their lives.

If the goal is for our kids to come to us with their hard stuff, like when they're teenagers navigating sex or substances, it starts now. It starts with how we respond when they misbehave or do something wrong, not just in the big moments but in the small stuff too—when they argue in the car, don't do their homework, or talk back to us. If we can't handle their small stuff, they won't bring us the big stuff.

Chapter 17

Where to Begin

With sixteen chapters behind us, you may find yourself wondering where to start. We have culled the three most important things to focus on first for families and for schools. These are the key elements necessary for having a foundation of trust, connection, regulation, and collaboration with children.

Families

1. Behaviors as communication of a need

If you take nothing else from this book, let it be this: all behavior communicates a need. Also, know this: it won't always seem that way in the moment. Sometimes the need is pretty clear—you went to a wedding, stayed out later than usual, pushed bedtime, and the kids are melting because they're tired. Sometimes it's less obvious—you carved out a special Saturday morning date with your eight-year-old who seems to always want your attention at home and she's whining the whole time because a group of her peers is at the breakfast spot you took her to and she wasn't invited with the group. She's afraid that this will lead to ongoing exclusion by her peers.

It's okay to be annoyed in the moment. It makes sense to feel frustrated that you went out of your way to plan this outing and she's being a brat through it all. As you show up for your children in ways that no one showed up for you, it can be both healing and triggering. A part of you might surface that wants to let her know that she is so lucky to have a parent who carved out this time with her because you didn't have that growing up. You aren't failing for feeling those things. In order to get to the next step of being able to be a detective and see what's driving her behavior, you have to start with yourself. Get granular. Go deeper. What is the story you're telling yourself about this behavior?

"I am being manipulated."
"He's so needy."
"She can't go through life being defiant. She needs to learn respect."

Those are the stories from your experience, from your childhood. If you want to move from a place of control and disconnection to a place of curiosity and connection, get curious with yourself first. Ask yourself these four questions:

1. What would it mean about me if my child was _____ (needy/defiant/manipulative)?
2. What am I afraid would happen if they were?
3. Do they have tools to navigate that if it did?
4. Did I have the tools to navigate that in childhood?

Answering these questions might sound like . . .

1. If my child is a spoiled brat who doesn't care about people doing special things for her, then it means that I am failing to teach her what she needs to know to be socially successful.
2. If she isn't socially successful, then she will have no friends and be lonely.
3. No, she doesn't know what to do when she feels lonely and often just mopes around the house or is rude to us at home.
4. No. When I felt lonely, I would cry or feel like I was stupid and no one liked me. There were times I had scary thoughts and often questioned my worth and value when I felt lonely.

Your child needs support in learning about what to do when she feels lonely, so she's equipped to handle this when it inevitably comes up throughout her life. You want to help her with the tools you didn't have for navigating those feelings.

Notice those barriers to going deeper into this work and start there. Your child will sometimes melt down or lie. They will be defiant or manipulative. They will choose the thing they know they aren't supposed to because they are curious and learning about the world involves making many mistakes along the way. It's not your job to prevent behaviors from occurring, and if you stay on the surface, focused on the behavior, their unmet need will continue to fester. New behaviors will pop up as you get others to disappear. It will feel like a game of whack-a-mole.

Remind yourself in the moment: all behavior is communication of a need. Allow yourself to pause and get curious about that need for sensory regulation or emotional support and connection.

2. Supporting the nervous system

Start with the FACTS.

Food
Activity
Connection
Tune-out
Sleep

In order for kids or adults to access self-control, we need to be in a regulated state. Focusing on supporting our nervous system regulation throughout the day and reactively when dysregulation inevitably occurs is crucial to responding with intention. Scan the following QR code to access a quiz to get to know your nervous system and your child's.

Now, pause and reflect on your unique life. Use this guide to create a plan for yourself and your family to proactively support regulation. That guide is your self-care plan for your family. It will not result in zero emotions and regulation all the time. No one lives like that. It will, however, support your family with more capacity to navigate the ups and downs that will inevitably show up in your day-to-day. It will help you move from reactive mode, where you are putting out fires left and right, to proactive regulation for a smoother experience of the challenges that come up. Someone will forget their uniform. Their sibling will annoy them. Their friends will hurt their feelings. And they will project that all onto you sometimes. Proactively supporting your nervous system allows you to have more energy and clarity to respond.

Build your in-the-moment toolbox. What is accessible in the moment? Check off all the items from the list that follows that apply and are helpful for your nervous system. Now, jot down three of them and hang them in places you need them most—the dashboard of your car, the refrigerator, the bathroom mirror.

Take a moment and write down three phrases or mantras that can help you regulate in the moment. Need help brainstorming? Find some of my favorites below:

They're not giving me a hard time; they're having a hard time.
Connection before correction.
I can handle their big feelings.
There is an emotion beneath the behavior.
I can pause and get curious.
This isn't an emergency.

Remember that most problems are not emergencies. Provide safety, but then pause and breathe. It's not a child's job to get calm for you, it's your job to get calm for them. You've got this.

In-the-Moment Toolbox

☐ Have a snack/meal

☐ Take a drink

☐ Rest/sleep

☐ Build/refine routines

Routines provide security and stability and allow your brain to switch into autopilot, which gives you more resources to devote to making bigger decisions. Having a reliable framework leaves space for flexibility.

☐ Ask for help

Advocate for yourself and get your needs met. This could sound like, "Will you swap duties with me?" or "I need advice on this behavior. Can we chat?"

☐ Tap into coping strategies as needed

Calming your body brings the regulation needed to respond with intention. Try one of the following strategies:

- Drawing/coloring/painting
- Movement/exercise
- Breathing
- Reading a book
- Journaling
- Playing music
- Gratitude practice
- Hugging
- Looking at the sky
- Talking to a support person

3. Be their safe space

We have to be the adult in the relationship. We have to take responsibility for our own emotions in order to support theirs. It's not their job to change their behavior so it's easy for us to be their safe space. It's our job to prioritize connection and relationship even in the face of the really annoying, really frustrating behaviors. Our role is to let them know they can bring their hard stuff to us, without fear of judgment, shame, or punishment. When they're upset or overwhelmed, starting with an approach like, "You're not in trouble. I'm here to help you figure this out," can go a long way in showing them that they truly can turn to us—even when they're feeling scared or embarrassed.

Following through is key: they need to know they won't be punished for coming to you, even when they make mistakes. Boundaries and expectations are important, of course. But punishment and shame don't have to be part of that picture. Instead, we can create a space where they feel safe to learn, grow, and seek our support no matter what they're facing.

Schools

Social emotional learning does not happen in a time block. You cannot put a Multi-Tiered System of Supports (MTSS) on your school schedule and expect to navigate skill building, behavior challenges, and dysregulation only in that time period. Let's look at some ways you can create emotionally supportive school environments that foster an opportunity for children to build the skills for regulation, emotion processing, and resilience.

1. Sensory-friendly classrooms

Every human has a nervous system and thus has needs for regulation. My husband sits in an office chair that spins and can rock a little. I have a walking pad under my desk and a notebook I often doodle in when I'm in meetings. When we can support children's nervous system regulation in school, they can spend less energy trying to regulate and have more capacity for learning and engagement. Every classroom, pre-K to twelfth grade, should have equipment for vestibular, proprioceptive, and tactile input. This could include seats that spin or bounce, a beanbag chair, rocking chair, exercise bands on chair legs or desks for kids to push against, a wobble board, fidgets, and the permission to stand versus sit. Classrooms should have an option for kids to have a break from stimuli by using noise-canceling headphones or a solo pod/spot they can go into proactively and reactively for nervous system regulation. If you have a child who is highly sensory sensitive, is there a behavior support specialist who could proactively give them a three- to five-minute break from the classroom environment into a low-lit, low-stimulation environment a few times a day? This can drastically decrease behavior challenges.

Sensory-friendly classrooms decrease visual stimulation, including decor on the walls. They also provide movement breaks that are not just screen based for children who are sound sensitive. Sensory-friendly classrooms allow kids to sit in the way that's most regulating for them. Some children may lie on their stomach on the carpet, while others will sit in their chairs for morning meeting or have an exercise band on their chair to push their feet against. They may have a seat that rotates or can rock. Sensory-friendly classrooms are mindful of who needs closeness in proximity to another versus who has a bigger space bubble and help each child advocate for those needs by being their co-advocate before expecting self-advocacy. These classrooms recognize that the child walking down the hall dragging their shoulder on the wall is not misbehaving, but instead trying to get the sensory input their nervous system needs to be regulated.

Sensory-friendly classrooms are curious spaces that ask, "What does this environment need for each child to thrive?" rather than expecting a child to conform to the environment. As my friend Heather Avis wrote in her book *Everyone Belongs*, "The space is the problem, not how [one] gets around."[1]

Sensory regulation is built into the culture of the day, not just expected to be fulfilled at recess, recognizing that if kids can't sit still or attend to a task, they need to pause and have their needs met first. You can try and power through, but it'll be far less effective for long-term learning than pausing to regulate first.

Start with the FACTS.

Food
Activity
Connection
Tune-out
Sleep

In order to access regulation and self-control, we need to begin here. When was the last time the child ate food that nourished them and gave them energy? When was the last time they moved their body in a way that is regulating for them? Note: If the only movement available is whole group movement breaks, where students follow along with a video, sensory-sensitive children may be overwhelmed and dysregulated by this. Do they feel like they belong, are included, and are loved in the classroom? What is their energy level—both from nighttime sleep and task demand throughout the day? If a child is working really hard to sit still or is stretching their cognitive rubber band, they will tire faster. When was the last time they had access to a calm, quiet space for a brain break?

When we start here, we can set our children up for success in the classroom. It also helps us understand the root of a behavior or emotion.

2. Emotions as a part of the culture

As I polled teachers while writing this book, the number one challenge they reported is meeting their academic instruction expectations if they incorporate social emotional learning into the culture of their classroom. Practicing this means being able to pivot from a lesson plan momentarily to allow for emotional expression. The lesson becomes social emotional learning in order to be able to focus on the academic expectations. We often shy away from acknowledging emotions as a whole class in fear of embarrassing the child, but what we are really doing is adding shame to the emotion. By trying to hide it or silence it without mentioning it, we inadvertently communicate that the child shouldn't be feeling what they're feeling. That doesn't stop them from experiencing their feeling, but it does make academic learning incredibly challenging. We know that the most crucial predictor of success in life isn't whether or not children know that mitochondria are the powerhouse of the cell, but if they know how to experience emotions without being overwhelmed by them. What matters is if they know how their nervous system works and how to regulate it to respond with intention. This is how we build resilience and foster skills for conflict resolution and problem-solving. This is also *how* they will learn *how* they learn, gaining self-awareness about their needs that will allow them infinite possibilities for academic growth.

Our school systems are so focused on quantitative data that we are losing opportunities for qualitative data. Rather than how many kids can pass that test, let's look at how many calls are made to the behavior support teams for kids who are dysregulated. Imagine removing clocks for the day from the classroom. What if teachers followed a daily rhythm rather than a schedule? I wonder if they'd slow down and respond to the energy of the room rather than moving from one thing to the next based on a specific time on the clock. Imagine if the whole class was moving into dysregulation during math, and instead of waiting for the movement break that follows, the teacher said, "You know what? It seems like we all need a breather from this, let's do our movement break now and come back to math in a couple of minutes." Or, if a student was having a hard time figuring something out and chucked their pencil across the room, imagine a teacher drawing attention to it by saying, "Whoa, you're working so hard to figure that out and it isn't working. Man, that's frustrating," then turning to the rest of the class to say, "Ian seems frustrated by this one. Does anyone have something helpful you do when you're frustrated that we could try before figuring out how to solve this math problem?" What if the class came together to co-regulate and later, when Ian was calm, the teacher talked to him about what he could do instead of throwing a pencil?

Children feel safe when they understand what's happening inside their bodies and in the environment around them. If a child is doing something in the classroom that feels scary or threatening, we can foster inclusion and empathy by talking about it, not hiding or shaming it. "His body is learning what it needs to calm and ask how to play with you. We are all helping him learn those things. Hm, what is your body still learning?" Kids are never too old or too young to have these conversations. We get to model what inclusion looks and sounds like in practice.

This requires a shift away from punishment and reward systems like school suspension and programs like Positive Behavioral Interventions and Supports (PBIS). Including emotion processing as a part of the culture means that we get to make mistakes and learn from them together. It also requires the adults to look beyond the behavior to find the need that's driving it. When we support that need, the behavior will cease. If we focus on reacting to the surface behaviors, punishing unwanted ones and rewarding those we hope to see more of, we miss the crucial step of understanding what's driving them. Soon that punishment won't matter to the child anymore or the reward will stop "working" and you'll need a different reward for the same results. It means we won't have quiet, calm, regulated classrooms all the time because children will feel safe to express their emotions and navigate conflict in a healthy way, knowing that all feelings are mentionable and manageable, as Mister Rogers taught us.

When we see a behavior on the surface, ask, "What is the child's need?" Until a school system is able to answer that question, responses will be Band-Aids on bullet holes and behaviors will continue to surface.

3. Power with instead of power over

There is a fear in classroom environments of losing control of the students. Children are supposed to see the adult as the authority figure and must be obedient. If we want to raise children who stand up for their values, who change systems that are unjust, or who dare to think for themselves and be innovators, we must allow them to practice these skills. We can hold respect as a value, while allowing for critique and critical thinking. When we shift the focus from "Here are my rules" to being a community with our students, we often see an increase in their trust and respect for all the humans around them, including their teachers.

This requires the adults to notice their biases. Are there certain ages at which you expect kids to stop crying? Do phrases like "They're old enough

It's not their job to get calm for me; it's my job to get calm for them.

There isn't one right way to be a parent.

Resting is a job too.

I am strong and capable.

I give myself permission to change my mind.

It's not my job to be perfect; it's okay to make mistakes.

I am the best version of myself when I meet my own needs.

I can handle hard things.

I am the best parent for my child.

I am fully present, here and now.

to know better" pop up for you in the moment? Notice these reminders of your social programming and practice self-regulation so they don't become barriers to your connection with the children.

Doing this work with our kids doesn't require perfection. I've never left the day as a teacher or a parent and said, "Wow, I was perfect today. I responded with intention all the time today." We can't expect kids to be perfect, but we often do because we expect perfection from ourselves. Research shows that we don't have to respond in an emotionally supportive way all of the time to create lasting results.[2] You get to drop the ball, make mistakes, and repair with your children. What would it look like to shift from perfection to being in a relationship with our children that allows all parties to be their full selves and dive into the messiness of being human together? What would it look like to allow ourselves and our children the grace to grow without perfection? As you move forward with this work, remember that you are enough. You are doing enough. Your child is enough just as they are today. They are lovable, worthy, and valued not because of any certain behaviors or traits, but because they are uniquely themselves.

Looking Ahead: Raising Connected, Compassionate Humans

The work of raising and teaching kids is layered and demanding, but it's also some of the most meaningful and impactful work we can undertake. It requires us to navigate complex emotions, respond to ever-changing needs, and reflect deeply on our own habits and patterns—all while showing up, day after day, for the children who depend on us. This work isn't about getting everything right or striving for perfection; it's about progress, presence, and the relationships we build along the way.

Whether you're a caregiver, an educator, or both, the effort you put into understanding and supporting children shapes who they are now and who they'll become in the future. It's in the countless small moments—when you choose to listen instead of dismiss, guide instead of control, and repair instead of retreat—that children learn what it means to trust, feel safe, and grow.

The future isn't built in grand gestures or sweeping changes but in these small, consistent acts of connection, trust, and care. Thank you for showing up, for choosing to do this work, and for continuing to learn and grow alongside the children in your care. Together, we're shaping not only their future but also a kinder, more empathetic world.

Acknowledgments

Alyssa: This book would not exist without the incredible people who have supported, challenged, and believed in me along the way.

Rachel, my coauthor—you have been an anchor and a thought partner through this entire process. Your insight, dedication, and shared passion for this work made this book better in every way. The Seed team—thank you for the countless ways you've shaped and strengthened this work, for every conversation, collaboration, and moment of encouragement. Beki, your visuals brought these ideas to life in a way words alone never could.

To our agent, Sally, and our editor, Sarah—thank you for your guidance, your belief in this book, and your patience as we shaped it into something meaningful.

To my village—you help me raise my kids with love and intention, making space for me to write and create. Without you, I wouldn't have the capacity to do this work.

Zach, my partner in life—thank you for your unwavering support, for holding space for my big feelings, and for always reminding me that this work matters. Sage and Mila, my greatest teachers—you are the reason I do this. Watching you navigate the world with curiosity, resilience, and so much heart inspires me every day.

And finally, to my tiny human self—the little girl with big feelings she didn't know what to do with. You found ways to cope, to grow, to keep going. And because of you, we are here.

This book is for all of us.

Rachel: Alyssa, thank you for inviting me to write this book with you. I'm deeply grateful for the opportunity to help make this work accessible to other caregivers. Thank you for creating Seed & Sew and for bringing me into this journey.

Erika, your support kept me going. Thank you for answering every phone call and text, for your feedback, and for your encouragement. I'm so grateful for our relationship.

To the Seed team, thank you for your support and for making time for me to write, even when there was other work to do.

And thank you to Sally, our agent, and Sarah, our editor, for believing in this project and its impact.

To my parents, for being a loving and supportive presence in my life. To Cody, for loving our family so well. And finally, to Nora and Abel—thank you for being exactly who you are. Being your mom is the greatest honor of my life. This work will always be for you.

Appendix
Reflective Self-Assessments

The self-assessments below are not about perfection—they are about awareness and reflection. Use the spaces below each prompt to pause, explore, and reconnect with the tools and insights from the book.

Parents and Caregivers

1. What was the last behavior that really challenged me?

   If that behavior didn't change, what would it have meant for me or my child?

   _____

   _____

   _____

2. How do I typically respond to challenging behaviors?

   What feels instinctive, and what do I want to be more intentional about?

   _____

   _____

   _____

3. What could help me respond differently in those moments?

   What tools do I have to calm my body? What scripts or mental reframes could I use to shift my thoughts?

   _____

   _____

   _____

4. What have I learned about the difference between sensory needs and emotional needs?

How has that shifted the way I interpret behavior?

_____

_____

_____

5. Which of the nine sensory systems is most draining for me? Which is most regulating? What about for my child?

Taste, touch, smell, sight, sound, proprioceptive (muscle activation), vestibular (movement), interoceptive (hunger, thirst, fatigue, etc.), neuroceptive (attunement to emotional and physical safety).

_____

_____

_____

6. How does my child receive connection? What makes me feel connected?

Are these different?

_____

_____

_____

7. What stories do I carry about boundaries?

How does my past shape the way I set or struggle with boundaries now?

_____

_____

_____

8. When I think about co-regulation, what feels accessible to me—and what still feels challenging?

What tools help me show up as a calm, connected adult?

_____

_____

_____

9. How do I care for my own nervous system?

Especially after meltdowns, power struggles, or emotionally charged moments.

_____

_____

_____

10. Which area of the FACTS framework do I feel most confident supporting? Which area feels the most challenging—for me and for my child?

Is there a way to shift my daily routine to more easily meet that need?

_____

_____

_____

11. What's one idea from the book that deeply resonated with me?

And one area where I still want to grow?

_____

_____

_____

Educators

1. What was the last behavior that really challenged me in the classroom?

   If that behavior didn't change, what would it have meant for the student, the learning environment, or for me as the educator?

   _____

   _____

   _____

2. How do I typically respond to challenging behaviors?

   What feels automatic, and what do I want to be more intentional about moving forward?

   _____

   _____

   _____

3. What could help me respond differently in those moments?

   What strategies or tools help me regulate? What scripts or mental reframes could I lean on?

   _____

   _____

   _____

4. What have I learned about the difference between sensory needs and emotional needs?

   How does that understanding shift the way I interpret student behavior?

   _____

   _____

   _____

5. Which of the nine sensory systems is most draining for me? Which is most regulating? What about for the student I'm thinking of?

Taste, touch, smell, sight, sound, proprioceptive (muscle activation), vestibular (movement), interoceptive (hunger, thirst, fatigue, etc.), neuroceptive (attunement to emotional and physical safety).

_____

_____

_____

6. How do my students receive connection—and how can I build relationships with many children at once?

What helps me feel connected to my class as a whole? Are there students whose connection needs I may be missing?

_____

_____

_____

7. What stories do I carry about boundaries in the classroom?

How might my own experiences or upbringing shape the way I approach boundaries with students?

_____

_____

_____

8. When I think about co-regulation, what feels accessible to me—and what still feels challenging?

What tools help me stay calm, grounded, and present during dysregulation?

_____

_____

_____

9. How do I care for my own nervous system—especially after hard days?

What do I need to recover after meltdowns, power struggles, or emotional moments in the classroom?

_____

_____

_____

10. Do I have a variety of tools and strategies in place to meet the needs of all learners?

Where might I need more support, resources, or ideas to build a more responsive classroom?

_____

_____

_____

11. Which area of the FACTS framework do I feel most confident supporting in my classroom?

Which area could be optimized in our daily routines to better support regulation—for both me and my students?

_____

_____

_____

12. What's one idea from the book that really resonated with me?

What's one area where I still want to grow or try something new?

_____

_____

_____

Notes

Chapter 1: What Is Emotional Intelligence?

1. Daniel Goleman, *Emotional Intelligence* (New York: Bantam Books, 1995).
2. Carol S. Dweck, *Mindset: The New Psychology of Success* (New York: Ballantine, 2007).
3. Katherine Olcoń, Youngmi Kim, and Lauren E. Gulbas, "Sense of Belonging and Youth Suicidal Behaviors: What Do Communities and Schools Have to Do with It?" *Social Work in Public Health* 32, no. 7 (2017): 432–42, https://doi.org/10.1080/19371918.2017.1344602.
4. Mohammad Alavi, Seyed Aliakbar Mehrinezhad, Mitra Amini, and Manjit K. A. Parthaman Singh, "Family Functioning and Trait Emotional Intelligence Among Youth," *Health Psychology Open* 4, no. 2 (December 17, 2017): 2055102917748461, https://doi.org/10.1177/2055102917748461.
5. Carolyn MacCann, Ying Wang Jiang, Luke E. Brown, Michelle Bucich, Kit S. Double, and Amirali Minbashian, "Emotional Intelligence Predicts Academic Performance: A Meta-Analysis," *Psychological Bulletin*, published online December 12, 2019.
6. Elizabeth Lando-King, Annie-Laurie McRee, Amy L. Gower, Rebecca J. Shlafer, Barbara J. McMorris, Sarah Pettingell, and Renee E. Sieving, "Relationships Between Social-Emotional Intelligence and Sexual Risk Behaviors in Adolescent Girls," *Journal of Sex Research* 52, no. 7 (2015): 835–40, https://doi.org/10.1080/00224499.2014.976782.
7. Hanan Faried Maghawry, Alaa M. Darwish, Naglaa Abd ElMegeed Mohammed, Nadia Abd El-ghany Abd El-hameed, and Gellen K. Ahmed, "Assessing Emotional Intelligence Domains and Levels in Substance Use Disorders," *Egyptian Journal of Neurology, Psychiatry, and Neurosurgery* 60 (2024): 19, https://doi.org/10.1186/s41983-024-00797-w.
8. Benito León-Del-Barco, Sandra Molero Lázaro, María Isabel Polo-Del-Río,

and Víctor Manuel López-Ramos, "Emotional Intelligence as a Protective Factor Against Victimization in School Bullying," *International Journal of Environmental Research and Public Health* 17, no. 24 (December 15, 2020): 9406, https://doi.org/10.3390/ijerph17249406.

9. "Psychology for Clinical Settings," *Frontiers in Psychology* 11 (January 30, 2020), https://doi.org/10.3389/fpsyg.2020.00093.

10. National Institute of Mental Health, "Any Anxiety Disorder," National Institute of Mental Health, accessed October 18, 2024, https://www.nimh .nih.gov/health/statistics/any-anxiety-disorder.

Chapter 2: Helping Children Understand and Process Their Emotions

1. "Our Epidemic of Loneliness and Isolation: The U.S. Surgeon General's Advisory on the Healing Effects of Social Connection and Community," US Department of Health and Human Services, 2023, https://www.hhs .gov/sites/default/files/surgeon-general-social-connection-advisory.pdf.

Chapter 3: Why Can't They Control Themselves?

1. Jennifer MacCormack, "Feeling 'Hangry': When Hunger Is Conceptualized as Emotion," master's thesis (University of North Carolina at Chapel Hill, 2016), https://doi.org/10.17615/0hgh-se19.

2. University of Maryland School of Medicine, "Children Who Lack Sleep May Experience Detrimental Impact on Brain and Cognitive Development That Persists Over Time, UM School of Medicine Study Finds," *University of Maryland School of Medicine News*, August 2022, https://www.medschool.umaryland.edu/news/2022/children-who-lack-sleep -may-experience-detrimental-impact-on-brain-and-cognitive-development -that-persists-over-time-um-school-of-medicine-study-finds.html.

3. F. N. Yang, W. Xie, and Z. Wang, "Effects of Sleep Duration on Neurocognitive Development in Early Adolescents in the USA: A Propensity Score Matched, Longitudinal, Observational Study," *Lancet Child & Adolescent Health* 6, no. 10 (October 2022): 705–12, https://doi .org/10.1016/S2352-4642(22)00188-2, epub July 30, 2022. PMID: 35914537; PMCID: PMC9482948.

4. Eli Harwood (@attachmentnerd), "A well-behaved child, isn't always an emotionally-well child," Instagram, February 5, 2024, https://www .instagram.com/p/C298K2lvvTJ/?hl=en.

5. Silvia Melero, Azucena Morales, José P. Espada, Isabel Fernández-Martínez, and Mireia Orgilés, "How Does Perfectionism Influence the Development of Psychological Strengths and Difficulties in Children?" *International Journal of Environmental Research and Public Health* 17, no. 11 (2020): 4081, https://doi.org/10.3390/ijerph17114081.

Chapter 5: Responding to Disrespect and Defiance

1. Robert J. Ellis and Julian F. Thayer, "Music and Autonomic Nervous System (Dys)function," *Music Perception* 27, no. 4 (April 2010): 317–26, https://doi.org/10.1525/mp.2010.27.4.317.
2. Kamilah B. Legette, Andrew Supple, Johari Harris, and Amy G. Halberstadt, "Teachers' Racialized Anger: Implications for Discipline Disparities," *Journal of School Psychology* 99 (2023): 101221, https://doi.org/10.1016/j.jsp.2023.05.004.
3. T. J. Sabol, C. L. Kessler, L. O. Rogers, A. Petitclerc, J. Silver, M. Briggs-Gowan, and L. S. Wakschlag, "A Window into Racial and Socioeconomic Status Disparities in Preschool Disciplinary Action Using Developmental Methodology," *Annals of the New York Academy of Sciences* 1508, no. 1 (February 2022): 123–36, https://doi.org/10.1111/nyas.14687.

Chapter 6: Sneaking and Lying

1. Aliza Pressman, "The Truth About Lying," Substack, October 28, 2024, https://dralizapressman.substack.com/p/the-truth-about-lying.
2. Liyang Sai, Siyuan Shang, Cleo Tay, Xingchen Liu, Tingwen Sheng, Genyue Fu, Xiao Pan Ding, and Kang Lee, "Theory of Mind, Executive Function, and Lying in Children: A Meta-Analysis," *Developmental Science* 24 (2021), https://doi.org/10.1111/desc.13096.

Chapter 7: Navigating Peer Pressure

1. Stuart Shanker and Teresa Barker, *Self-Reg: How to Help Your Child (and You) Break the Stress Cycle and Successfully Engage with Life* (New York: Penguin Press, 2016).
2. Tasia Stone, "Are We Too Quick to Cry 'Bully'?" CNN Wire, WTVR CBS 6 News, October 5, 2013, https://www.wtvr.com/2013/10/05/are-we-too-quick-to-cry-bully.
3. Kristin Borgwald and H. Theixos, "Bullying the Bully: Why Zero-

Tolerance Policies Get a Failing Grade," *Social Influence* 8 (2013): 149–60, https://doi.org/10.1080/15534510.2012.724030.

4. S. Whitson, "Is It Rude, Is It Mean, or Is It Bullying?" *Psychology Today*, November 25, 2012, https://www.psychologytoday.com/intl/blog/passive -aggressive-diaries/201211/is-it-rude-is-it-mean-or-is-it-bullying.

5. Tracy E. Waasdorp, Catherine P. Bradshaw, and Philip J. Leaf, "The Impact of Schoolwide Positive Behavioral Interventions and Supports on Bullying and Peer Rejection: A Randomized Controlled Effectiveness Trial," *Archives of Pediatrics & Adolescent Medicine* 166, no. 2 (2012): 149–56, https://doi.org/10.1001/archpediatrics.2011.755.

6. Stuart Shanker and Teresa Barker, *Self-Reg: How to Help Your Child (and You) Break the Stress Cycle and Successfully Engage with Life* (New York: Penguin Press, 2016).

7. Lucy Bowes, Louise Arseneault, Barbara Maughan, Amber Taylor, Avshalom Caspi, and Terrie E. Moffitt, "School, Neighborhood, and Family Factors Are Associated with Children's Bullying Involvement: A Nationally Representative Longitudinal Study," *Journal of the American Academy of Child & Adolescent Psychiatry* 48, no. 5 (2009): 545–53, https:// doi.org/10.1097/CHI.0b013e31819cb017.

8. Stuart Shanker and Teresa Barker, *Self-Reg: How to Help Your Child (and You) Break the Stress Cycle and Successfully Engage with Life* (New York: Penguin Press, 2016).

Chapter 8: Tackling Taboos

1. Stephanie Burnett, Stephanie Thompson, Geoffrey Bird, and Sarah-Jayne Blakemore, "Pubertal Development of the Understanding of Social Emotions: Implications for Education," *Learning and Individual Differences* 21, no. 6 (2011): 681–89, https://doi.org/10.1016/j .lindif.2010.05.007.

2. S. F. Witchel, B. Pinto, A. C. Burghard, and S. E. Oberfield, "Update on Adrenarche," *Current Opinion in Pediatrics* 32, no. 4 (2020): 574–81, https://doi.org/10.1097/MOP.0000000000000928.

3. Shalon Nienow, "Seven Steps to Teaching Children Body Autonomy," Rady Children's Hospital–San Diego, December 2019, https://www.rchsd .org/2019/12/seven-steps-to-teaching-children-body-autonomy/.

4. Melissa Pintor Carnagey, *Sex Positive Talks to Have with Kids: A Guide*

to Raising Sexually Healthy, Informed, Empowered Young People, independently published, October 14, 2020.

5. NC Solutions, "Sober Curious Nation Alcohol Survey," last modified August 17, 2023, accessed October 23, 2024, https://ncsolutions.com/the -goods/sober-curious-nation-alcohol-survey/.

6. Jessica Lahey, *The Addiction Inoculation: Raising Healthy Kids in a Culture of Dependence* (New York: Harper, 2021).

7. Jessica Lahey, *The Addiction Inoculation: Raising Healthy Kids in a Culture of Dependence* (New York: Harper, 2021).

8. Jessica Lahey, *The Addiction Inoculation: Raising Healthy Kids in a Culture of Dependence* (New York: Harper, 2021).

Chapter 9: Tech Boundaries in a Connected World

1. K. Ray, "Here's What the Research Says About Screen Time and School-Aged Kids," *EdTech Magazine,* January 3, 2023, https://edtechmagazine .com/k12/article/2023/01/heres-what-research-says-about-screen-time-and -school-aged-kids.

2. B. Chaarani, J. Ortigara, D. Yuan, H. Loso, A. Potter, and H. P. Garavan, "Association of Video Gaming with Cognitive Performance Among Children," *JAMA Network Open* 5, no. 10 (2022): e2235721, https://doi .org/10.1001/jamanetworkopen.2022.35721.

3. "Interactive Screen Use Reduces Sleep Time for Kids, Researchers Find," *Penn State University News,* May 23, 2022, https://www.psu.edu/news /research/story/interactive-screen-use-reduces-sleep-time-kids-researchers -find/.

4. American Academy of Child and Adolescent Psychiatry, "Children and Watching TV," last modified 2024, accessed July 15, 2024, https://www .aacap.org/AACAP/Families_and_Youth/Facts_for_Families/FFF-Guide /Children-And-Watching-TV-054.aspx.

5. Common Sense Media, The Common Sense Census: Media Use by Tweens and Teens, 2022, accessed October 23, 2024, https://www .commonsensemedia.org/sites/default/files/research/report/8-18-census -integrated-report-final-web_0.pdf.

6. Jonathan Haidt, *The Anxious Generation: How the Great Rewiring of Childhood Is Causing an Epidemic of Mental Illness* (New York: Penguin Press, 2024).

7. K. Braune-Krickau, L. Schneebeli, J. Pehlke-Milde, M. Gemperle, R. Koch, and A. von Wyl, "Smartphones in the Nursery: Parental Smartphone Use and Parental Sensitivity and Responsiveness Within Parent-Child Interaction in Early Childhood (0–5 Years): A Scoping Review," *Infant Mental Health Journal* 42, no. 2 (March 2021): 161–75, https://doi .org/10.1002/imhj.21908.

8. "Why Parents Really Need to Put Down Their Phones," *Psychology Today*, November 27, 2017, https://www.psychologytoday.com/us/blog /going-beyond-intelligence/201711/why-parents-really-need-put-down-their -phones.

Chapter 11: Navigating Heavy Topics

1. "School Shootings Database," *Washington Post*, accessed October 23, 2024, https://www.washingtonpost.com/education/interactive/school-shootings -database/.

2. Everytown Research, The Impact of Active Shooter Drills in Schools, accessed October 23, 2024, https://everytownresearch.org/report/the -impact-of-active-shooter-drills-in-schools/.

3. K. K. Henry, R. M. Catagnus, A. K. Griffith, and Y. A. Garcia, "Ending the School-to-Prison Pipeline: Perception and Experience with Zero-Tolerance Policies and Interventions to Address Racial Inequality," *Behavior Analysis in Practice* 15, no. 4 (2021): 1254–63, https://doi.org/10.1007/s40617-021 -00634-z.

4. Britt Hawthorne and Natasha Yglesias, *Raising Antiracist Children: A Practical Parenting Guide*, (New York: Simon Element, 2022).

Chapter 12: Anxiety

1. Tori DeAngelis, "Anxiety Among Kids Is on the Rise. Wider Access to CBT May Provide Needed Solutions," *Monitor on Psychology* 53, no. 7 (October 1, 2022), https://www.apa.org/monitor/2022/10/child-anxiety -treatment.

2. Jonathan Haidt, *The Anxious Generation: How the Great Rewiring of Childhood Is Causing an Epidemic of Mental Illness* (New York: Penguin Press, 2024).

3. "U.S. Surgeon General Issues Advisory on Mental Health and Well-Being of Parents," US Department of Health and Human Services, August 28,

2024, https://www.hhs.gov/about/news/2024/08/28/us-surgeon-general
-issues-advisory-mental-health-well-being-parents.html.

4. Alexander J. Scott, Thomas L. Webb, Marrissa Martyn-St James, Georgina Rowse, and Scott Weich, "Improving Sleep Quality Leads to Better Mental Health: A Meta-Analysis of Randomised Controlled Trials," *Sleep Medicine Reviews* 60 (2021): 101556, https://doi.org/10.1016/j.smrv.2021.101556.

5. E. R. Lebowitz, C. Marin, A. Martino, Y. Shimshoni, and W. K. Silverman, "Parent-Based Treatment as Efficacious as Cognitive-Behavioral Therapy for Childhood Anxiety: A Randomized Noninferiority Study of Supportive Parenting for Anxious Childhood Emotions, *Journal of the American Academy of Child and Adolescent Psychology* 59, no. 3 (March 2020): 362–72, https://doi.org/10.1016/j.jaac.2019.02.014, epub March 7, 2019. PMID: 30851397; PMCID: PMC6732048.

6. Richard C. Schwartz, *No Bad Parts: Healing Trauma and Restoring Wholeness with the Internal Family Systems Model* (Louisville, CO: Sounds True, 2021).

Chapter 13: ADHD, Dyslexia, and Learning Differences

1. Margy MacMillan, Mark Tarrant, Charles Abraham, and Chris Morris, "The Association Between Children's Contact with People with Disabilities and Their Attitudes Towards Disability: A Systematic Review," *Developmental Medicine & Child Neurology* 56, no. 6 (2014): 529–46, https://doi.org/10.1111/dmcn.12326.

2. George W. Hynd, Robert Marshall, and Jeanette Gonzalez, "Learning Disabilities and Presumed Central Nervous System Dysfunction," *Learning Disability Quarterly* 14, no. 4 (1991): 283–96, https://doi.org/10.2307/1510664.

3. V. T. Shimizu, O. F. Bueno, and M. C. Miranda, "Sensory Processing Abilities of Children with ADHD," *Brazilian Journal of Physical Therapy* 18, no. 4 (July–August 2014): 343–52, https://doi.org/10.1590/bjpt-rbf.2014.0043.

Chapter 14: Respecting Diversity

1. Andrew N. Meltzoff and Walter S. Gilliam, "How Children Acquire Racial Biases," *The MIT Press Reader*, December 14, 2024, https://thereader.mitpress.mit.edu/how-children-acquire-racial-biases/.

2. "Implicit Association Test," Harvard University, accessed October 23, 2024, https://implicit.harvard.edu/implicit/takeatest.html.

Chapter 15: Raising a Kind Human

1. L. Rowland and O. S. Curry, "A Range of Kindness Activities Boost Happiness," *Journal of Social Psychology* 159, no. 3 (2019): 340–43, https://doi.org/10.1080/00224545.2018.1469461, epub May 15, 2018. PMID: 29702043.
2. "The Art of Kindness," Mayo Clinic Health System, accessed October 23, 2024, https://www.mayoclinichealthsystem.org/hometown-health/speaking-of-health/the-art-of-kindness.
3. L. Brimbal and A. M. Crossman, "Inconvenient Truth-Tellers: Perceptions of Children's Blunt Honesty," *Journal of Moral Education* 52, no. 3 (2022): 275–90, https://doi.org/10.1080/03057240.2022.2109606.

Chapter 16: Creating Connection with Your Child

1. Eli Harwood, *Raising Securely Attached Kids* (Seattle: Sasquatch Books, 2024).
2. Heidi Priebe (@heidipriebe), "To love someone long-term is to attend a thousand funerals of the people they used to be," Instagram, January 22, 2020, https://www.instagram.com/p/B7pLNtylaFK/?hl=en.

Chapter 17: Where to Begin

1. Heather Avis and Sarah Mensinga, *Everyone Belongs* (Colorado: WaterBrook, 2022).
2. John M. Gottman and Joan DeClaire, *Raising an Emotionally Intelligent Child: The Heart of Parenting* (New York: Simon & Schuster, 1997).

Index

About the Authors

Alyssa Blask Campbell is a leading voice in emotional development. As the founder and CEO of Seed & Sew, she has dedicated her career to helping families, educators, and caregivers raise emotionally intelligent children. Alyssa is the coauthor of *Tiny Humans, Big Emotions*, which explores the intersections of emotional intelligence, childhood development, and practical strategies for navigating big feelings in young children. A sought-after public speaker, Alyssa has shared her expertise at events like the United Nations International Congress on Brain Sciences and has been featured in publications such as the *Washington Post* and on CNBC, empowering audiences with tools to manage their own emotional regulation while fostering healthy relationships. With a master's degree in early childhood education, Alyssa brings a wealth of knowledge and a refreshing, down-to-earth approach to her work. She has reached hundreds of thousands through workshops, online courses, social media, and the S.E.E.D. Certification Program, where she provides professionals with research-based strategies to support social and emotional growth. Alyssa's mission is rooted in the belief that sensory and emotional regulation is at the heart of raising kind, confident humans who thrive in a complex world. When she's not teaching or writing, Alyssa enjoys family time with her husband and two children, leaning into the lessons of parenting in real time.

Rachel Stuart Lounder is a mom of two elementary-school-age children, a cancer survivor, and an advocate for children's emotional wellness. Her interest in fostering emotional intelligence grew during her own parenting journey, particularly after navigating the challenges of parenting through her cancer diagnosis. Rachel's work at Seed & Sew is rooted in a deep curiosity about the why behind behavior, combining personal experience with a research-driven approach to understanding child development and emotional health. She believes in equipping both kids and parents with the tools to handle life's difficulties, fostering resilience and empathy along the way. Rachel lives in Maine with her husband and their two children.